COMPUTER PROGRAMMING
IN
BASIC
THE
EASY
WAY

SECOND EDITION

An Introduction to Computer Programming

Douglas Downing, PhD
Seattle Pacific University

BARRON'S

Barron's Educational Series, Inc.

Dedication

This book is for my grandmother, Hannah Hayland.

Acknowledgments

I would like to thank Charlie Roberts, Linda Roberts, Ruth Roberts, Bill Roberts, Marlys Downing, Peggy Downing, Robert Downing, Mark Yoshimi, and Michael Covington for their help in developing and testing the programs contained in this book.

All inquiries should be addressed to:
Barron's Educational Series, Inc.
250 Wireless Boulevard
Hauppauge, New York 11788

Library of Congress Catalog Card No.   89-6675

International Standard Book No. 0-8120-4253-0

Library of Congress Cataloging-in-Publication Data

Downing, Douglas.
    Computer programming in BASIC the easy way: an introduction to computer
programming/Douglas Downing.—2nd ed.
        p.   cm.
    Includes index.
    ISBN 0-8120-4253-0
    1. BASIC (Computer program language) I. Title.
QA76.73.B3D69 1989
005. 13'3—dc20   89-6675
                                                                 CIP

PRINTED IN THE UNITED STATES OF AMERICA
3456   100   98765

Contents

INTRODUCTION

A computer is a very literal-minded servant. It will do exactly what you tell it to. This book is all about how to get a computer to do exactly what you want. The computer will be glad to do many boring tasks that you would rather not do. Also, because it can work very fast, it can do many tasks that would be impossible without computers simply because they are too long. The only requirement is that the computer needs to receive very clear-cut instructions. These instructions must be written in a *computer programming language*. Learning a computer language is a bit like learning a foreign language, but it is much easier because there are not nearly as many words to learn.

There are several programming languages in common use. This book teaches the language BASIC, which stands for Beginners All Purpose Symbolic Instruction Code. The BASIC language was developed by John Kemeny and Thomas Kurtz in the 1960s. In many ways it is the best language for beginners. BASIC is simple enough that many small computers are able to understand it. Once you've mastered BASIC, you are in a good position to study more complicated languages such as FORTRAN, PL/1, PASCAL, COBOL, and APL.

What we'll do in this book is *create* the BASIC language ourselves. We'll imagine that we've been given a computer that will do whatever we want it to do, provided that we figure out how to give it instructions. Each time we come across a new problem, we will find that it will help to add a new instruction to our computer programming language. The purpose of this approach is to show the logic and motivation for each BASIC command as it is introduced. The main reason for introducing new commands is to save work (even if it looks as though new commands are introduced to torment you by making life more complicated). If you enjoy lots of drudgery and menial calculations, then you won't appreciate computers. However, if, like me, you'd like some relief from boring, repetitive tasks, then you'll realize the value of each new command as it is introduced. If you were to create your own simple programming language, it would probably look something like BASIC. Of course, your job is easier because BASIC has already been invented and you just have to learn it.

Before you start work with computers, you should be familiar with pocket calculators. In Chapter 1 we describe a machine that has the same capabilities as a pocket calculator. In Chapter 2 we make the big jump to developing a real computer when we develop a way for the machine to store its own instructions. In Chapters 3 through 9 we slowly develop the building blocks needed to write programs.

There are two main aspects to learning computer programming. Learning the commands and syntax of a particular language is one of them. The other is learning how to develop a method for solving a problem (called an *algorithm*). Once you have created an algorithm, you need to translate it into a particular computer language so it can be executed by a computer.

The main text of each chapter covers the essential material you need to know in order to start writing BASIC programs. The notes at the end of each chapter contain additional information on BASIC features. One advantage of BASIC is that you don't need to know the more complicated options when you're just getting started. (However, you should read the notes, since they mention features that are used later in the book.)

The text includes examples of the usage of each command, and it also includes boxes in which there are descriptions of the general form of the commands. In the general form description, the parts written in capital letters need to be typed exactly as shown. The parts written in *italics* can be replaced by any appropriate item of your own choosing. For example, the general form of the FOR command

FOR *counter* = *start* TO *stop* STEP *increment*

indicates that FOR, =, TO, and STEP need to be typed exactly as shown, but you can choose what you want for *counter, start, stop,* and *increment*.

BASIC is available on many different types of computers. Large computers offer BASIC on *time-sharing* systems, that is, computer systems on which the operating terminals of many users are connected to the computer simultaneously. BASIC is also widely available on microcomputers: personal computers and small business computers. Because there are many different types of computers, there are many different versions of BASIC. The essential BASIC commands are the same in almost all versions. However, each different version handles some tasks in its own special way, and as manufacturers have added unique features to their computers, they have added unique commands to their versions of BASIC.

You will need to have a computer available (at home, at school, or at work) in order to learn to write computer programs. You will be most interested in learning the version of BASIC that runs on the computer available to you. Thus, you will need to have the BASIC manual for your computer available so that you can learn the specific features of your own version of BASIC. There are three especially popular versions of BASIC that will be presented in this book: Commodore 64 BASIC, Applesoft BASIC, and Microsoft

BASIC. Microsoft BASIC runs on the IBM PC, where it is known as BASICA, and several other computers, where it is known as MBASIC or GWBASIC. There is also a version of Microsoft BASIC available for the Apple Macintosh.

There is only one way to learn computer programming: practice. The book includes many exercises that give suggested computer programming applications. The exercises near the beginning of the book ask you to write short programs. Suggested answers to many of these exercises are included in Appendix A-3. There is seldom only one answer to a computer programming problem. You are quite likely to come up with a perfectly correct solution that differs from the one suggested in the back of the book.

Learn the concepts of BASIC by writing many short programs, and then you will have confidence when you start writing long programs. The exercises near the end of the book provide you with suggested projects for you to work out on your own. A wide variety of possible programming applications are discussed. You should find some exercises that interest you, but you're not likely to be interested in all of them.

The book contains some practical programs that you are free to use as you wish. These include programs for personal financial record keeping (Chapter 11); notecard box information storage (Chapter 12); and financial table calculation (answer section for Chapter 11). Two game programs are included in Chapter 13—a quick-recall trivia game and a two-person football strategy game. There is also a program that helps write programs by printing an alphabetical list of all variables used in a Microsoft BASIC program (answer section for Chapter 9).

You don't need to know much mathematics to learn computer programming, although you do need to know some algebra and trigonometry to understand some of the applications discussed here. You may skip over sections that seem too advanced mathematically for you. Most of the mathematical material is contained in Chapter 8 (Mathematical Operations) or Chapter 15 (Scientific Applications).

You don't need to learn to program in order to use computers, since you can buy programs that are already written by someone else. However, you need to learn to program if you are to appreciate the full power and versatility of computers and if you want to get your computer to do exactly what *you* want it to do. After reading this book, you'll be able to write your own game programs, design your own graphics, and develop your own applications.

You are now about to embark on the journey of learning computer programming.

CHAPTER 1

GETTING STARTED

I f you like to do a lot of boring work yourself, then this book is not for you. However, if you're like me, you would much rather have somebody else do the boring work for you. The ideal boring work servant would be able to do routine tasks very quickly, without making mistakes and without complaining. The servant wouldn't have to be very creative since we would give all the instructions. Unfortunately, people don't really fit this description. However, if we could build a *machine* to do the work, then we would be in good shape.

COMPUTER HARDWARE

We'll call the machine a *computer*. First, we need the *hardware*. Most computers will look like a typewriter keyboard joined to a television screen. The keyboard will be used to provide *input* into the machine. The keyboard has keys for letters, numbers, and some special symbols, along with an ON switch. The screen is a *cathode-ray-tube (CRT)* screen. The screen will be used by the computer to display messages for us. Somewhere in the middle of the computer is the actual brain, that is, the *central processing unit (CPU)*. It is the CPU that controls the operations of the computer.

Flip the switch to ON, and a small blinking dash will appear on the screen. The dash is called the *cursor*. It tells us where on the screen the next symbol that we type will appear.

THE NEED FOR INSTRUCTIONS

The computer hardware by itself is no good. The hardware without the instructions is about as useless as a helper who can't understand a word you say.

We will now figure out how to give instructions to our computer. We will pretend that we are starting from scratch, making our own list of instructions. When we are finished, we will have created a whole new type of language (called a *computer programming language*). There are many different computer programming languages available. The language that we will develop in this book is called BASIC, one of the easiest languages to learn. BASIC is widely available on most microcomputers as well as on many big computers. However, the situation is complicated because there are many different dialects of BASIC. Many types of computers are available, and they understand slightly different versions of the BASIC language. When you learn BASIC, you will need to concentrate on the version of BASIC that is available to you. You will need to learn its own special features, capabilities, and limitations. In this book we will focus as much as possible on the general features of BASIC that are common to almost all computer systems. We will also pay special attention to some popular versions of BASIC:

• Commodore BASIC, available on Commodore 64 computers;

• Microsoft BASIC, available on the IBM PC (where it is known as BASICA) and on many other types of computers (where it is known as MBASIC or GWBASIC);

• Quick BASIC, also produced by Microsoft;

• Applesoft BASIC, available on the Apple II family of computers.

As you are reading this book, you will want to type the programs on your own computer. The first thing to learn is how you tell the computer that you are going to be writing BASIC programs. Many computers are "multilingual"—that is, they understand many different languages. You will generally need to tell your machine that you are speaking BASIC. You may be wondering, How can I tell the computer what language I will be using if the computer can't understand a word I say until after I've told it what language I will be using? When the computer is first turned on, it will expect you to type an *operating system command*. This command will tell the computer what language you wish to use or what program you wish to execute. For example, if you are using an IBM PC, you will first need to find the disk that contains BASIC and put it in disk drive A. (We will say more about disks and drives later.) After you turn on the computer, it will ask you for the date and time and then you will see this symbol on the screen: A>
This symbol is called the *operating system prompt*. Type BASICA (or MBASIC or GWBASIC, depending on what your particular version of BASIC is called), and the computer will then be prepared for you to communicate with it in BASIC. The computer will display the message "Ok" when it is ready for you to speak BASIC to it.

On Commodore computers it is even easier to use BASIC, since the computer will automatically assume that you will be using BASIC unless you tell it otherwise. When you first turn the machine on, you will see the message "Ready." This means that the computer is ready for you to use BASIC.

If you are using an Apple computer, you will find your Applesoft BASIC in one of three places: on a disk, on a cassette tape, or on a card that plugs directly into the computer. You will need to determine which type you have and then read the computer's instructions to tell you how to start BASIC. When it is started, you will see a bracket,], which is the prompt telling you the computer is ready for a BASIC command.

ARITHMETIC CALCULATIONS

Now we'll set to work imagining that we can create the language. First, we'll use our computer for arithmetic calculations. You probably are familiar with performing arithmetic calculations on a pocket calculator. We will see that a computer can be used as a sophisticated calculator. We'll want the symbol 1 to stand for the number 1, the symbol 2 to stand for the number 2, and so on. We also need some symbols to stand for arithmetic operations. We can use the symbols on the keyboard that are as close as possible to ordinary arithmetic notation. The symbol + will stand for plus, and the symbol – will stand for minus. The keyboard does not contain a multiplication symbol, ×, since that symbol is too easily confused with the letter x. We will use an asterisk, *, to stand for multiplication. The keyboard does not contain a division symbol, ÷, so we will let a slash, /, stand for division. For example, the expression $12/3$, which looks a bit like the fraction $\frac{12}{3}$ is used to input $12 ÷ 3$.

Suppose we need to find the answer to the problem 2 + 2. If we were using a pocket calculator, we would find the answer by pressing the following keys:

2 + 2 =

We would like the computer to work in much the same way. The command 2 + 2 will indeed tell the computer to add 2 and 2. However, a typical computer is not smart enough to know that after it has performed the calculation it should present the result (instead of keeping it for itself). Therefore, we need to tell the computer to display the answer on the screen. In the old days (back in the 1960s), most computer output went directly to a printer. So, when BASIC was first developed, the command PRINT told the computer to send the output (the result of its calculation) to the printer. The command PRINT is still used as the main output command in BASIC, only now the PRINT command causes the output to appear on the screen. (You may be wondering, What if we really do want the output to go to the printer? We will discuss that question later.) Therefore, type this command:

PRINT 2 + 2

There is one special key about which we need to learn. At the end of each line, we have to press the key marked <RETURN> (which is located on the lower right-hand side of the keyboard). The <RETURN> key tells the computer that we have completed the line. (It is similar to the <RETURN> key on a typewriter. On some computers the key that fulfills this function is called the ENTER key, or it may be marked with a symbol like this: ↵.)

Now we're ready to try our first calculation. Type

PRINT 2 + 2 <RETURN>

and the screen will display

PRINT 2 + 2

4

(This type of calculation is called an *immediate mode* calculation. On some computers it is not necessary to type the word PRINT in front of the command.)

Try an example of subtraction:

PRINT 100 – 64 <RETURN>

36

and multiplication:

PRINT 3 * 18 <RETURN>

54

and division:

PRINT 72/9 <RETURN>

8

Now, suppose we need to find the total amount we spent on groceries for the last seven weeks. Type in the seven numbers like this:

PRINT 34 + 50 + 35 + 66 + 34 + 37 + 41 <RETURN>

297

If a baseball player has 168 hits in 546 at-bats, we can find the batting average by division:

PRINT 168/546

.307692

We'll let an on-line dot, ., represent the decimal point on the computer just as it does in arithmetic. (The answer shown here is displayed with six digits. Try this calculation on your computer and see how many digits are displayed in the answer. Depending on which computer you have, you may see six, seven, nine, or ten digits.)

If you put \$1 in the bank today and leave it there for 10 years, assuming it earns 5% compound interest each year, then you will have 1.05^{10} dollars at the end of 10 years. It will be very valuable for our computer to be able to do exponentiations. To remind us that exponentiation means raising a number to a power, we can use an upward pointing arrow , ↑, to stand for exponentiation. For example, the computer will interpret 10 ↑ 3 to mean $10^3 = 10 * 10 * 10 = 1,000$. Type in this formula:

PRINT 1.05 ↑10 <RETURN>

and the answer is

1.62889

(On some computers the upward pointing arrow looks like this: ^.)

We'd also like the computer to be able to calculate square roots. The expression *SQR(X)* will be equal to the square root of *X*. For example:

PRINT SQR(9)

3

PRINT SQR(25)

5

PRINT SQR(2)

1.4142136

Suppose you throw a baseball straight up, and you need to know how high it will be at any time. The height will be given by a formula similar to this:

$$-0.5 * 9.8 * t^2 + 100 * t + 15$$

where *t* is the time since the ball was thrown. If we want to know the height when $t = 2$, we can type it into the computer like this:

PRINT −0.5 * 9.8 * 2 ↑ 2 + 100 * 2 + 15 <RETURN>

The answer is

195.4

When the computer is given a long expression like this with several different operation symbols, the order in which it will perform the operations depends on certain rules of precedence. Exponentiations are always done before any other operations, and then multiplications and divisions are always done before additions or subtractions. This order corresponds to the way that normal algebraic notation works. In our example, the computer will first perform the exponentiation $2 \uparrow 2$ (result: 4), then it will perform the multiplications $-0.5 * 9.8 * 4$ (result: -19.6) and $100 * 2$ (result: 200). Finally, it will perform the additions $-19.6 + 200 + 15$ (result: 195.4.) We will discuss the precedence of operations further in Chapter 8. You can always change the precedence with the parentheses if you don't want the computer to follow its normal precedence. For example, in the expression

PRINT 2 + 3 $*$ **4**

the computer will perform the multiplication first and the result will be $2 + 12 = 14$. In the expression

PRINT (2 + 3) $*$ **4**

the computer will perform the addition first and the result will be $5 * 4 = 20$.

USING LETTERS TO STAND FOR NUMBERS

It saves a lot of work to have a machine that does arithmetic operations. However, we still need to type the numbers into the machine each time we want to use them in a calculation. This can get bothersome. For example, suppose we need to calculate the height of our baseball exactly 7.043295 seconds after launch. We can use the expression

−0.5 $*$ **9.8** $*$ **7.043295** $\uparrow$ **2 + 100** $*$ **7.043295 + 15**

476.25028

But this method requires us to type the long number twice. If you ever used a calculator with a memory, then you already know a better way. First, you can store the complicated number in the memory using a MEMORY STORE key. The, when you need to get the number out of memory, you can use the MEMORY RECALL key. Sophisticated pocket calculators will have two or three memories, so you can store more than one number at a time. You can use the computer as you would use a calculator with very many different memories. Each memory will be identified by a *variable name*. For now, we will use letters as variable names. For example, A, B, C, X, Y, and Z are all possible variable names. In our example we will use the letter T to stand for 7.043295 since T will remind us that 7.043295 is a time. (Later, we will use variable names that are longer than one letter.) We will use the equal sign, =, to stand for assignment. For example, if we type the command

T = 7.043295

it means that we are storing the value 7.043295 under the letter T. Then, whenever the computer comes across the letter T in an arithmetic expression, it will pretend that it really came across the number 7.043295.

Now we can calculate the height in a way that involves less typing, although it now requires two lines of computer instructions:

T = 7.043295 <RETURN>

(There will be no response from the computer after we type this part.)

PRINT −0.5 ∗ 9.8 ∗ T ↑ 2 + 100 ∗ T ∗ 15 <RETURN>

The computer responds with

476.25028

Here's another example:

T = 0 <RETURN>

PRINT −0.5 ∗ 9.8 ∗ T ↑ 2 + 100 ∗ T + 15 <RETURN>

15

Here is the general form for an assignment statement:

ASSIGNMENT STATEMENT

$$x = expression$$

where x is any letter, and *expression* is an arithmetic formula involving additions, multiplications, exponentiations, and so on.

Note that the letter to which the value is being assigned must always be written on the left. In algebra you can reverse the two sides of an equation if you wish, but you cannot reverse the order of a computer assignment statement.

CHARACTER STRINGS

A pocket calculator can store only numbers in its memories. Computers are much more versatile because they can store not only numbers but letters and other characters as well. A group of characters stored in a computer is called a *character string* (or just a *string*). For example, suppose we would like to store the string, "Hello. How are you?" We will use a letter to represent this string. You may be wondering how the computer can tell the difference between a letter that represents a numeric value and a letter that represents a string? To make things easier for the computer, we will always put a dollar sign, $, at the end of a string name. (Remember: $ looks like S, and S stands for "string".) For example, A$ can be the name of a string. We can use assignment statements for strings just as we did for numeric values:

H$ = "Hello. How are you?"
Now type:

PRINT H$

and the screen will display:

Hello. How are you?

(Note that we are no longer showing <RETURN> at the end of each line. However, you should remember that you always type the <RETURN> key when you have completed a line.)

A letter followed by $ is called a *string variable*. String variables can save a lot of typing, particularly if there is a string that we will be using a lot. Many computers allow you to use lower-case letters as well as upper-case letters in strings. You will have to check your computer, though, since some computers have only upper-case letters.

You can assign values to strings and print them out, just as you can for numeric variables. However, you clearly cannot perform arithmetic operations on strings. For example, if you try

A$ = "Hello"

B$ = "Goodbye"

PRINT A$ * B$

the result will be a message similar to this:

Type mismatch

This is an example of an error messsage. Don't panic; you have not done any harm to the computer. If the computer is given an instruction that it can't handle, it will simply refuse to do anything with the instruction, giving a cryptic message explaining why it can't. (One annoying feature of Microsoft BASIC is that the computer will cheerfully display the messsage "Ok" immediately after the error messsage. This does not mean that the computer thinks everything is fine. It just means that it is ready for you to type a new command.) Errors are an unfortunate fact of computer life, and you will probably see many error messages in your computer career. Error messages are valuable learning aids, however, since they can help you learn how to avoid the error. We will discuss other types of error messsages later.

What if you realize that you have typed a wrong key before you hit <RETURN>? When you type the wrong key on a typewriter, the mistake appears on the paper, and it can be a nuisance to erase. A mistake on a computer is much easier to correct. Your keyboard should have a key labeled BACK SPACE or ← (leftward-pointing arrow). When you press this key, the cursor will move back over what you have typed, mowing down all the characters in its path. When you have moved back to the point where the mistake began, you can start typing the correct version.

You cannot perform arithmetic operations on strings even if the strings themselves contain numeric characters. For example:

PRINT "2" * "2"

will once again give the "Type mismatch" messsage.

However, there are some operations that can be performed on character strings. For example, suppose you have

A$ = "GEORGE"

B$ = "WASHINGTON"

We can join these two strings into one string using a plus operator (+):

PRINT A$ + B$

GEORGEWASHINGTON

(The technical term for joining two character strings like this is *concatenation*.)

We probably would like a space between the names, so we can type

PRINT A$ + "" + B$

GEORGE WASHINGTON

We can also use the plus operator in an assignment statement:

C$ = A$ + "" + BS

PRINT C$

GEORGE WASHINGTON

D$ = A$ + "" + C$ + "" + B$

PRINT D$

GEORGE GEORGE WASHINGTON WASHINGTON

There will be more about tricks with strings in Chapter 7.

NOTES
- When people write numbers, they like to insert commas. For example, 216034129 is written as 216,034,129. On the computer, however, you cannot insert commas when you type numbers.

- In this chapter we used only single letters for numeric variable names, and we used only single letters followed by a $ for string variables. As we will see, it helps to give variables longer descriptive names. For example, if a variable represents the height of something, it would be best to give it the name HEIGHT. Some versions of BASIC allow you to write variable names as long as six characters or longer. Microsoft BASIC allows variable names up to 40 characters long. It is easier to write programs when you are allowed to use longer variable names. However, some versions of BASIC restrict the lengths of names. In some versions, variable names are not allowed to be longer than two characters. In Commodore BASIC and Applesoft BASIC, a variable name can be several characters long, but the computer only pays attention to the first two characters. For example, the two variables HEIGHT and HELP would be treated as the same variable. Therefore, if you use variable names longer than two characters, you must be very careful to make sure that all variables differ in their first two characters. In all versions, the first character in a variable name must be a letter, but the other characters can be either letters or numeric digits.

- The computer would be confused if you gave a variable the same name as one of the special key words used by the BASIC language. For example, the word PRINT is a BASIC key work, so you would suffer an error message if you tried these statements:

PRINT = 10 * 2

PRINT PRINT

The words that cannot be used as variable names are called *reserved words*. We will learn many reserved words in BASIC: RUN, SAVE, LOAD, LIST, and others. You will need to check with your particular computer to find the complete list of reserved words for your version of BASIC. In some versions you will get an error message if you include a reserved word in the middle of a variable name. For example, the name BASERUNNER includes the reserved word RUN, so it would be illegal in some versions.

- When an assignment statement is executed, the computer completely forgets the old value of the variable involved. For example, after the assignment statement

A = 103.5

the variable A has the value 103.5. If you then type in the assignment statement

A = 10

the variable A now has the value 10 and the value 103.5 is lost forever. You can think of the variable A as being a box labeled A. The box can store only one number at a time, so when you put a new number in, the old number has to come out.

However, you can use the *old* value of a variable to help you calculate the new value. For example, suppose A is 10 and you want to make the value of A go up by 1. You can type in the assignment statement

A = A + 1

First, the computer will calculate the value of the expression on the right (in this case, A + 1, which will be 10 + 1, which will be 11). Then, after it has finished the calculation, it will assign the new value to the variable A and the old value will be lost.

• In some versions of BASIC, there are abbreviations that can be used in the place of many of the key words. For example, in some versions the question mark, ?, can be used as an abbreviation for the word PRINT.

• If you are using Microsoft BASIC and you would like to tell the computer that you have completed your work with BASIC, type the command SYSTEM. Then the computer will be ready for you to type an operating system command or to begin using another type of program, such as a word processing program or a spreadsheet program.

EXERCISES   *Write BASIC equivalents of these algebraic expressions:*

1. $$\dfrac{\dfrac{10}{4}}{\dfrac{16}{3}}$$

2. $$\dfrac{12}{\dfrac{3}{2}}$$

3. $$\dfrac{1}{1-x}$$

4. $$\dfrac{1}{1+x^2}$$

5. $$ax^2 + bx + c$$

6. $(1 + w)^{1/w}$

7. $$\dfrac{1}{\dfrac{1}{a} + \dfrac{1}{b}}$$

8. $$\dfrac{1}{1 + \left(\dfrac{x^2}{a}\right)}$$

9. 6.02×10^{23}

10. $x^a y^{1-a}$

11. $[ax^p + (1 - a)y^p]^{1/p}$

12. $$\dfrac{Pr\,(1 + r)^{n-1}}{(1 + r)^{n-1} - 1}$$

13. $$\dfrac{4\,\pi\,r^3}{3}$$

14. $4\,\pi\,r^2$

15. $16x^2 y^3$

Are these legal BASIC expressions? If they are, what will their values be? (Let A = 10, B = 6, C = 4.)

16.   **2 + 2**

17.   **6 * 5**

18.   **6 * 4 + 5**

19.   **(6 * 4) + 5**

20.   **6 * (4 + 5)**

21.   **10 + (20 * 3**

22.   **2 * 4**

23.   **(−1) ↑ (0.5)**

24.   **2 * ((3 + 5) − (2/4))**

25.   **3.14159 * 10 ↑ 2**

26.   **0.6 ↑ 0.3 * 0.4 ↑ 0.7**

27.   **(0.6 ↑ 0.3) * (0.4 ↑ 0.7)**

28.   **(4 + 20 + 5 + 36 + 4 + 7 + 11)/7**

29.   **10 * 1 + 5/100 ↑ 6**

30.   **10 * (1 + 5/100) ↑ 6**

31.   **4A + 10B**

32.   **14 ÷ 2**

33.   **A/B/C**

34.   **A/B * C**

35.   **A/(B * C)**

36.   **(A/B)/C**

37.   **(A/B) * C**

For exercises 38–43, trace the execution of the statements by hand and then determine what the result will be.

38.   **A = 30**

B = 2 * A

A = A + B

C = 2 * A + B

B = B + 1

A = A/2

PRINT A + B + C

39.   **A$ = "ABC"**

B$ = A$ + "DEF"

A$ = "Z" + A$ + "Z"

B$ = B$ + A$

PRINT A$

```
                    PRINT B$
40.   A = 10
      B = 5 * A
      A = B
      B = 5 *A
      A = B
      B = A/10
      PRINT A
      PRINT B
41.   X$ = "HELLO"
      Y$ = "GOODBYE"
      Z$ = X$ + "  " + Y$ + "."
      A$ = Z$ + Z$
      PRINT A$
42.   M$ = "JANUARY"
      N$ = "FEBRUARY"
      M$ = N$
      N$ = M$
      PRINT M$
      PRINT N$
43.   A = 1
      B = 2
      A = A/(A + B)
      B = B/(A + B)
      PRINT A
      PRINT B
```

CHAPTER 2

WRITING PROGRAMS

The machine that we developed in Chapter 1, which has the same capabilities as a pocket calculator, can solve an amazing variety of problems. It has one severe limitation though. To make it work, we need to type in new instructions every time we want to use the machine. When we come to calculations that involve many instructions, this can get to be a real problem. Historically, this limitation was the motivation for the development of computers. During World War II the army had to hire a lot of people to perform the tedious task of calculating ballistics tables. The ENIAC, the first true computer, was developed to make this task much easier.

Here are some examples of problems that can be solved with a calculator, but the solutions would be tedious. If you're having a pancake breakfast and you need to count calories, you will need to know the area of each pancake. You can easily measure the radius of a pancake, but you will have to calculate the area from the formula

$$A = \pi r^2$$

(Remember π is a symbol called pi, which stands for the number 3.14159....)

As another example, suppose you need to know how far your bicycle goes during each rotation of the front wheel. You will need to calculate the circumference of the wheel, using the formula

$$C = 2\pi r$$

If, for example, we have a circle of radius 10, we can easily solve this problem on the calculator:

2 * 3.14159 * 10

62.8318

If we have to repeat this calculation for many different-sized circles, it will help to store the value 3.14159, perhaps under the variable name P. Then we can perform the calculations with less typing:

P = 3.14159

PRINT 2 * P * 10

62.8318

PRINT P * 10 ↑ 2

314.159

However, if we have many different circles, even this much typing can become a bother.

Here's another problem. If you measure the temperature of the air with an ordinary thermometer, it will read the temperature in degrees Fahrenheit. However, if you need to use the air temperature in a physics formula, such as the ideal gas law, you will have to convert that temperature into degrees Kelvin. (The Kelvin temperature scale is a scale on which zero occurs at absolute zero and each degree is the same size as 1 degree in the Celsius system. Absolute zero occurs at –273.2°C, or –459.7°F.) Fortunately, there is a simple formula that relates temperatures in the Fahrenheit system to temperatures in the Kelvin system:

$$K = 273.2 + \tfrac{5}{9} \ (F - 32)$$

You can easily handle that formula on the calculator, but it will be a lot of work if you have to perform too many temperature-conversion calculations.

In Chapter 1 we calculated the height of our baseball from the formula

$$h = -\tfrac{1}{2} \times 9.8t^2 + 100t + 15$$

If you have to repeat this calculation many times, your fingers will get very tired. There's also the possibility you could make a mistake.

THE NEED TO STORE INSTRUCTIONS

Fortunately for us the computer has been invented, and all we need to do is figure out a way to have the computer remember the instructions that are typed in. We've already seen how we can use an assignment statement, such as P = 3.14159, to store numbers in the computer. Now we need a similar type of command to store instructions.

Let's look at the three instructions that we want the computer to save in order to calculate the area and circumference of a circle of radius R:

P = 3.14159

A = P * R ↑ 2

C = 2 * P * R

(A group of computer instructions is called a *program*.)

We have two problems now. First, how do we tell the computer to save the instructions, instead of executing each one immediately after it is typed in? Second, how do we make sure that the computer executes instructions in the correct order? We can solve both of these problems at once by putting a number in front of each statement:

1   P = 3.14159

2   A = P * R ↑ 2

3   C = 2 * P * R

Whenever you type a command without putting a line number in front of it, the computer will execute the command immediately. But when the line number is included, the computer will not execute the command. Instead, it will store the statement inside its main memory.

Now we need to decide what command will cause the computer to run the program. When the command RUN is typed, the program currently in the main computer memory will be executed. The line with the smallest number will be executed first, and thereafter each line will be executed in order according to its number. (In the next chapter we will see how to change the order of execution.)

We now have two more problems. First, the computer's main memory cannot store anything permanently. Whenever the power is shut off, the computer's memory goes completely blank. We don't want to retype the program every time we turn the computer on, so we need some permanent way to store the program. Second, we will write many programs in this book, and we can't have them all loaded in the computer's memory at the same time. We need to be able to save each program in a place where we can find it again.

STORING PROGRAMS ON DISKS

Fortunately, the computer can also store information on external storage devices: disks or tapes. Many computers can be connected to cassette tape recorders and can store information on ordinary cassette tapes. If you have cassette storage with your computer, then you will need to learn how to store programs and other information on the tapes and how to get that information back to the computer. It is faster and easier to store information on disks, so if you use your computer a lot you will likely find it would be worthwhile for you to acquire a disk-reading device (called a *disk drive.*) Computer disks for microcomputers are called *floppy disks*. They look like small phonograph records encased in protective jackets. The two most common sizes are 5¼ inches and 3½ inches across. The disks need to be placed into a slot in the disk drive, which will either be part of the computer or a separate device connected to the computer by a cable. Some computers have a high-capacity disk, called a *hard disk*, built into the computer. Unlike a floppy disk, a hard disk remains permanently inside the machine. The computer can store more information and retrieve it more quickly when it is equipped with a hard disk. There are several operations you will need to learn how to perform in order to use the disk drive that comes with your particular computer:

- how to open the drive door and insert the disk in the drive

- how to prepare a new disk so that it is ready for the computer to store data on it

- how to distinguish between the drives if you have more than one (if there are two drives, they are usually labelled A: and B:)

Now, suppose the floppy disk is in the disk drive and is ready for data to be stored on it. The command SAVE will cause the program to be saved on the disk. You must give the program a name so you will know what to ask for when you want it back. We will call our program CIRCLE since it is about circles. Type SAVE "CIRCLE". There will be a brief humming noise from the disk drive, and then the computer will be silent. Now let's make sure that the program really is stored on the disk. Type NEW. (That command will erase all of the program that is currently stored in the computer's main memory.) Type LIST to make sure that the program is gone. (The LIST command causes the current program to be displayed.) If the screen is blank, there are no programs currently in the main computer. (Don't panic—you won't have to type the program again.) We can use the command LOAD "CIRCLE" to get the program back. Type LOAD "CIRCLE". There will be another brief hum from the disk reader. Now if you type LIST, the following will appear on the screen:

1 P = 3.14159

2 A = P ∗ R ↑ 2

3 C = 2 ∗ P ∗ R

THE REM COMMAND

If you look at that program, you should be able to remember that P stands for pi, R stands for radius, A stands for area, and C stands for circumference. However, we wrote the program only minutes ago. By next week, you'll quite likely forget what the letters mean. It is a good idea to keep a record of how the program works on a piece of paper, but it is even more helpful if we can somehow include an explanation of the program on the display screen itself. We can do that, provided we think of a command that tells the computer to ignore a particular statement. (We don't want the computer to try to execute the explanation.) We'll use the keyword REM (short for REMARK) to tell the computer that the rest of that statement is for people to read, not for the computer to execute. That means we can type anything we want in a REM statement, but the most logical thing to include is an explanation of the program. A REM statement is often called a *comment*.

What we want to do now is to put the statement

REM P STANDS FOR PI

at the start of the program. However, because the first statement of the CIRCLE program has the number 1, there is no way we can put any other statement in front of it. In fact, there will often be times when we will want to insert a new statement between two existing statements. Therefore it is a good idea to leave gaps in the statement numbers so we can insert new statements later. As a general rule, it is a good idea to give most main statements numbers that are multiples of 10. For example, we can rewrite the CIRCLE program with new statement numbers as follows:

```
10  P = 3.14159

20  A = P * R ↑ 2

30  C = 2 * P * R
```

(Remember that when it runs the program the computer will execute the statements in the order of their statement numbers, regardless of the order in which the statements were typed in.)

Now we can add comments to the CIRCLE program to explain what the variables mean:

```
 9  REM  P STANDS FOR PI

10  P = 3.14159

18  REM  R STANDS FOR THE RADIUS

19  REM  A STANDS FOR THE AREA

20  A = P * R ↑ 2

29  REM  C STANDS FOR THE CIRCUMFERENCE

30  C = 2 * P * R

40  END
```

We also need a command that we can put at the end of each program to tell the computer that it is finished and can take a rest. Thus, the statement END will be placed at the conclusion of the program to tell the computer that the program is over.

Now type RUN to see the CIRCLE program work. Unfortunately, when you type RUN the screen will stay blank. The computer is actually still working—it is calculating the area and circumference of the circle just as you told it to do. However, you never told the computer that you wanted it to tell *you* the answer. The computer will not do any work unless you tell it *exactly* what to do. That means that we now need a command that causes the computer to display the result of a calculation. Even the most elaborate computer program is useless if it does not contain any way to deliver the results (the output) in some form where people can read them.

THE PRINT AND INPUT COMMANDS

The command PRINT A will cause the value of the variable A to be displayed on the screen.

We can rewrite the circle program as follows:

9   REM P IS THE VALUE OF PI

10   P = 3.14159

18   REM R IS THE RADIUS OF THE CIRCLE

19   REM A IS THE AREA OF THE CIRCLE

20   A = P * R ↑ 2

29   REM C IS THE CIRCUMFERENCE OF THE CIRCLE

30   C = 2 * P * R

40   PRINT A

50   PRINT C

60   END

However, before we're ready to run this program, we have another snag. If the program is written the way it is now, the computer won't know what the value of R is. We could, of course, add an assignment statement at the beginning of the program, like this:

5 R = 10

We would have to change that line whenever we run the program for a different-sized circle, so the program would not be very versatile in that case. The whole point of designing a computer that could memorize its instructions was that we could use exactly the same instructions without having to change them each time. We need a way to tell the computer the value for R without having to use an assignment statement. What we need is a command that does the opposite of the PRINT command. The PRINT command causes the computer to tell us what the value of a variable is. We need a new command that allows us to tell the computer what the value of a variable should be. We'll call this command the INPUT command since we're putting a number *in*to the computer. For example, the command INPUT R means that the computer will stop and wait for us to type in a value for the variable R.

The new version of the circle program looks like this:

```
1   REM  PROGRAM TO CALCULATE THE AREA

2   REM  AND CIRCUMFERENCE

9   REM  P IS THE VALUE FOR PI

10  P = 3.14159

14  REM  R IS THE RADIUS OF THE CIRCLE

15  INPUT R

19  REM  A IS THE AREA OF THE CIRCLE

20  A = P * R ↑ 2

29  REM  C IS THE CIRCUMFERENCE OF THE CIRCLE

30  C = 2 * P * R

40  PRINT A

50  PRINT C

60  END
```

Now type RUN. The screen will display

?

The computer looks confused, but what it is doing is waiting for you to type in the value for R. The question mark is a signal to you that the computer has reached an INPUT statement and that it is now ready for you to type in a value. Type

10

Then after you press RETURN, the screen will display these values:

314.159

62.8318

Surely enough, they are the answers. The first number is the area of the circle, and the second number is the circumference of the circle. We can try it some more times:

RUN

?

7

153.83804

43.982297

RUN

?

20

1256.637061

125.6637

RUN

?

24

1809.55737

150.796447

PRINTING WORDS

The answers are all here, but it is getting a bit confusing. We're probably going to forget which numbers mean what. What we need is some way to label the output. For example, we could create a command that causes the computer to print THE AREA IS above the number that stands for the area. We could try the command

PRINT THE AREA IS

but that won't work because we need to give the computer some way to differentiate between when we want it to print the value of a variable and when we want it to print a group of letters exactly as we wrote them. For example, when we type PRINT R, we want the computer to print the value of the variable R instead of just the letter R. What we'll do is put a group of letters in quotation marks when we want them printed exactly the way we wrote them. For example, the command

PRINT "THE AREA IS:"

will cause the computer to print this:

THE AREA IS:

In general, the command

PRINT "*xxxxxx*"

will cause the characters *xxxxxx* to be printed. The *x*'s can be any computer characters (except for the " character.) Blanks also count as characters. The command PRINT "" will cause the computer to print a blank line.

Now we can make the program much easier to use by adding labels to the output. Also, just as important, we can add a label to the input command. Since we have only one input command in our program, we'll be able to remember that whenever the computer types the question mark on the screen, we're supposed to type in the value of the radius. However, we'll have nightmares if we're in the middle of a complicated program, and all of a sudden a ? appears on the screen and we've forgotten what variable we're supposed to type in. Here's a new version of the circle program with labels for both the input and the output:

```
1    REM  PROGRAM TO CALCULATE THE AREA

2    REM  AND CIRCUMFERENCE

9    REM  P IS THE VALUE OF PI

10   P = 3.14159

14   PRINT "INPUT THE VALUE OF THE RADIUS"

15   INPUT R

19   REM  A IS THE AREA OF THE CIRCLE

20   A = P * R ↑ 2

29   REM C IS THE CIRCUMFERENCE OF THE CIRCLE

30   C = 2 * P * R
```

Continued

```
40    PRINT "THE AREA IS:"

50    PRINT A

60    PRINT "THE CIRCUMFERENCE IS:"

70    PRINT C

80    END
```

Now, when we type RUN, the screen will look like this:

INPUT THE VALUE OF THE RADIUS:

?

If we type 10, the following will appear:

THE AREA IS:

314.159

THE CIRCUMFERENCE IS:

62.8318

If we run the program a few more times, we will see that it is now much easier to understand what the results mean.

```
      RUN
```

INPUT THE VALUE OF THE RADIUS:

?

```
      7
```

THE AREA IS

153.93804

THE CIRCUMFERENCE IS:

43.982297

```
      ` RUN
```

INPUT THE VALUE OF THE RADIUS:

?

12

THE AREA IS:

452.38896

THE CIRCUMFERENCE IS:

75.39816

RUN

INPUT THE VALUE OF THE RADIUS:

?

16

THE AREA IS:

804.24704

THE CIRCUMFERENCE IS:

100.53088

This program fills up the screen very quickly. It would be useful if we could compress the output by putting more than one result on a line. We'll add this modification to the PRINT command. When two items in a PRINT statement are separated by a comma, both items will be printed on the same line. We can make a new version of the CIRCLE program:

```
 1  REM  PROGRAM TO CALCULATE THE AREA
 2  REM  AND CIRCUMFERENCE
 9  REM  P IS THE VALUE OF PI
10  P = 3.14159
14  PRINT "INPUT THE VALUE OF THE RADIUS:"
15  INPUT R
20  A = P * R ↑ 2
30  C = 2 * P * R
40  PRINT "AREA", "CIRCUMFERENCE"
```

Continued

        50   PRINT A, C

        60   END

   Now we can run this program:

   RUN

   INPUT THE VALUE OF THE RADIUS:

   ?

      16

   AREA   CIRCUMFERENCE
   804.24704   100.53088

      RUN

   INPUT THE VALUE OF THE RADIUS

   ?

      13

   AREA   CIRCUMFERENCE
   530.92871   81.68134

   When two items in a PRINT command are separated by commas, the computer will automatically decide how far apart to space them. Most computers will divide the screen into *print zones*, each 15 or 16 characters wide, and then print each new item in the next free print zone.

   Sometimes we'd like two items to be displayed right next to each other. In that case we will separate them with a semicolon, ;, instead of a comma. For example,

   PRINT "Hello";"Goodbye"

causes the output

HelloGoodbye

whereas the statement

   PRINT "Hello","Goodbye"

causes the output

Hello   Goodbye

Now we have all the commands we need to write our other programs. The temperature-conversion program looks like this:

1   REM TEMPERATURE-CONVERSION PROGRAM

10   PRINT "INPUT TEMPERATURE IN DEGREES F"

20   INPUT F

30   K = 273.2 + 5 ∗ (F−32)/9

40   PRINT "TEMPERATURE IN DEGREES K IS" ;K

50   END

Now we can run this program:

RUN

INPUT TEMPERATURE IN DEGREES F:

?

   0

TEMPERATURE IN DEGREES K IS: 255.4222

  RUN

INPUT TEMPERATURE IN DEGREES F:

?

  −459

TEMPERATURE IN DEGREES K IS: 0.4222

  RUN

INPUT TEMPERATURE IN DEGREES F:

?

  32

TEMPERATURE IN DEGREES K IS: 273.2

  RUN

INPUT TEMPERATURE IN DEGREES F:

Continued

?

212

TEMPERATURE IN DEGREES K IS: 373.2

And we can write the final version of the program that prints the height of the baseball:

```
 1  REM   PROGRAM TO CALCULATE HEIGHT OF
 2  REM   BASEBALL
10  PRINT "INPUT THE TIME:"
20  INPUT T
30  H = -0.5 * 9.8 T ↑ 2 + 100 * T + 15
40  PRINT "THE HEIGHT IS:" ;H
50  END
```

We can run this program:

RUN

INPUT THE TIME:

?

0

THE HEIGHT IS: 15

RUN

INPUT THE TIME:

?

5

THE HEIGHT IS: 392.5

RUN

INPUT THE TIME:

?

10

THE HEIGHT IS: 525

RUN

INPUT THE TIME:

?

20

THE HEIGHT IS: 55

THE <u>USING</u> COMMAND

There's one more useful feature we'd like to add to the PRINT command. It would help if we could control the number of decimal places the computer prints in its answers. We'll add an instruction with the keyword USING to tell the computer what *format* to use when it comes to a PRINT statement. The USING command needs to be followed by a *format string*. In the format string, the symbol # represents a numerical digit, and the symbol . represents a decimal point. The entire format string needs to be surrounded by quotation marks. Here's an example:

```
10  REM  PROGRAM TO DEMONSTRATE USE OF

11  REM  USING COMMAND

20  A = 100/3

30  PRINT USING "###";A

40  REM  IN THE FIRST EXAMPLE, 0 DIGITS

41  REM  WILL BE PRINTED TO THE RIGHT OF

42  REM  THE DECIMAL POINT

43  REM  NOTE THAT THE FORMAT STRING

44  REM  IS FOLLOWED BY A SEMICOLON

50  PRINT USING "###.#";A

60  REM  ONE DECIMAL PLACE WILL BE PRINTED

61  REM  IN THE SECOND EXAMPLE

70  PRINT USING "###.##";A
```

Continued

80 PRINT USING "###.####";A

90 END

The output is:

RUN

33

33.3

33.33

33.3333

If your version does not include a USING command, it is trickier to control the format of the output. We will see how to round numbers in Chapter 8.

SWAPPING VALUES

Let's try another example program to provide practice with assignment statements. We'll write a program that reads in values for two character strings and then swaps their values.

1 REM PROGRAM THAT (ALLEGEDLY) SWAPS THE VALUES OF

2 REM A$ AND B$

10 INPUT A$, B$

20 PRINT "A$=";A$;" B$=";B$

30 B$ = A$

40 A$ = B$

50 PRINT "A$=";A$;" B$=";B$

60 END

Note that we can put more than one variable in a single input command. When we see the question mark, we need to type in two strings separated by commas. However, this program does not work. Here is an example:

RUN

?

After you see the question mark, type:

GEORGE, WASHINGTON

The result is:

A$= GEORGE   B$=WASHINGTON

A$=GEORGE   B$=GEORGE

The program did not swap the values of A$ and B$. Instead, both A$ and B$ ended up with the same value ("GEORGE"). The problem occurred in line 30. When the computer executes the assignment B$ = A$, the old value of B$ is lost. Here is a new version of the program that will work:

```
1   REM  PROGRAM TO READ IN TWO STRINGS AND SWAPS THEIR VALUES

10  INPUT A$,B$

20  PRINT "A$=";A$;"  B$=";B$

30  T$ = B$

31  REM   T$ WILL TEMPORARILY HOLD THE ORIGINAL VALUE OF B$

40  B$ = A$

50  A$ = T$

60  PRINT "A$=";A$;"  B$=";B$

70  END
```

```
         RUN

     ? GEORGE, WASHINGTON

     A$=GEORGE B$=WASHINGTON

     A$=WASHINGTON B$=GEORGE
```

Microsoft BASIC makes it even easier to swap two variables since it comes with a built-in SWAP command. The command SWAP A$,B$ will swap the values of the two variables, just as our program did.

PRINTING OUTPUT

Now suppose that you would like some of the computer output to be sent to the printer instead of the screen. When you perform complicated calculations on a computer, you often like to have the results stored permanently on paper. The commands to print output vary considerably, depending on the type of computer you have. In Microsoft BASIC, the command LPRINT works exactly the same as PRINT except that the output is sent to the printer. The command LLIST will cause the program to be listed on the printer.

With Commodore computers type these commands:

OPEN 3,4

CMD3

Here, 4 is the device number for the printer, and 3 is a *file number*. (We will say more about file numbers in Chapter 9.) The command CMD3 directs the screen output to file number 3, which has been defined to be the printer in the OPEN statement. To return output to the screen, type

PRINT#3

CLOSE 3

An Apple computer contains several slots. The printer will be connected to one of these slots. If, for example, the printer is connected to slot 1, the command PR#1 will cause all subsequent output to be sent to the printer. The command PR#0 will cause output to return to the screen.

No matter what kind of computer you have, you must make sure that the printer is connected properly and turned on before you attempt to send output to it.

We have now achieved a very important advance—we have a machine that can remember its own instructions. Throughout the rest of the book we will see what a powerful and flexible tool the computer can be because of this capability. Before we move on, there are several more important points about BASIC programs that we will cover in the following notes.

NOTES

• The keyword LET is sometimes used at the beginning of an assignment statement. The use of LET is optional. For example, the command

P = 3.14159

does exactly the same thing as the command

LET P = 3.14159

The use of LET helps clarify the difference between an assignment statement and a mathematical equation

• Normally, whenever the computer comes to a new PRINT

statement, it will automatically start putting the output on a new line. However, if you put a comma or semicolon at the end of a PRINT statement, the computer will stay on the same line when it displays the output from the *next* PRINT statement. For example, if A is 35 and B is 64, then the commands

100 PRINT A

110 PRINT B

will produce the output

35

64

The commands

100 PRINT A,

110 PRINT B

will produce the output

35 64

• If we get tired of having all the answers start at the left-hand edge of the screen, we can add a command that will control the column where the output of a PRINT statement will be placed. We call this the TAB command since it acts like the tab key on a typewriter. For example, the command

PRINT TAB(20)X

will cause the value for X to be printed starting in column 20.

• Normally, in BASIC, we put one statement on each line. We can, however, put more than one statement on a line by separating the statements with colons (:). For example,

100 P = 3.14159 : C = 2 ∗ P ∗ R : A = P ∗ R ↑ 2

means exactly the same thing as:

100 P = 3.14159

110 C = 2 ∗ P ∗ R

120 A = P ∗ R ↑ 2

Putting more than one statement on a line often makes the

program difficult to read, but sometimes it is a good idea to do so.

• Many versions of BASIC provide a quicker way to attach a label to an input command. After the word INPUT, type a message (surrounded by quotation marks), then put in a comma or a semicolon, then type the name of the variable whose value you want to be read in. For example, when the computer reaches the command

INPUT "TYPE IN THE VALUE OF THE RADIUS";R

It will display the message

TYPE IN THE VALUE OF THE RADIUS

Then the computer will stop and wait for you to type in the value.
    If this feature is available on your computer, you will need to find out whether you need to use a comma or a semicolon after the message string. In Microsoft BASIC, you may use either a semicolon or a comma. If you use a semicolon, then a question mark is displayed after the message string.

• On a Commodore computer, you will need to specify a device number when you use the SAVE or LOAD command to store a program on a disk. The device number for a disk drive is usually 8, so the commands would look like:

SAVE "CIRCLE",8

and

LOAD "CIRCLE",8

• Once you start storing programs on disks, you will find that it is important to be able to keep track of what programs have been put on a particular disk. Each computer has a way of examining the *directory* of a disk. The directory is a list of the *files* contained on that disk. BASIC programs are stored as files, but files can also contain other information, such as data to be used by programs or documents for word processing.

    In Microsoft BASIC, type the command FILES to view a list of all files in the current drive. If the current drive is drive A: and you want to look at the list of files on drive B:, then type

FILES "B:*.*"

    A file name consists of the first part of the name followed by a period followed by three letters called the *file extension*. The file extension generally describes the type of the file. BASIC programs have the extension BAS. If you would like to see a list of only those files that are BASIC programs, then type

FILES " * .BAS"

On a Commodore computer, the directory is stored in a special file called $. To look at the directory, type

LOAD "$",8

(Here, 8 is the device number for the disk drive.) Then type LIST to see the directory. The BASIC programs will have the three letters PRG (for program) at the end of their file names. On an Apple computer, type the command CATALOG to see a list of the files on a disk.

• In Microsoft BASIC, you can put comments at the end of a program line by using a single quotation mark ' as a signal to start the comment. For example:

10   X = 0 ' THE COMPUTER WILL IGNORE EVERYTHING TO THE RIGHT

20   Y = 0 ' OF A SINGLE QUOTATION MARK

We will use single quotation marks for comments in some of the big programs in this book. If your computer does not allow the use of single quotation marks, you can still put a comment at the end of a line by using a colon and a REM statement. For example:

10   X = 0 : REM THIS IS A COMMENT

• The command LIST causes the entire program to be displayed, but you can easily direct the computer to list only part of the program. For example, the command LIST 30-60 will cause the computer to list only those program lines between line 30 and line 60, inclusive.

• Some computers, such as the Commodore, have a built-in key that represents the number pi.

• Some Commodore and Apple computers have screens that are only 40 characters wide. If you type a line longer than 40 characters, the computer will display the rest of the characters on the next screen line, but it will still treat them as if they comprised one line.

EXERCISES

1. Write a program that reads in the number of earned runs a pitcher has given up (*ER*), the number of whole innings he has pitched (*IP*), and the number of extra thirds of innings (*TI*) he has pitched, and then calculates the earned run average (*ERA*) from the formula

$$ERA \ = \ 9 \ \frac{ER}{IP + TI/3}$$

2.   Write a program that reads in put-outs (PO), assists (A), and errors (E), and then calculates the fielding average (FA) from the formula:

$$FA = \frac{PO + A}{PO + A + E}$$

3. Write a program that calculates slugging average from the formula:

$$SA = \frac{4HR + 3TR + 2DB + SI}{AB}$$

where HR = home runs, TR = triples, DB = doubles, SI = singles, and AB = times at bat.

4.   Write a program that reads in a distance in kilometers and converts it into a distance in miles.

5.   Write a program that reads in the price per liter of a brand of gasoline and then calculates the equivalent price per gallon of the same brand of gasoline.

6.   Write a program that reads in the base radius and altitude of a right circular cone and then calculates the volume from the formula

$$V = \frac{1}{3} \pi r^2 h$$

7.   Write a program that reads in the monthly inflation rate and converts it into an annual inflation rate.

8.   Write a program that reads in a character string and then creates a new character string consisting of three copies of the original string, one right after the other.

9.   Write a program that reads in a character string and then creates a new character string consisting of the original string surrounded by asterisks.

10. Write a program that reads in a distance and then calculates one-quarter of that distance, one-half of that distance, and three-quarters of that distance.

11. Write a program that reads in the speed you travel and the length of the trip and then calculates the time the trip will take.

12. Write a program that reads in the speed you travel and the time you have been traveling and then calculates the distance you have traveled.

13. Write a program that reads in the distance you have traveled and the time you have been traveling and then calculates the speed.

14. Write a program that reads in the mileage on your car at the time of your previous fillup, the amount of gas you purchased at your current fillup, and the mileage on your car at your current fillup, and then calculates the mileage performance of your car (in miles per gallon) during the time between the two fillups.

15. Write a program that reads in a person's hourly wage rate and then calculates annual income.

16. Write a program that reads in the vote totals for three candidates in an election and then calculates the percent of the total vote for each candidate.

17. Write a program that reads in the total population and the total area of a country and then calculates the population density of that country.

18. Write a program that calculates the total calories in a meal. Use assignment statements to assign values for the calories per unit for several foods, and then read in the quantity of each of those foods at this particular meal.

19. Write a program that reads in the price of three items purchased by a customer and then calculates the sales tax and the total amount due. Use an assignment statement at the start of the program to set the tax rate.

20. Write a program that reads in the price and the quantity sold for four items sold by a small store, and then calculates the total sales revenue for those four items.

21. Write a program that reads in the principal amount for a home loan (P), the monthly interest rate measured as a decimal fraction (r), and the number of months to repay the loan (n). Then have the program calculate the amount of the monthly payment from this formula:

$$\frac{Pr(1+r)^n}{(1+r)^n - 1}$$

CHAPTER 3

IF AND GOTO STATEMENTS

CALCULATING A PAYROLL

Suppose you have the job of computing the amount of pay earned by each of a large group of workers. To do that, you will need to write a program that reads in the number of hours a worker has worked during a particular week and then multiplies that number by the wage rate. If the wage is $7.00 per hour, the program might look like this:

```
1    REM   PAYROLL PROGRAM

10   INPUT "HOURS WORKED:" ;H

11   REM   NOTE THE COMMAND THAT PUTS THE LABEL

12   REM   ON THE SAME LINE AS THE INPUT STATEMENT

20   P = 7 * H

30   PRINT "PAY IS:" ;P

31   REM   NOTE THE USE OF THE SEMICOLON TO CAUSE

32   REM   THE TWO PRINT ITEMS TO BE PRINTED

33   REM   RIGHT NEXT TO EACH OTHER

40   END
```

This program works fine, except for one complication. Employees who work more than 40 hours per week get overtime pay at 1½ times the regular rate. However, you can write a new program that will calculate the pay for the workers that work overtime:

```
1    REM PAYROLL PROGRAM—FOR WORKERS WHO WORK OVERTIME

10   INPUT "HOURS WORKED:" ;H

20   P = 7 * 40 + 1.5 * 7 * (H – 40)

21   REM  EACH WORKER WORKS 40 HOURS AT THE REGULAR RATE
```

38

22   REM   AND (H – 40) HOURS AT THE OVERTIME RATE

30   PRINT "PAY IS:" ;P

40   END

In order to know which program to use, all we have to do is look at the number of hours worked. If H is greater than 40, we use the overtime program; otherwise we use the regular program. That method is cumbersome, though. It would be nice to find some way to write *one* program that handles both situations. To do this, we need to write a program that contains the word IF. We will use the word IF when we want the computer to do one action only if a specific condition is true. Here is a new version of the payroll program:

1   REM   PAYROLL PROGRAM

2   REM   FOR BOTH REGULAR AND OVERTIME WORKERS

10   INPUT "HOURS WORKED:" ;H

20   IF H > 40 THEN P = 7 * 40 + 1.5 * 7 * (H – 40)

30   IF H < = 40 THEN P = 7 * H

40   PRINT "PAY IS:" ;P

50   END

IF STATEMENTS

Lines 20 and 30 contain IF statements. An IF statement must contain a condition (which comes after IF) and an action (which comes after THEN). When the computer reaches line 20, it will check to see if the condition H>40 is true. The > symbol means "greater than," so the condition will be true if the number of hours typed in was greater than 40. If the condition is true, the computer will execute the action part of the statement:

$$P = 7 * 40 + 1.5 * 7 * (H – 40)$$

If the condition is false (in other words, the number of hours typed in is less than 40), the computer will ignore the action part of the statement and then proceed to the next statement. In our program, line 30 also contains a condition: H <= 40. The <= symbol means "less than or equal to." (Note that less than or equal to is normally written ≤ in mathematics, but that character is not normally available on a computer keyboard.) In our example, the condition in line 30 will be true only if the condition in line 20 was false, so the computer will execute the action part of either 20 or 30, depending on whether the worker has earned any overtime hours or not.

The general form of an IF statement is:

IF *condition* **THEN** *action*

where *condition* can be one of these:

expression1 = *expression2*

expression1 > *expression2* (greater than)

expression1 < *expression2* (less than)

expression1 >= *expression2* (greater than or equal to)

expression1 <= *expression2* (less than or equal to)

expression1 < > *expression2* (not equal to)

In some versions of BASIC, the word THEN is not used; in these cases condition statements can be written like these:

IF H<= 40 LET P = 7 ∗ 40

IF H<0 GOTO 100

Run our program a few times to make sure that it works:

RUN

HOURS WORKED: 40

PAY IS: 280

RUN

HOURS WORKED: 48

PAY IS: 364

RU N

HOURS WORKED: 24

PAY IS: 168

However, if there are many workers, you will have to run the program many times. It would be much more efficient if you didn't have to type RUN every time. We need a command that tells the computer to return to the beginning of the program when it has finished the calculations for each worker. We can add a new command: a GOTO command, which tells the computer to go to a different location in the program. The general form of the GOTO command is

> **GOTO** *statement number*

where *statement number* is the number of the next statement that you wish to have the computer execute.

1   REM PAYROLL PROGRAM

2   REM FOR BOTH REGULAR AND OVERTIME WORKERS

10   INPUT "HOURS WORKED:" ;H

20   IF H>40 THEN P = 7 * 40 + 1.5 * 7 * (H − 40)

30   IF H<= 40 THEN P = 7 * H

40   PRINT "PAY IS:" ;P

50   GOTO 10

60   END

This program allows you to do the payroll faster because you do not need to type RUN each time. For example:

RUN

HOURS WORKED: 42

PAY IS: 301

HOURS WORKED: 27

PAY IS: 189

HOURS WORKED: 50

PAY IS: 385

HOURS WORKED:

TRAPPED IN AN INFINITE LOOP

However, after you've done all the payroll and are ready to go home, the computer still displays this messasge:

HOURS WORKED:

It is waiting for you to type in the number of hours for another worker. The program will go around in circles forever, never reaching the END statement. We can call this type of program an *infinite loop* program. We need a way to avoid this, since you don't want to type an infinite number of numbers. Fortunately, every computer provides a way to interrupt a program so that you can escape the clutches of an endless loop. In Microsoft BASIC, Applesoft BASIC, and other versions, you can interrupt a program by holding down the control key and typing C.

The control key on the left side of the keyboard does not do anything when it pressed by itself. When pressed with another key, it sends a code to the computer. Pressing control and C is called "control-C." You will find other uses for the control key, depending on what software package you are using. The execution of a program on a Commodore computer can be interrupted by pressing the key marked RUN/STOP on the left side of the keyboard. Other types of computers have a key marked BREAK to fulfill this function. In some versions of BASIC, a program can be interrupted by pressing the control and break keys together. You will have to learn how to interrupt a program on your own computer.

In order to illustrate what is happening, we can represent the program with a diagram, using arrows to show what is next to be executed. (See Figure 3–1.) This type of diagram is called a *flow-*

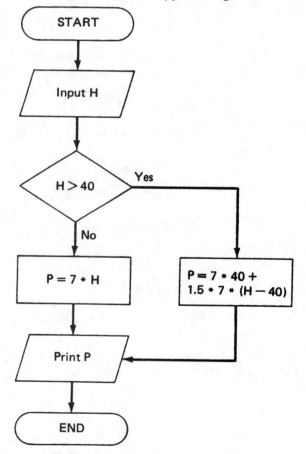

Figure 3–1

chart. A flowchart can be used to represent a computer program, with different actions represented by different shapes. An oval represents starting or ending; a parallelogram represents input or output; a diamond represents a decision such that one action is executed if the given condition is true and another path is followed if the condition is false; and rectangles represent other types of actions taken by the computer.

There should be a way to write the program without the infinite loop. We can use an IF statement to break out of the loop. Since no worker will have a negative number of hours, we can use a negative number as a signal that it is time to go to the end of the program. We write a new flowchart such as the one in Figure 3–2.

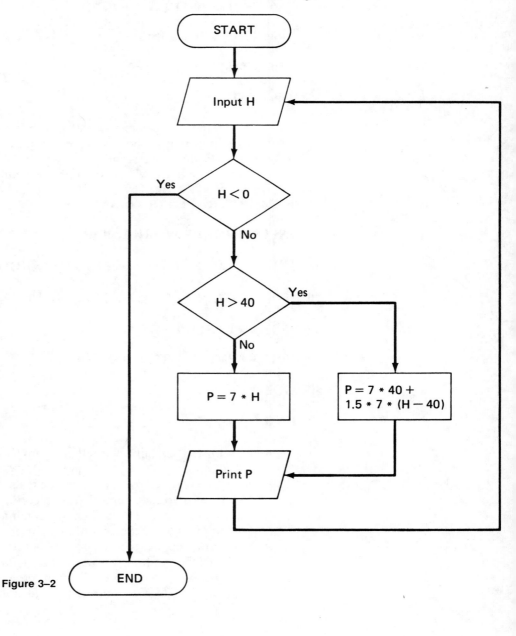

Figure 3–2

The program now looks like this:

```
1   REM  PAYROLL PROGRAM

2   REM  FOR BOTH REGULAR AND OVERTIME WORKERS

10  INPUT "HOURS WORKED:";H

15  IF H<0 THEN GOTO 60

20  IF H>40 THEN P = 7 * 40 + 1.5 * 7 * (H – 40)

30  IF H<= 40 THEN P = 7 * H

40  PRINT "PAY IS:";P

50  GOTO 10

60  END
```

Suppose we want to have more than one action executed if the condition is true. For example, we may wish to have a special message displayed identifying each worker who has worked overtime. Here is a new version of the program:

```
1   REM  PAYROLL PROGRAM

10  INPUT "HOURS WORKED:";H

15  IF H<0 THEN GOTO 60 : REM  STOP IF HOURS ARE NEGATIVE

20  IF H>40 THEN P = 7 * 40 + 1.5 * 7 * (H – 40) : PRINT "OVERTIME"

30  IF H<= 40 THEN P = 7 * H

40  PRINT "PAY IS:";P

50  GOTO 10

60  END
```

Line 20 contains two action commands after the word THEN: P = 7 * 40 + 1.5 * 7 * (H – 40) and PRINT "OVERTIME". Note that they are separated by a colon, which is the symbol we use in order to separate two statements that are placed on the same line. Both of these actions will be executed if the condition H>40 is true; neither will be executed if the condition is false.

Now, suppose we have several actions that need to be accomplished if the condition is true. If these actions will not all fit on one line, then we need to use a different programming tactic: we will need to use GOTOs to direct the execution of the program into different blocks, depending on the conditions.

```
1    REM   PAYROLL PROGRAM

10   REM   THIS PROGRAM COUNTS THE NUMBER OF WORKERS

11    REM   AND THE NUMBER OF HOURS FOR BOTH OVERTIME

12   REM   AND REGULAR WORKERS

20   W = 7  : REM   WAGE RATE

30   T = 0  : REM   TOTAL VALUE OF PAYROLL

40   N1 = 0 : REM   NUMBER OF REGULAR WORKERS

50   N2 = 0 : REM   NUMBER OF OVERTIME WORKERS

60   H1 = 0 : REM   NUMBER OF REGULAR HOURS

70   H2 = 0 : REM   NUMBER OF OVERTIME HOURS

80   INPUT "HOURS WORKED:";H

90   IF H>70 THEN PRINT "MISTAKE": GOTO 80

100   IF H<0 THEN GOTO 270  :  REM   STOP IF HOURS ARE NEGATIVE

110   IF H>40 THEN GOTO 170  :  REM   GOTO OVERTIME SECTION

119   REM

120   REM —— REGULAR PAY SECTION ——

130   P = W * H

140   N1 = N1 + 1

150   H1 = H1 + H

160   GOTO 230  :  REM   GOTO PRINT PAY SECTION

169   REM

170   REM —— OVERTIME PAY SECTION ——

180   P = W * H + 1.5 * W * (H − 40)

190   N2 = N2 + 1

200   H1 = H1 + 40
```

Continued

```
210   H2 = H2 + (H - 40)

220   GOTO 230  :  REM   GOTO PRINT PAY SECTION

229   REM

230   REM ——— PRINT PAY SECTION ———

240   PRINT "PAY IS:";P

250   T = T + P : REM   T REPRESENTS THE TOTAL PAYROLL

260   GOTO 80  : REM   READ IN HOURS FOR NEXT WORKER

269   REM

270   REM ——— CONCLUDING SECTION ———

280   PRINT "NUMBER OF WORKERS WITH NO OVERTIME:";N1

290   PRINT "NUMBER OF WORKERS WITH OVERTIME:";N2

300   PRINT"TOTAL NUMBER OF REGULAR HOURS:";H1

310   PRINT "TOTAL NUMBER OF OVERTIME HOURS:";H2

320   PRINT "TOTAL PAYROLL:";T

330   END
```

This program is more complicated because several new features have been added. Notice how the program is divided into sections, with a REM statement identifying the start of each section. We will find that as our programs become more and more complicated, it is crucial to write them as a collection of smaller pieces. Lines 119, 169, 229, and 269 are blank REM statements included to separate the different sections. The computer doesn't care if these blank REM statements are included, but it helps to include them because it makes the program easier for people to read. If you look closely at the program, you will see that the GOTO statement in line 220 could have been left out; however, by including it we have made it more clear to a human reader where the overtime pay section ends.

In this program, we have used the variable W to represent the wage rate. This will make it much easier to use the program if the wage rate changes at some point in the future. In that case, all we would need to do is change line 20.

Suppose that we accidentally typed in 400 as the number of hours for a worker. Clearly that must be a mistake, so it would help if the computer would tell us that such a mistake had been made and then ask us to enter the correct value. The computer has no way of knowing what the correct input should be, so we cannot include a line in the program that will catch every possible error. However, it helps to have the computer let us know if we make a very obvious error.

In our example, suppose we have a rule that no worker may work more than 70 hours per week. In that case, we know that an error must have been made if the number of hours that is typed in is greater than 70. Line 90 is included in the program to check for this error. If the condition H>70 is true, then two actions are performed: the word "MISTAKE" is printed, and the computer will return to line 80 and ask the user to type in a new value.

AND/OR

Suppose we decide that any worker who works more than 50 hours per week should be paid at twice the regular rate for every hour over 50. We now need to divide the workers into four groups according to the number of hours worked:

less than 40 hours:	**regular pay**
greater than 40 and less than 50:	**overtime pay**
greater than 50 and less than 70:	**double-time pay**
greater than 70:	**mistake**

In order to test for conditions like this, we will use the key word AND. The use of AND makes it possible to include two conditions in an IF statement; thus, the action part of the statement will be executed only if both conditions are true. For example, in this IF statement:

IF (A>10) AND (B$="GEORGE") THEN PRINT"HI THERE!"

the command PRINT "HI THERE" will be executed only if both conditions are met: A>10 *and* B$="GEORGE".

Here is a rewritten version of the payroll program.

```
1   REM   PAYROLL PROGRAM

10  INPUT "HOURS WORKED";H

14  REM   IF H<0, THEN IT IS TIME TO GO TO THE END

15  IF H<0 THEN GOTO 70

20  IF H<40 THEN P = 7 * H

30  IF (H>40) AND (H<=50) THEN P=7*40+1.5*7*(H−40)

40  IF (H>50) AND (H<=70) THEN P=7*40+1.5*7*10+2*7*(H−50)

50  IF H>70 THEN PRINT "MISTAKE! ENTER AGAIN":GOTO 10
```

Continued

60   PRINT "PAY IS:";P

65   GOTO 10

70   END

The pay of the regular workers will be processed in line 20; the pay of the overtime workers will be processed in line 30; and the pay of the double-time workers will be processed in line 40.

We can use the word OR if we would like an action to be executed if either of two conditions is true. For example:

10   INPUT X

20   IF (X=7) OR (X=11) THEN PRINT "WE WON!"

These lines will then print the messsage WE WON! if the value typed in for X is either 7 or 11.

One very useful feature found in some versions of BASIC, such as Microsoft BASIC, is the ELSE clause. If your version contains an ELSE clause, you can tell the computer to do one thing if a condition is true and do something else if the condition is false. The general form of an ELSE clause is:

IF *condition* **THEN** *statement1* **ELSE** *statement2*

Statement1 will be executed if the *condition* is true, and *statement2* will be executed if the condition is false. Either *statement1* or *statement2* can be a GOTO command. If neither one is a GOTO command, the next program line will be executed after the computer has performed *statement1* or *statement2*, whichever was appropriate for this instance.

Here is an example:

20   IF H<40 THEN P=7 * H ELSE P=7 * 40 + 1.5 * 7 * (H − 40)

Unfortunately, many versions of BASIC do not allow ELSE clauses, so we will not use ELSE very much in this book. If you cannot use ELSE, then you are often forced to fill your programs with crisscrossed GOTO commands, which can be confusing if you are not careful.

ON/GOTO

The IF/GOTO command only gives us two choices: either go or not go somewhere. When it would be helpful to allow for several different choices, the ON/GOTO command can be used. The general form of an ON/GOTO command is:

> ON *variable* GOTO *sn1, sn2, sn3,...*
>
> IF *variable* has the value 1, the computer will go to statement number *sn1*; if *variable* has the value 2, the computer will go to statement number *sn2*; and so on.

Here is an example:

```
10     INPUT "ENTER YOUR PLACE:";P

20     ON P GOTO 30,40,50,60

25     GOTO 70  ' IN MICROSOFT BASIC THE "ON GOTO" STATEMENT WILL

26     REM        BE IGNORED IF P DOES NOT HAVE ONE OF THE VALUES 1,2,3, OR 4

30       PRINT "FIRST PLACE! ******** "

35       GOTO 80

40       PRINT "SECOND PLACE"

45       GOTO 80

50       PRINT "THIRD PLACE!"

55       GOTO 80

60       PRINT "FOURTH PLACE!"

65       GOTO 80

70       PRINT "NOT ONE OF THE TOP FOUR FINISHERS"

80       END
```

Line 10 asks you to type in the value of P. Line 20 contains the ON/GOTO command. If P is 1, the computer will go to line 30; if P = 2, it will go to 40; if P = 3, it will go to 50; if P = 4, it will go to 60. You may be wondering what happens if the value of P is not 1, 2, 3, or 4. The result in that case depends on the version of BASIC you are using. In some versions, an error message may be printed; in other versions, the computer will simply ignore the ON/GOTO command and proceed to execute the next line. We are assuming that this is what the computer will do for this program. We will see later that use of the ON/GOTO command is very helpful in writing programs with menus that give the user a choice of what the computer should do.

NOTE
• Some versions of BASIC, such as Microsoft BASIC, provide a special command to direct the computer to execute a set of statements while a specific condition is true. Type

WHILE *condition*

before the statements to be executed, and type

WEND

at the end of those statements. The *condition* can be any true-or-false expression, such as X>10 or A$="YES". When the computer first reaches the WHILE condition, it will check to see that the *condition* is true. If it is, the computer will execute all of the statements until it reaches the WEND statement. At that point, the computer will check again to see if the *condition* is true. If it is, the statements will be executed again; if not, the computer will jump to the first line following the WEND statement.

Here is an example:

```
1   REM  THE COMPUTER WILL KEEP READING H AND CALCULATING

2   REM   P UNTIL A NEGATIVE NUMBER IS ENTERED FOR H

5   INPUT "W:";W

10  INPUT "H:";H

20  WHILE H>0

30  P = H * W

40  PRINT "PAY IS:";P

50  INPUT "H:";H

60  WEND
```

EXERCISES
1. Write a program that compares the unit prices of several types of cereals in different-sized boxes. For each type of cereal, have the program read in the price of the box and the number of grams of cereal contained in that box. After all the items have been read in, have the computer print the price of the item with the lowest price per gram.

2. Write a program that reads in a number and then calculates the square root of that number. Have the computer print a warning message if a negative number is entered.

3. Rewrite the program in exercise 2 so that the computer will automatically repeat the calculation until the user types in the number 0.

4. Write a program that reads in a temperature. If the temperature is less than 32°, print the message "It's freezing!"; if the temperature is between 32° and 60°, print the message "Too cold!"; if the temperature is between 60° and 80°, print the message "Just right!"; if the temperature is greater than 80°, print the message "Too hot!"

5. Write a number-guessing program. The first person types a secret number. Then the second person types a guess for the number. The computer responds by stating if the guess is equal to the secret number, greater than that number, or less than that number. Have the computer continue to ask for new guesses until the second person has learned the value of the secret number.

6. Write a program that reads in the win-loss record of the first-place team, then reads in the win-loss record of another team, and then prints out how many games the other team is behind the first-place team.

7. Write a program that reads in the win-loss record of the first-place team and of the second-place team, then reads in the number of games remaining for each team, and then calculates the first-place team's "clinching" number; in other words, the number of first-place team wins plus second-place team losses that will be required for the first-place team to clinch first place.

8. Write a program that calculates powers of 2, such as 2, 4, 8, 16, 32, and so on. After each result is displayed, have the computer read in a number. If the number is 1, the program will continue to the next power of 2; if the number is 0, the program will stop.

9. Write a program that reads in a number from 3 to 5 and prints one of these messages: "TRIANGLE", "QUADRILAT-ERAL", or "PENTAGON". Write the program three different ways:

(a) using ON/GOTO
(b) using several GOTOs
(c) using no GOTOs

10. Consider a firm whose workers are divided into four classifications: class 1 (paid $4 per hour), class 2 (paid $6), class 3 (paid $8), and class 4 (paid $10). Write a program that reads in the classification for a worker and the number of hours and then calculates the rate of regular and overtime pay.

11. Here is an income tax table, showing the amount of tax owed by a single taxpayer:

If taxable income is over this amount:	but not over this amount:	then your tax is this amount:	plus this percent:	of the amount of your income that is over this amount:
0	17,850	0	15%	0
17,850	43,150	2,677.50	28%	17,850
43,150	89,560	9,761.50	33%	43,150
89,560	—	25,076.80	28%	89,560

Write a program that reads in the value of taxable income and then calculates the amount of tax due.

12. It is often useful to determine if one number is divisible by another number. For example, 12 is divisible by 2, 3, 4, and 6, but it is not divisible by 5. Here is an expression that determines if A is divisible by B:

IF INT(A/B) = (A/B)

INT stands for "Integer Part." Write a program that reads in two numbers and determines if the first number is divisible by the second number.

13. Write a program that reads in a year and determines if it is a leap year.

14. Write a program that calculates the number of trailing zeros in a whole number. For example, 1050 has one trailing zero; 9,000,000 has six trailing zeros; and 327 has no trailing zeros.

15. Write a program that reads in a number and determines if it is a prime number. (A prime number is a number that is not divisible by any numbers except itself and 1.)

16. Write a program that prints all the *prime factors* of a number. For example, the prime factors of 12 are 2 * 2 * 3, and the prime factors of 60 are 2 * 2 * 3 * 5.

CHAPTER 4

LOOPS

CALCULATING AVERAGES

Suppose the following are the figures for how many dollars you spent on groceries each day last week: Sunday, 0; Monday, 10; Tuesday, 12; Wednesday, 45; Thursday, 6; Friday, 7; and Saturday, 5. To figure out your normal daily consumption, you need to calculate the average of these seven numbers. One way is to type on the computer

PRINT (0 + 10 + 12 + 45 + 6 + 7 + 5)7

and the computer will show the result:

12.142857

A better way is to write a program that will automatically calculate the average of any seven numbers. Then you can use the same program for *next* week's grocery bill as well.
Here's one possibility:

```
1   REM  PROGRAM TO CALCULATE THE AVERAGE OF 7 NUMBERS

10  INPUT X

20  T = X

25  INPUT X

30  T = T + X

40  INPUT X

45  T = T + X

50  INPUT X

55  T = T + X

60  INPUT X

65  T = T + X
```

```
70    INPUT X

75    T = T + X

80    INPUT X

90    T = T + X

100   PRINT "THE AVERAGE IS:";T/7

110   END
```

At first you should be suspicious of the statement T = T + X, because T can't be equal to T + X, unless X happens to equal 0. However, remember that the statement is not an equation; it's a computer assignment statement. This is the way it works. First it calculates the value of the expression on the right of the equal sign. Then it stores that value in the box labeled by the variable name on the left of the equal sign. There's no reason why we can't use the old value of a variable to help calculate its new value.

The main problem with this program is that it is too long. We shouldn't have to type the instruction INPUT X seven times. Let's try this program:

```
1    REM PROGRAM TO CALCULATE THE AVERAGE OF 7 NUMBERS

9    REM  FIRST, SET T EQUAL TO 0

10   T = 0

20   INPUT X

30   T = T + X

40   GOTO 20

50   PRINT "THE AVERAGE IS";T/7

60   END
```

LOOPS

This program will execute the instruction INPUT X 7 times. But there's nothing to make it stop after the seventh time. *Every* time the computer gets to line 40, it will jump back to line 20. This is another infinite loop program. To avoid the infinite loop, we need some way to count the number of times the computer has gone around the loop. Suppose we take a particular variable, start it at 0, and then add 1 to it every time we go through the loop. That variable will then count the number of times we have gone through the loop.

Figure 4–1 shows a flowchart using this idea. Here is the program:

1   REM PROGRAM TO CALCULATE THE AVERAGE OF 7 NUMBERS

2   REM I TELLS HOW MANY TIMES THE COMPUTER HAS

3   REM   GONE AROUND THE LOOP

4   REM I IS INITIALLY SET TO 0

5   I = 0

9   REM T IS INITIALLY SET TO 0—T IS THE TOTAL

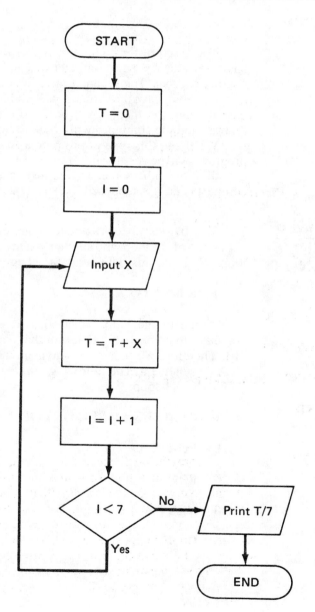

Figure 4–1

```
10    T = 0

20    INPUT X

30    T = T + X

40    I = I + 1

50    IF I < 7 GOTO 20

60    PRINT "THE AVERAGE IS:";T/7

70    END
```

The first time the computer reaches line 50, the variable I will have the value 1, so the computer will go back to line 20 and input another number. The second time, I will have the value 2; subsequently, it will have the values 3, 4, 5, and 6. Finally, on the seventh pass through the loop, I will be 7, so the IF instruction will be ignored and the computer will go on to line 60.

We'll call this type of program a *loop* program. These loop programs will be very useful. However, the instructions for the loop are still too cumbersome. There must be a simpler way to tell the computer that it's supposed to execute a loop seven times.

THE FOR AND NEXT COMMANDS

We obviously need two statements: one statement to mark the beginning of the loop, and another statement to mark the end of the loop. We'll put this statement at the beginning of the loop:

FOR I = 1 TO 7

At the end of the loop, we need a statement that will tell the computer to go back to the start of the loop and use the *next* value of I. Therefore we'll call the statement at the end of the loop the NEXT I statement. The following program is a simple example of a FOR-NEXT loop:

```
1     REM   EXAMPLE OF FOR-NEXT LOOP

10    FOR A = 1 TO 5

20    PRINT A

30    NEXT A

40    END
```

The output is:

RUN

1

2

3

4

5

It's easy to write a program to find an average by using a FOR-NEXT loop:

```
1   REM   PROGRAM TO FIND THE AVERAGE OF 7 NUMBERS

2   REM      USING A FOR-NEXT LOOP

10   T = 0

20   FOR I = 1 TO 7

21           REM  STATEMENT 20 IS THE START OF THE LOOP

30           INPUT X

40           T = T + X

50   NEXT I

51   REM   STATEMENT 50 IS THE END OF THE LOOP

60   PRINT "THE AVERAGE IS:";T/7

70   END
```

(Since we are free to put blanks in the program wherever we wish, we'll indent the statements in the middle of the loop to make the program easier to read.)

Run this program with some different sets of numbers to make sure that it works.

Numbers	Average
1,2,3,4,5,6,7	4
3,3,3,3,3,1,5	3
16, −2, 27, 4, −8, 35, 3	10.71428
0.96, 0.83, 0.51, 0.89, 0.04, 0.86, 0.47	0.6514285

Now we need to write out the general form for the loop command. We won't always want to use the letter I as the counter variable, or always execute the loop exactly seven times.

LOOP COMMAND

> FOR *counter* = *start* TO *stop*
>   *statements in middle of loop*
> NEXT *counter*

Here *counter* is the variable that will be increased by 1 each time; *start* is the initial value of the counter variable; and *stop* is the final value of the counter variable. (In the program shown above to calculate averages, *counter* is I, *start* is 1, and *stop* is 7.) Note that *start* and *stop* can be numbers, variable names, or expressions; but *counter* must be a variable name.

The loop command greatly increases the value of the computer. Now we only have to type in the set of instructions once, and the computer executes those instructions as many times as we want.

As another example of a loop, let's write a program that prints a table of the numbers from 1 to 10 with their square roots.

```
1   REM  PROGRAM TO PRINT TABLE OF SQUARE ROOTS
10  PRINT "NUMBER","SQUARE ROOT"
20  FOR X = 1 TO 10
30  PRINT USING "###.###";X,SQR(X)
40  NEXT X
50  END
```

The output looks like this:

NUMBER	SQUARE ROOT
1.0000	1.0000
2.0000	1.1414
3.0000	1.7320
4.0000	2.0000
5.0000	2.2360
6.0000	2.4494
7.0000	2.6457
8.0000	2.8284
9.0000	3.0000
10.000	3.1622

THE **STEP** COMMAND

It's boring to make the counter variable go up by 1 each time, so let's make a command that allows us to change the amount by which the counter variable is incremented. The keyword STEP will fulfill this function. For example, the command

FOR K = 0 TO 30 STEP 5

causes the counter variable K to take on the values 0, 5, 10, 15, 20, 25, and 30. Here is a program that prints a table of the heights of the baseball at different times:

```
1    REM  PROGRAM TO PRINT TABLE OF HEIGHT OF BASEBALL

10   PRINT "TIME""HEIGHT"

20   FOR T = 0 TO 20 STEP 2

30         H = –0.5 * 9.8 * T ↑ 2 + 100 * T + 15

40         PRINT T, H

50   NEXT T

60   END
```

The output is:

TIME	HEIGHT
0	15
2	195.4
4	336.6
6	438.6
8	501.4
10	525
12	509.4
14	454.6
16	360.6
18	227.4
20	55.0001

Here is the general form of the STEP command:

STEP COMMAND

FOR *counter =start* TO *stop* STEP *increment*
        statements in middle of loop

NEXT *counter*

The first time the loop is executed, the variable *counter* will be equal to *start*. The second time, *counter* will be equal to (*start* + *increment*), and during each subsequent pass through the loop the value of *counter* will be increased by *increment*. (If the phrase STEP *increment* is left out, *counter* will automatically be increased by 1 each time, just as it was in the programs earlier in this chapter.)

LOOPS INSIDE LOOPS

Here's another clever device with loops. We can put one loop inside another. Suppose you need to know what your bank balance will be at the end of each of 10 years, using several possible values of the interest rate. If you put $100 in the bank today, after *n* years you will have $100(1 + r)^n$, where *r* is the interest rate. Consider seven possible values for the interest rate: $r = 0.03, 0.04, 0.05, 0.06, 0.07, 0.08,$ and 0.09. Here's a program to print a table of compound interest:

```
1    REM  PROGRAM TO PRINT TABLE OF COMPOUND INTEREST

2    REM  R IS THE INTEREST RATE

3    REM  N IS THE NUMBER OF YEARS MONEY HAS BEEN IN BANK

4    REM  M IS THE BALANCE IN THE ACCOUNT

5    REM  THE INITIAL BALANCE IS 100

10   FOR N = 1 TO 10

20       PRINT

21       REM   LINE 20 CAUSES A BLANK LINE TO BE PRINTED

30       FOR R = 0.03 TO 0.09 STEP 0.01

40           M = 100 * (1 + R) ↑ N

50           PRINT USING "####.##";M,

51           REM   NOTE THAT THE COMMA AT THE END

52           REM      OF LINE 50 CAUSES THE OUTPUT

53           REM      FROM THE NEXT PRINT COMMAND TO

54           REM      BE PRINTED ON THE SAME LINE

60       NEXT R

70   NEXT N

80   END
```

Following is the output from the program. (We have to add the labels for the rows and columns manually. We can write a program that has the computer add the labels automatically. See exercise 2.)

N	R:0.03	0.04	0.05	0.06	0.07	0.08	0.09
1	103.00	104.00	105.00	106.00	107.00	108.00	109.00
2	106.09	108.16	110.25	112.36	114.49	116.64	118.81
3	109.27	112.48	115.76	119.10	122.50	125.97	129.50
4	112.55	116.98	121.55	126.24	131.07	136.04	141.15
5	115.92	121.66	127.62	133.82	140.25	146.93	153.86
6	119.40	126.53	134.00	141.85	150.07	158.68	167.71
7	122.98	131.59	140.71	150.36	160.57	171.38	182.80
8	126.67	136.85	147.74	159.38	171.81	185.09	199.25
9	130.47	142.33	155.13	168.94	183.84	199.90	217.18
10	134.39	148.02	162.88	179.08	196.71	215.89	236.73

We'll call the inside loop a *nested loop* since it is nested inside the outer loop. Here's another program that is an example of a nested loop:

```
10    FOR I = 1 TO 2
20        PRINT
30        PRINT "******"
40        PRINT
50        FOR J = 1 TO 3
60            PRINT I,J
70        NEXT J
80    NEXT I
90    END
```

The output is:

```
******

1         1

1         2

1         3

******

2         1

2         2

2         3
```

Note that the counter variable for the outer loop stays at its initial value while the computer runs through the entire inner loop. Then, after the inner loop is completed, the value of the outer counter variable is increased, and the entire inner loop is run again. If the outer loop has m repetitions and the inner loop has n repetitions, the statements in the middle of the inner loop will be executed $m \times n$ times.

Here are two rules that need to be followed when using loops.

LOOP RULE 1

> A GOTO statement can never cause the computer to jump inside a loop from outside a loop.

[If a GOTO statement did cause a computer to jump into a loop, it would reach the NEXT statement and not know what the next value of the counter variable is supposed to be. (A GOTO statement can cause the computer to jump around inside a loop, or a GOTO statement can cause a computer to leave the loop before reaching the last value of the counter variable.)

LOOP RULE 2

> If the FOR statement of one loop is inside another loop, then the NEXT statement for the inner loop must come before the NEXT statement for the outer loop.

For example,

```
FOR A = 1 TO 10
    FOR B = 2 TO 6
    NEXT B
NEXT A
```

is allowed, but

```
FOR A = 1 TO 10
    FOR B = 2 TO 6
NEXT A
    NEXT B
```

is not allowed.

NOTE

• The STEP value can be negative, in which case the counter variable will be *decreased* during every pass through the loop. (In that case make sure that the final value is *smaller* than the initial value.) For example, the program

```
10  FOR I = 10 TO 0 STEP -2
20  PRINT I
30  NEXT I
40  END
```

has the output

10

8

6

4

2

0

EXERCISES

1. Write a program that reads in a value for n, then reads in n numbers, and then prints the average of the n numbers.

2. Write a program identical to the program to calculate interest given in this chapter, except have the computer automatically print headings for the interest rate and the number of years.

3. The Tourist Trap Souvenir Manufacturing Firm, Inc., is a monopolist. There is the following relationship between the price it charges (p) and the quantity (q) of output it can sell:

$$q = 100 - \tfrac{1}{2}p$$

The cost (c) of making each souvenir is given by

$$c = \tfrac{1}{2}q^2 + 10$$

Write a program that calculates the firm's profits for each possible value of the price from $p = 0$ to $p = 200$. Have the program identify the price that leads to the maximum profits.

4. Suppose p is the principal amount currently owed on a home mortgage. If s is the monthly payment on the mortgage and r is the monthly interest rate, then the amount rp is the amount of interest paid in a given month and $(s - rp)$ is the amount that is subtracted from the principal that month. Write a program that reads in the initial value of the principal, the interest rate, and the monthly payment amount. Then, for each month, have the program print out the principal amount remaining after that month. Finally

have the computer tell how many months it will take until the principal amount is reduced to zero (until the house is paid for).

5. Print a table listing the areas and circumferences of circles that have radii of 1, 2, 3, 4,...,20.

6. Write a program that reads in at-bat totals and the number of hits for nine baseball players and then prints their batting averages.

7. Write a program that reads in the interest rate and the initial balance in a bank account and then prints a list of how much money will be in the account for each year for the next 30 years.

Are the programs in exercises 8 to 13 valid BASIC programs? If not, tell what is wrong.

```
8.  10   FOR I = 1 TO 20

    20   T = 0

    30   FOR J = 15 TO 21

    40   Q = (I + J)/20 * (I/J)

    50   T = T + Q

    60   NEXT I

    70   PRINT T,Q,I,J

    80   NEXT J

    90   END

9.  10   T = 0

    20   U = 0

    30   FOR I = 1 TO 17 STEP 2

    40   T = T + I ↑ 2

    50   PRINT I,T

    60   NEXT I

    70   NEXT I

    80   FOR I = 2 TO 18 STEP 2

    90   U = U + I ↑ 2
```

```
100   PRINT I,U
110   NEXT I
120   END
```

10.
```
10   FOR R = 0 TO 90 STEP 10
20   IF COS(R) = 0 GOTO 60
30   T = SIN(R)/COS(R)
40   PRINT R,T
50   GOTO 70
60   PRINT R,"INFINITY"
70   NEXT R
80   END
```

11.
```
10   PRINT "INPUT N:"
20   INPUT N
40   FOR A = 5 TO 27
30   IF N<50 GOTO 60
50   Q = A ↑ 2
60   T = Q * N
70   PRINT T,Q,A
80   NEXT A
90   END
```

12.
```
10   FOR A = 1 TO 10
20   FOR B = 1 TO 10
30   C = A * B
40   PRINT C
50   NEXT B
60   PRINT
```

Continued

```
70    NEXT A

80    END
```

13.
```
10    FOR Q = 2 TO 4 STEP 0.01

20    X = (Q ↑ 2/3.45) ↑ Q

30    IF X < 1 GOTO 70

40    PRINT X

50    NEXT Q

60    GOTO 80

70    PRINT "X IS LESS THAN 1"

80    END
```

14. For teams that have played 1, 2, 3, 4,...20 games, print a table showing their winning percentages for every possible value of their won-loss records.

15. Write a program that reads in a number n and then calculates $n!$ (*n factorial*), which is equal to

$$n! = n * (n{-}1) * (n{-}2) * (n{-}3) * ... * 4 * 3 * 2 * 1$$

16. Write a program that calculates the *present value* of a stream of future receipts. If r is the interest rate and X_i is the amount that will be received in year i, then the present value (PV) can be found from the formula

$$PV = X_0 + \frac{X_1}{(1+r)} + \frac{X_2}{(1+r)^2} + \frac{X_3}{(1+r)^3} + \frac{X_4}{(1+r)^4} + ...$$

(Note: The interest rate r is measured as a decimal fraction. For example, an interest rate of 8 percent is written 0.08.) Present-value calculations are very important in financial decision-making situations.

17. Suppose you are planning to save s dollars every year for n years. Suppose that the interest rate is r, and that the bank pays interest once a year at the end of each year. You will leave all of the interest you earn during that time in the bank. What will be the balance in your account at the end of the n years?

18. Write a program that (1) reads in a value for n; (2) reads in n numbers (call them $x_1, x_2, x_3, ... x_n$); (3) calculates the *expected*

value of x:

$$E(x), = \frac{x_1 + x_2 + \dots + x_n}{n}$$

(4) calculates the expected value of x^2:

$$E(x^2) = \frac{x_1^2 + x_2^2 + \dots + x_n^2}{n}$$

(5) calculates the *standard deviation* (σ) from the formula:

$$\sigma = \sqrt{E(x^2) - [E(x)]^2}$$

CHAPTER 5

ARRAYS

Computers can be very useful for keeping track of financial data. Suppose that you divide your expenditures into six broad categories, and the following table tells you how much you spent on each category last week:

	Category	Amount Spent
(food)	1	36
(clothing)	2	64
(transportation)	3	11
(entertainment)	4	17
(books)	5	14
(other)	6	12

It would be useful to know what fraction of the total expenditure goes to each of these six categories.

Here is one possible program:

```
1   REM   PROGRAM TO CALCULATE FRACTION OF SPENDING
2   REM      BY CATEGORY
10  T = 0
20  FOR I = 1 TO 6
30          PRINT "INPUT AMOUNT FOR CATEGORY";I
40          INPUT X
50          T = T + X
60  NEXT I
70  PRINT "TOTAL IS:";T
80  FOR J = 1 TO 6
90          PRINT "INPUT AMOUNT FOR CATEGOR";J
100         INPUT X
110         S = X/T
120         PRINT "SHARE OF EXPENDITURES OF CATEGORY";J
130         PRINT S
140 NEXT J
150 END
```

This program has one problem, though: each amount must be typed in twice. We can, however, store the amount for each category the first time it is read in, and then we won't have to input all the amounts the second time. All we need to do is pick a letter for each category.

We can use A to stand for expenditures in category 1, B for expenditures in category 2, and so on.

Here's the new program:

```
1    REM  PROGRAM TO CALCULATE FRACTION OF EXPENDITURES
2    REM      BY CATEGORY
10   INPUT "INPUT CATEGORY 1 AMOUNT:";A
20   INPUT "INPUT CATEGORY 2 AMOUNT:";B
30   INPUT "INPUT CATEGORY 3 AMOUNT:";C
40   INPUT "INPUT CATEGORY 4 AMOUNT:";D
50   INPUT "INPUT CATEGORY 5 AMOUNT:";E
60   INPUT "INPUT CATEGORY 6 AMOUNT:";F
70   T = A + B + C + D + E + F
80   PRINT "CATEGORY 1 SHARE:";A/T
90   PRINT "CATEGORY 2 SHARE:";B/T
100  PRINT "CATEGORY 3 SHARE:";C/T
110  PRINT "CATEGORY 4 SHARE:";D/T
120  PRINT "CATEGORY 5 SHARE:";E/T
130  PRINT "CATEGORY 6 SHARE:";F/T
140  END
```

SUBSCRIPTS

It's good that each number has to be inputted only once with this program. But look at how long the program itself is! And suppose you ever wanted to add more categories. You would then have to make the program even longer than it is now.

We need to think of a better way to write our program, but there's nothing we can do that uses the commands we've developed up to now. We need some way to store six values other than the cumbersome way of using a different letter for each value. Perhaps we can think of a way where we can use *one* letter to stand for six values. However, we will have to find some way to tell the different values apart. (Think how confusing it would be if everyone in your family had the same first name.) Therefore we'll identify each value by its own number. For example, suppose we use the letter A to stand for the six values. Then we can say that $A_1 = 36$, $A_2 = 64$, $A_3 = 11$, $A_4 = 17$, $A_5 = 14$, and $A_6 = 12$. The small numbers written below the letters are called *subscripts*. We can't actually print subscripts on the screen, but we can enclose the subscripts in parentheses. For example, the computer can represent the expenditure data as shown below.

A(1) = 36

A(2) = 64

A(3) = 11

A(4) = 17

A(5) = 14

A(6) = 12

We'll still call the number in the parentheses a subscript, even though it is not actually written below the main line.

We can use a variable name in place of the number in the subscript. For example, the two statements

I = 3

A(I) = 11

will do exactly the same thing as the one statement

A(3) = 11

However, the computer will give us an error message if the value of the variable used as a subscript is not a natural number. For example, the statements

K = −1

A(K) = 25

will generate an error message because the computer cannot execute the statement A(−1) = 25.

Now we need a set of statements that will input the six values of A. We can use a FOR/NEXT loop:

20   FOR I = 1 TO 6

30   INPUT A(I)

40   NEXT I

Now it will be easy to write a short program that requires us to type in the numbers only once to calculate the expenditure shares:

1   REM   EXPENDITURE SHARE PROGRAM

10   T = 0: REM   T WILL BE THE TOTAL EXPENDITURES

20   FOR I = 1 TO 6

30   PRINT "INPUT AMOUNT FOR CATEGORY";I

```
40    INPUT A(I)
50    T = T + A(I)
60    NEXT I
70    FOR I = 1 TO 6
80    S = A(I)/T
90    PRINT "CATEGORY";I
100   PRINT "EXPENDITURE SHARE I";S
110   NEXT I
120   END
```

ARRAYS

We'll call a variable name that stands for more than one value an *array*. For example, in the expenditure-share program, A is an array. Each particular value in the array is called an *element* or *component* of the array. If each component of the array can be identified with only one subscript, as is the case with array A, we call it a *one-dimensional array*. A one-dimensional array is also sometimes called a *list* or *vector*. (We'll later use arrays that have more than one dimension.) Now we need to tell the computer that A is supposed to be a one-dimensional array with six elements. Otherwise, the computer won't know what to do when it comes to the expression A(I).

THE <u>DIM</u> COMMAND

We'll use the keyword DIM (short for DIMension) to indicate the size of an array. For example, in the expenditure-share program, we should add the statement

5 DIM A (6)

at the beginning of the program. The DIM statement tells the computer that A is an array. The general form for a one-dimensional array follows:

<u>DIM</u> STATEMENT
(One-Dimensional Array)

> DIM *arrayname (size)*

where *arrayname* is the name of the array that is being defined by the DIM statement, and *size* is the maximum subscript allowed in the array *arrayname*. *Arrayname* must be a legal variable name, and *size* must be a natural number.

In many versions of BASIC, you may leave out the DIM statement if the subscript value will always be less than 10. For example, supose the computer reaches the statement

A(9) = 310

without having previously reached a DIM command for A. In that case the computer will act as if the statement

DIM A(10)

had been included in the program.

Here's a run of the expenditure-share program:

CATEGORY 1

EXPENDITURE SHARE IS   0.234

CATEGORY 2

EXPENDITURE SHARE IS   0.416

CATEGORY 3

EXPENDITURE SHARE IS   0.071

CATEGORY 4

EXPENDITURE SHARE IS   0.110

CATEGORY 5

EXPENDITURE SHARE IS   0.091

CATEGORY 6

EXPENDITURE SHARE IS   0.078

The development of arrays greatly increases our capabilities for handling and processing data. Now we can write a more complicated program to take care of personal finances.

Suppose you have decided that your expenditures can be classified into 30 different categories. Here are some possible categories:

Category	Item Purchased
category 1	ice cream
category 2	pizza
category 3	gasoline
category 4	fun books
category 5	boring books
category 6	chocolate ice cream cones

Every time you spend any money, you should keep track of the amount and the category number on which it was spent. It will also be useful to record the date of the expenditure. Then you'll have a record that looks like this:

Date	Category	Amount
2/5	10	6.45
2/5	1	0.68
2/6	29	10.04
2/9	3	1.04

The list will go on as you add your expenses each month.

We can use E as an array for the amount spent in each category. Since there are 30 categories, E must contain 30 elements. At the start of the program, we need to make sure that all of the elements of E are set to zero. When the program is being run, first we'll type in the category number (represented by C), and then we'll type in the amount for each item (represented by A). We'll then add A to E (C). We have only one problem: How do we tell the computer to stop? We cannot use a FOR-NEXT loop since we don't know how many items there are on the list (and since the number of items will probably change next month anyway). If 0 is typed for the category number, the computer will use that as a signal that it is time to stop. The full program now looks like this:

```
1    REM  FINANCIAL RECORD PROGRAM
2    REM  THIS PROGRAM READS IN A LIST OF EXPENDITURE
3    REM      ITEMS AND THEIR CATEGORIES, AND THEN
4    REM      PRESENTS THE TOTAL FOR EACH OF THE 30 CATEGORIES
10   DIM E (30)
11   REM E IS THE ARRAY THAT HOLDS THE TOTALS FOR EACH CATEGORY
19   REM  FIRST, ALL THE ELEMENTS OF E ARE SET TO 0
20   FOR I = 1 TO 30:E(I) = 0: NEXT I
21   REM  NOTE THAT LINE 20 CONTAINS 3 STATEMENTS
22   REM      SEPARATED FROM EACH OTHER WITH COLONS(":")
30   INPUT "INPUT CATEGORY NUMBER";C
40   IF C = 0 THEN GOTO 80
50   INPUT "INPUT AMOUNT";A
60   E(C) = E(C) + A
70   GOTO 30
80   REM  NOW THE OUTPUT IS PRINTED
90   PRINT "CATEGORY","AMOUNT"
100  FOR I = 1 TO 30
110  PRINT I,E(I)
120  NEXT I
130  END
```

WHICH IS LARGEST?

Let's add another clever device to the program. It will help to know on which of the 30 categories you spend the most money. Here's a quick addition to the program that will identify the largest element in the array E:

```
200   B = E (1):J = 1
201   REM  B IS THE BIGGEST ELEMENT OF THE ARRAY THAT
202   REM     WE HAVE LOOKED AT SO FAR
210   FOR I = 2 TO 30
220       IF E (I) < B GOTO 250
230       B = E (I)
240       J = I
250   NEXT I
260   PRINT "THE MOST MONEY WAS SPENT IN CATEGORY";J
270   PRINT "THE AMOUNT WAS";B
280   END
```

THE BUBBLE SORT METHOD

We will add many more features to our financial record program later. (See Chapter 12.)

It is often helpful to arrange the elements of an array in order. There are several different procedures that can be used. We will write a program that uses the *bubble sort* method. There are other methods that can sort more quickly, but the bubble sort method is one of the easiest methods to program.

Here is how the method works. Suppose we are sorting a list named A containing N elements. First, look at the first two elements in the array. If they are in the proper order—that is, if A(2) >= A(1)—then don't do anything. If they are not in order, swap their values. Next, look at the second and third elements in the array and see if they are in order. If not, swap them. Keep repeating the same procedure until you reach the end of the list. After you have passed through the entire list, you are guaranteed that the largest element in the list is now the last element. However, the first N–1 elements are not likely to be in order. Therefore, we will have to repeat the entire procedure, starting at the beginning of the list. However, this time we only need to check the first N–1 elements. After we have passed through the list the second time, then we are guaranteed that the second-largest element is the second-to-the-last element. Repeat the entire procedure with the first N–2 elements to make sure that the third-largest element becomes the third-to-the-last element. By repeating this procedure N times we can guarantee that the entire list has been sorted. It is called the bubble-sort method because during each pass the largest remaining element "bubbles" to the end.

To program a bubble sort in BASIC, we will need to use nested loops. The outer loop (with subscript I) will go from 1 to N. The inner loop (with subscript J) will go from 1 to N – I. Here is the program:

```
10    REM   PROGRAM TO READ IN A LIST OF NUMBERS
11    REM       AND SORT THE LIST USING THE
12    REM       BUBBLE SORT METHOD
20    DIM A(100)   'ASSUME THAT LESS THAN 100 NUMBERS WILL BE SORTED
30    INPUT "HOW MANY NUMBERS";N
40    FOR I = 1 TO N: INPUT A(I): NEXT I
100   REM   BEGIN BUBBLE SORT PROCEDURE
110   FOR I = 1 TO N
120      FOR J = 1 TO N – I
130          IF A(J)>A(J+1) THEN T=A(J+1):A(J+1)=A(J):A(J)=T
140   NEXT J
150   NEXT I
200   REM   OUTPUT
210   FOR I=1 TO N: PRINT I,A(I):NEXT I
220   END
```

Line 130 checks to see if A(J) and A(J+1) are in order. If not, their values are swapped, using T as a temporary variable. In Microsoft BASIC, line 130 can be written like this:

130 IF A(J)>A(J+1) THEN SWAP A(J),A(J+1)

CALENDAR PROGRAM

We will often need to convert a date expressed as the number of days that have elapsed since the beginning of the year into normal month/date notation. We will call the number of days that have elapsed since the beginning of the year the *yeardate* for that date. For example, suppose we need to know the month and date for the 100th day of the year. This problem is tricky because the months are not all of the same length. We will need to form an array to keep track of the number of days that have elapsed in all months prior to the current month:

Month	Number of days that have elapsed in all previous months
January	0
February	31
March	59

April	90
May	120
June	151
July	181
August	212
September	243
October	273
November	304
December	334

When we have read in the yeardate, we will need to check through the elements of the array, starting at the beginning, until we find the month such that the number of days that have elapsed up to the end of that month is greater than, or equal to, the yeardate. For example, when the yeardate is 100, we will read through the array, noticing that 100 is greater than 0, 31, 59, and 90. But 100 is not greater than 120, so the 100th day of the year must be in April. To find the exact date we can subtract: 100–90 to tell us that the 100th day of the year is April 10.

Here is the program:

```
10    REM - - CALENDAR PROGRAM
20    DIM M1(13)
30    M1(1)=0: M1(2)=31: M1(3)=59: M1(4)=90
40    M1(5)=120: M1(6)=151: M1(7)=181: M1(8)=212
50    M1(9)=243: M1(10)=273: M1(11)=304: M1(12)=334
60    M1(13)=365
70    INPUT T 'T IS THE YEAR DATE
80    FOR M=1 TO 12
90        IF T<=(M1(M+1)) THEN GOTO 110
100   NEXT M
110   D = T – M1(M)
120   PRINT "MONTH:";M;"DAY:";D
130   END
```

M1 is the array that contains the number of days that have elapsed in all months prior to a given month. Note that M1(13) is 365, since 365 days have elapsed in the first 12 months. Lines 80–100 contain the loop that keeps checking the entries in M1 until it finds one that is greater than the yeardate. Then it leaves the loop. The variable M is the number of the current month. This program only works for ordinary years, but we could easily modify it to handle leap years as well.

THE **READ** AND **DATA** COMMANDS

Once again we can find something about this program that is needlessly long. Lines 30–60 contain nothing but assignment statements to the array M1. It seems wasteful to type M1 each time. It would be very convenient if we could include a list of values in the program and then have the computer read from that list, one at a time, assigning values to the variables we indicate. BASIC provides a way to do this, using the commands READ and DATA. The DATA command tells the computer that all of the values that follow on that line are to be treated as a data list. When the computer reaches a READ command, such as READ X, it knows that it must take the next value in the data list and assign it to the indicated variable (in this case X.) Here is the new version of the calendar program.

```
10    REM  CALENDAR PROGRAM
20    DIM M1(13)
30    FOR I2=1 TO 13:READ M1(I2):NEXT I2
40    DATA 0,31,59,90,120,151,181
50    DATA 212,243,273,304,334,365
60    INPUT T 'T IS THE YEAR DATE
70    FOR M=1 TO 12
80        IF T<=(M1(M+1)) THEN GOTO 100
90    NEXT M
100   D = T - M1(M)
110   PRINT "MONTH:";M;"DAY:";D
120   END
```

Lines 40–50 set up the data list. The loop in line 30 causes the computer to read the values from the data list into the array M1. The computer first hits the READ command when the counter variable I2 is equal to 1. Then it executes the command READ M1(1). Since the first value in the data list is 0, it assigns the value 0 to M1(1). The second time it reaches the READ command, it will assign the value 31 to M1(2). The next time, it will assign the value 59 to M1(3), and so on, until it has assigned the value 365 to M1(13). This program will do exactly the same thing as the earlier version of the calendar program, but the use of READ and DATA makes it easier to write the program.

Here is another example of a program using READ and DATA:

```
1    REM   EXAMPLE OF READ/DATA
10   READ A,B
11   REM  NOTE THAT READ A,B IS THE SAME AS THE
12   REM     TWO STATEMENTS  READ A  READ B
20   IF A = –1 GOTO 80
21   REM  –1 IS A SIGNAL TO STOP THE PROGRAM
30   PRINT "A =";A
40   PRINT "B =";B
50   GOTO 10
60   DATA 6, 10, 13.5, 4
70   DATA 12, 11, 6.365, 4.21, –1, 0
80   END
```

The output for the foregoing program is

A = 6

B = 10

A = 13.5

B = 4

A = 12

B = 11

A = 6.365

B = 4.21

The DATA statements create a large stack of input data, similar to a stack of blocks with numbers on them. (See Figure 5–1.)

The DATA statements can be placed anywhere in the program. Whenever the computer comes to a READ command, it will look for the next element in the data stack, no matter where the DATA statements happen to be located. If the data list is to be read into an array, then it is convenient to put the DATA statements immediately after the READ loop, as we did in the calendar program. Otherwise it is convenient to put the DATA statements near the end of the program, as we did in the previous example.

There is no harm in including extra data items, because the computer will simply ignore any elements left in the data stack after it has executed all of the READ commands. However, you will cause an "Out of Data" error if the computer comes to a READ command after it has used up all elements in the data stack. Normally the computer will never use an element in the data stack more than once. However, if you would like to have the computer

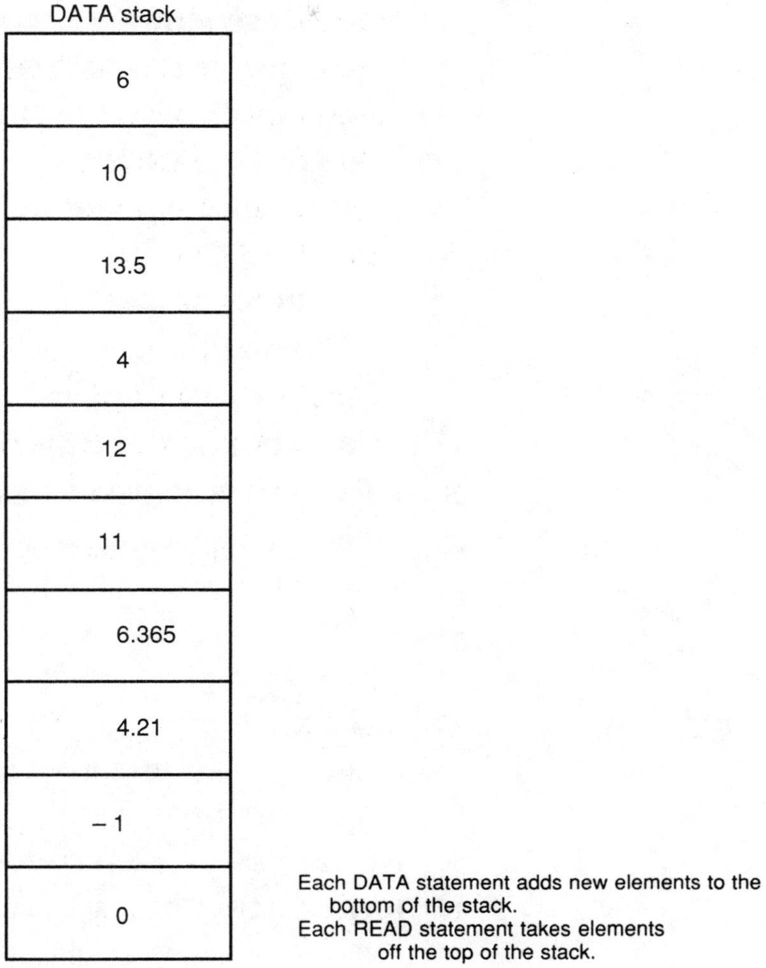

DATA stack

6
10
13.5
4
12
11
6.365
4.21
− 1
0

Each DATA statement adds new elements to the
bottom of the stack.
Each READ statement takes elements
off the top of the stack.

Figure 5–1

start over at the beginning of the data stack, you may use the command RESTORE. Here are three example programs:

```
1   REM  IN THIS PROGRAM THE DATA LIST CONTAINS
2   REM   EXTRA ELEMENTS THAT WILL BE IGNORED
10  READ A,B,C
20  PRINT "A=";A;" B=";B;" C=";C
30  DATA 100,200,300,400,500,600,700
40  END
    RUN
  A = 100   B = 200   C = 300
```

  *   *   *   *

```
1    REM    IN THIS PROGRAM THE DATA LIST CONTAINS
2    REM    TOO FEW ELEMENTS SO AN
3    REM     OUT OF DATA ERROR MESSSAGE WILL OCCUR
10   READ A,B,C
20   PRINT "A=";A"  B";B"  C";C
30   DATA 100,200
40   END
        RUN
        Out of data in 10
```

                    * * * *

```
10   REM    NOTE THE USE OF THE RESTORE COMMAND
20   REM      THAT CAUSES THE COMPUTER TO RETURN TO
30   REM      THE BEGINNING OF THE DATA STACK
40   READ A,B,C
50   READ D,E
60   RESTORE
70   READ X,Y,Z
80   PRINT "A=";A;"  B=";B;"  C";C
90   PRINT "D=";D;"  E=";E
100  PRINT "X=";X;"  Y=";Y;"  Z=";Z
110  DATA 100,200,300,400,500,600
120  END
        RUN
        A= 100  B= 200  C=300
        D= 400  E= 500
        X= 100  Y= 200  Z= 300
```

We can also use the computer to keep track of the statistics for our favorite basketball team. If there are five people on the team, we can store all their point totals in a one-dimensional array with five components called P:

10 DIM P (5)

Then P (1) will be the point total for player 1, P (2) will be the point total for player 2, and so forth. However, we don't want to keep track of just points. We want to keep track of field goals, field goal attempts, free throws, free throw attempts, and rebounds, as well as points. We need to keep track of six statistics for each player. That will be more difficult since we can't store all the statistics in one one-dimensional array. We can use six arrays, however. We can say that S2 is the array that stores field goal attempts, S3 is the array that stores free throws, and so forth. That means that the statistics for one game can be represented on the computer as follows:

Category	Player 1	Player 2	Player 3	Player 4	Player 5
FG	S1 (1)=4	S1 (2)=10	S1 (3)=11	S1 (4)=9	S1 (5)=13
FGA	S2 (1)=12	S2 (2)=22	S2 (3)=25	S2 (4)=19	S2 (5)=20
FT	S3 (1)=0	S3 (2)=4	S3 (3)=3	S3 (4)=3	S3 (5)=3
FTA	S4 (1)=0	S4 (2)=7	S4 (3)=5	S4 (4)=6	S4 (5)=3
Reb	S5 (1)=4	S5 (2)=6	S5 (3)=12	S5 (4)=0	S5 (5)=3
Pts	S6 (1)=8	S6 (2)=24	S6 (3)=25	S6 (4)=21	S6 (5)=29

TWO-DIMENSIONAL ARRAYS

This method will work, but we will have to add a DIM statement to declare the size of six arrays. And if we look closely at the statistics, we will notice an interesting pattern. We can use the letter S to stand for all the statistics, and then let *two* subscripts identify the element that we need. To do that, we need to add the statement DIM S (5,6) at the beginning. An array like this is called a *two-dimensional array*. The general form for two-dimensional arrays follows:

DIM STATEMENT
(Two-Dimensional Array)

DIM *arrayname (n1,n2)*

This command means that the computer will treat *arrayname* as a two-dimensional array, with *n1* rows and *n2* columns. *Arrayname* must be a legal variable name. (The maximum value of *n1* and *n2* will depend on the particular computer being used.) Two subscripts are needed to identify any one element in *arrayname*. The expression *arrayname (subscript , subscript2)* will mean the element in *arrayname* that is in row *subscript* and column *subscript2*. The *subscript 1* and *subscript 2* may be numbers, variable names, or expressions, but their values must be positive integers. The *subscript 1* must be less than or equal to *n1*, and the *subscript 2* must be less than or equal to *n2*. Note that the subscripts are enclosed by parentheses and separated by commas. In our array, the player number is written first and the statistic number is written second. It would really confuse matters if we wrote the subscripts in the wrong order.

We can use nested FOR-NEXT loops to write a program that reads the statistics into the computer:

```
1   REM   BASKETBALL STATISTICS PROGRAM

10   DIM S(5,6)

20   FOR P = 1 TO 5
```

Continued

```
21        REM   P IS THE PLAYER NUMBER
30        PRINT "INPUT STATISTICS FOR PLAYER";P
40        FOR J = 1 TO 6
41            REM   J IS THE STATISTIC NUMBER
50            PRINT "INPUT STATISTIC";J
60            INPUT S(P,J)
61            REM   NOTE THAT S(P,J) IS NOT THE SAME AS S(J,P)
70        NEXT J
80    NEXT P
```

Once the statistics are read into the computer, there are three things we want to do. We want to calculate field goal percentage (fg/fga) and free throw percentage (ft/fta) for each player, and we want to add up each statistic to find the total for the team. Once again we use loops:

```
100   DIM F(5)
101   REM   F IS AN ARRAY THAT WILL HOLD FIELD GOAL PERCENT
110   FOR P = 1 TO 5
120           F(P) = S(P,1)/S(P,2)
121           REM   S(P,1) IS FIELD GOALS FOR PLAYER P
122           REM   S(P,2) IS FIELD GOALS ATTEMPTED FOR PLAYER P
130   NEXT P
140   DIM G (5)
141   REM   G IS AN ARRAY THAT HOLDS FREE THROW PERCENT
150   FOR P = 1 TO 5
160           G(P) = S(P,3)/S(P,4)
170   NEXT P
180   DIM T (6)
181   REM   T IS AN ARRAY THAT WILL HOLD THE TOTALS FOR THE TEAM
190   FOR J = 1 TO 6
191           REM   J IS THE STATISTIC NUMBER
200           T(J) = 0
210           FOR P = 1 TO 5
211               REM   P IS THE PLAYER NUMBER
220               T(J) = T(J) + S(P,J)
230       NEXT P
240   NEXT J
```

The only remaining task for the basketball program is to direct the computer to print the output. (See exercise 31.)

There will often be times when we will want to print a two-dimensional array along with the totals for each of the rows and each of the columns. For example, if you have a record of your expenditures for each of four categories for 12 months, it would help to know the total expenditures in all categories for each month and the total expenditures in each category for the whole year. Here is a general program that calculates row totals and column totals:

```
1    REM  THIS PROGRAM READS ELEMENTS INTO A
2    REM      TWO-DIMENSIONAL ARRAY A AND THEN PRINTS
3    REM      OUT THE ARRAY SHOWING THE TOTALS FOR EACH
4    REM      COLUMN, THE TOTALS FOR EACH ROW, AND THE GRAND TOTAL
10   DIM A(30,4) 'WE ARE ASSUMING THE ARRAY DOES NOT
20   REM          CONTAIN MORE THAN 30 ROWS AND 4 COLUMNS
30   DIM CT(4)    'CT IS THE ARRAY THAT HOLDS THE COLUMN TOTALS
40   FOR C=1 TO 4:CT(C)=0:NEXT C
50   REM — READ IN NUMBERS
60   INPUT "NUMBER OF ROW";NR
70   INPUT "NUMBER OF COLUMN";NC
80   FOR R=1 TO NR
90   PRINT "ENTER ITEMS FOR ROW";R
100  FOR C=1 TO NC
110      PRINT C;
120      INPUT A(R,C)
130  NEXT C
140  NEXT R
150  REM — CALCULATE TOTALS AND PRINT OUTPUT
160  FOR R=1 TO NR
170      T=0 'T WILL BE THE TOTAL FOR THIS ROW
180      FOR C=1 TO NC
190      PRINT USING "#########";A(R,C);
200      T=T+A(R,C)
210      CT(C)=CT(C)+A(R,C)
220      NEXT C
230      PRINT USING "#########";T
240  NEXT R
```

Continued

```
250        T=0 'NOW T WILL BE THE GRAND TOTAL
260   FOR C=1 TO NC
270        PRINT USING "#########";CT(C);
280        T=T+CT(C)
290   NEXT C
300   PRINT USING "#########";T
310   END
```

The program as it is written allows for a maximum of four columns. You can easily increase that, but you are subject to the limitation provided by the width of your screen (or your paper if you are sending the output to a printer).

NOTES

• In some versions of BASIC, the DIM statements can be placed anywhere in the program, just as DATA statements can. In other versions, the DIM statement for an array must be placed so that it is reached before the computer first encounters another statement using that array. And in some versions, the computer will signal an error if it reaches a DIM statement that refers to an array that has already been dimensioned. In Microsoft BASIC, you may use the command ERASE A if you want to cancel the effect of a previous DIM statement dimensioning the array A. You are then free to use another dimension statement if you want A to stand for a different array.

• It is also possible to have arrays with more than two dimensions. For example:

DIM A(2,3,4)

declares that A will be a three-dimensional array of size 2 by 3 by 4. You will need three subscripts to identify a particular element in that array. The maximum number of dimensions allowed per array varies with different computers, but the practical size limit for arrays of any dimension is determined by the amount of computer memory available.

• It is possible to establish the size of more than one array in a single DIM statement. For example, the statement

10 DIM A(20), B(6,5)

has exactly the same effect as the two statements

10 DIM A(20)

20 DIM B(6,5)

• Some computers allow us to use a zero subscript in an array. In that case the command DIM X(6) means that the array X will have seven elements: X(0), X(1), X(2), X(3), X(4), X(5), and X(6).

In some versions of BASIC, you may use the command

OPTION BASE 1

to tell the computer that 1 is the lowest subscript allowed. The command

OPTION BASE 0

will tell the computer that 0 subscripts are allowed.

EXERCISES

1. Write a program that reads in a value for N and then reads in N values for the one-dimensional array A. (Assume $N \leq 50$.)

2. Write a program that reads in values for N1 and N2 and then reads in $N1 \times N2$ values for the two-dimensional array B. Read in the first row first, then the second row, and so on. (Assume that $N1 \leq 50$ and $N2 \leq 50$.)

In all the exercises that follow, assume that the necessary arrays have already been read into the computer.

3. Write a program that checks to see whether a list of numbers is arranged in ascending order.

4. Write a program that prints all the elements of a list A in the opposite order from the order in which they are contained in A.

5. H is a 162-element list consisting of the number of hits by a major league baseball player in each game during a season. Write a program that calculates the longest consecutive string of games during which the player had at least one hit during each game. (If the result is larger than 56, have the computer print: "This player has just broken Joe DiMaggio's record hitting streak.")

6. N is a list containing the digits 0, 1, 2, 3, ... 9. Write a program that calculates how many times each digit occurs in N.

7. M is a list of arbitrary numbers. Write a program that prints each number that occurs in M and then prints how many times that number occurs in M.

8. A is a list of *N* natural numbers. Write a program that tests to see whether A contains every integer from 1 to *N*.

9. Write a program that removes all the zeros from a list of numbers but leaves all the nonzero elements of the list in the same order.

10. S is a 20-by-2 array. The first column consists of the score for your team in the big football game each year for the past 20 years. The second column contains the scores for your archrival each year. Write a program that calculates how many games your team has won, how many games the archrivals have won, and how many games have been ties.

11. Write a program that checks to see whether the list A contains a particular number X. Have the program read through every element of A until it comes to X, and then have it print where in A the number X occurs. Have the computer print an appropriate message if X is not contained in A.

12. A much faster method to locate a particular item in a list can be used if the list has already been sorted into numerical order. This method is called the *binary search* method. Start at the middle element of A. If X is larger than this element, then you know that X must be contained in the last half of the list; otherwise it must be in the first half of the list. Once you have narrowed X's location down to the correct half, you can repeat the procedure to find out what quarter of the list X is in. After enough repetitions of this method you can narrow down the exact location of X, or else prove that X is not contained in the list. Write a program that executes a binary search.

13. Consider two lists, A and B, each with n elements. Each list is sorted in numerical order. Write a program that merges A and B into a new array C (with $2n$ elements) that contains all the elements from A and B arranged in numerical order.

14. Write a program that sorts a list of numbers using the *merge-sort* method. First, arrange each pair of numbers in the list in order. Next, use the merge technique from exercise 13 to merge all the pairs of numbers into groups of four. Then merge the groups of four into groups of eight. Keep repeating this process until all of the elements have been merged into one sorted list. (Assume that the entire list contains 2^k elements, where k is an integer.)

15. Write a calendar program that works for leap years as well as other years. Have the program ask whether or not this is a leap year before it reads in the yeardate.

16. Write a program that does the opposite of our calendar program. Have the program read in a month and day and then calculate the yeardate for that day.

If necessary, refer to a book on algebra to do exercises 17 to 20.

17. Write a program that calculates the *matrix product* of two 4-by-4 arrays A and B.

18. Write a program that calculates the *determinant* of a 4-by-4 matrix A.

19. Write a program that calculates the *inverse* of a 4-by-4 matrix A.

20. Write a program that identifies which elements of a list A are turnaround points. [A(I) is a turnaround point if $A(I) > A(I + 1)$ and $A(I) > A(I - 1)$, *or* if $A(I) < A(I + 1)$ and $A(I) < A(I - 1)$.]

21. A and B are two lists. Write a program that calculates how many elements are contained in both array A and array B.

22. Write a program that calculates the total number of elements in either array A or array B. (If an element occurs in both A and B, count it only once.)

23. Write a program to calculate how many items are contained in every single one of 10 different arrays.

24. Given an array A, write a program that calculates an array B such that

$B(1) = 0$

$B(I) = 1$ if $A(I) > A(I - 1)$

$B(I) = 0$ if $A(I) = A(I - 1)$

$B(I) = -1$ if $A(I) < A(I - 1)$

25. Write a program that calculates the five-term moving average of the elements in A. Store the moving averages in an array B. For $3 < I < (n - 2)$, the elements of B can be found from the formula:

$$B(I) = \frac{A(I - 2) + A(I - 1) + A(I) + A(I + 1) + A(I + 2)}{5}$$

26. X is a 2-by-10 array. Each row of X contains the two endpoints of an interval. Write a program that reads in a number N and then creates a 10-element list A such that

$A(I) = 1$ if $X(I,1) < N < X(1,2)$

$A(I) = 0$ otherwise

27. Write a program to print the output from the basketball statistics program described in the chapter.

CHAPTER 6

SUBROUTINES

L et's write a new financial record program that keeps track of our cumulative year-to-date expenditures in each category as well as our expenditures in the current month. Here is the program:

```
1     REM    FINANCIAL RECORDS PROGRAM
10    INPUT "DATE:";D$
20    N=6   'N IS THE NUMBER OF CATEGORIES
25    DIM E1(6), E2(6)
27    T1=0 : T2=0
30    FOR I=1 TO N
40         PRINT "INPUT CURRENT AMOUNT FOR CATEGORY";I;
50         INPUT E1(I)
60         PRINT "INPUT PAST CUMULATIVE AMOUNT FOR CATEGORY";I;
70         INPUT E2(I)
80    NEXT I
100   FOR I=1 TO N
105        T1=T1+E1(I)  'TOTAL CURRENT EXPENDITURES
110        E2(I)=E2(I)+E1(I)   'ADD CURRENT AMOUNT TO OLD
                                      CUMULATIVE TOTAL
115        T2=T2+E2(I)   'TOTAL CUMULATIVE EXPENDITURES
120   NEXT I
200   PRINT "FINANCIAL REPORT"
210   PRINT D$
220   PRINT "CURRENT EXPENDITURES"
230   PRINT "CATEGORY", "AMOUNT", "SHARE"
240   FOR I=1 TO N
250        PRINT I,E1(I),
```

```
260         PRINT USING "######.###";E1(I)/T1
270   NEXT I
300   PRINT "FINANCIAL REPORT"
310   PRINT D$
320   PRINT "CUMULATIVE EXPENDITURES"
330   PRINT "CATEGORY", "AMOUNT", "SHARE"
340   FOR I=1 TO N
350         PRINT I,E2(I),
360         PRINT USING "#####.###";E2(I)/T2
370   NEXT I
380   END
```

To operate this program you must type in the current amount and the past cumulative amount for each category. (Later we will write a program that is able to remember the past cumulative amounts so that you will not need to type them in again each time.) The program will print two reports: one showing the current expenditures and one showing the cumulative expenditures.

SUBROUTINES

By now you should realize that we want our computer to save us from unnecessasry work. Thus, looking at the above program, you can see that lines 200–230 are almost exactly the same as lines 300–330. It seems a shame to type the same set of lines more than once. What we need is a command that causes the computer to jump to a small set of instructions and then, when it's done with that set of instructions, return to where it was originally. We'll call the little block of instructions that we jump to a *subroutine*. We can easily write a subroutine that does the same as lines 200–230 and 300–330:

```
400   REM  SUBROUTINE TO PRINT HEADINGS
410   PRINT "FINANCIAL REPORT"
420   PRINT D$
430   PRINT T$;"EXPENDITURES"
440   PRINT "CATEGORY","AMOUNT","SHARE"
```

D$ is a string variable showing the date. T$ is a string variable that will be "CURRENT" if it is a current expenditure report and "CUMULATIVE" if it is a cumulative report.

THE GOSUB AND RETURN COMMANDS

We need to decide what to put at the end of the subroutine. We can't put END, because that's what we put at the end of the main program to tell the computer it's done. We don't want the computer to stop when it reaches the end of the subroutine; we want it to continue running. Specifically, we want the computer to return to the main program. Let's put the command RETURN at the end of the subroutine.

Next we need a command that causes the computer to go to the subroutine and start executing it. We will use the command

GOSUB 400

to cause the computer to start executing the subroutine that begins at statement number 400.

The new version of the program to keep track of our expenditures looks like this:

```
1     REM    FINANCIAL RECORDS PROGRAM
10    INPUT "DATE:";D$
20    N=6  'N IS THE NUMBER OF CATEGORIES
25    DIM E1(6), E2(6)
27    T1=0 : T2=0
30    FOR I=1 TO N
40       PRINT "INPUT CURRENT AMOUNT FOR CATEGORY";I;
50       INPUT E1(I)
60       PRINT "INPUT PAST CUMULATIVE AMOUNT FOR CATEGORY ";I;
70       INPUT E2(I)
80    NEXT I
100   FOR I=1 TO N
105      T1=T1+E1(I) 'TOTAL CURRENT EXPENDITURES
110      E2(I)=E2(I)+E1(I) 'ADD CURRENT AMOUNT TO OLD CUMULATIVE TOTAL
115      T2=T2+E2(I)  'TOTAL CUMULATIVE EXPENDITURES
120   NEXT I
200   T$="CURRENT"
201   REM   THE VARIABLE T$ TELLS WHAT TYPE OF REPORT WE ARE PRINTING
202   REM      WHETHER IT IS A CURRENT REPORT OR A CUMULATIVE REPORT
210   GOSUB 400   'THIS STATEMENT CAUSES THE COMPUTER TO GO TO THE
211   REM        SUBROUTINE THAT PRINTS THE HEADINGS
240   FOR I=1 TO N
250      PRINT I,E1(I),
260      PRINT USING "######.###";E1(I)/T1
270   NEXT I
```

```
299   REM    NOW PRINT THE CUMULATIVE REPORT
300   T$="CUMULATIVE"
310   GOSUB 400
340   FOR I=1 TO N
350       PRINT I,E2(I),
360       PRINT USING "#####.###";E2(I)/T2
370   NEXT I
380   END
399   REM
400   REM    SUBROUTINE TO PRINT HEADINGS
410   PRINT "FINANCIAL REPORT"
420   PRINT D$
430   PRINT T$;"EXPENDITURES"
440   PRINT "CATEGORY","AMOUNT,"SHARE"
450   RETURN
```

When the computer reaches line 210, it will jump to line 400 and then begin executing the subroutine that starts there. When it reaches the RETURN command in line 450, the computer remembers that it is supposed to return to line 210, so it will return there and then begin executing the next statement immediately following the GOSUB. The computer is sent to the subroutine again in line 310. In these instances, it is said that the subroutine is being "called." Note that the END command occurs in line 380. The END statement does not have to be the last statement of the program. In fact, you need to put the END statement before the beginning of the subroutines, or else use a GOTO statement to detour the computer around the subroutines. The computer becomes very confused if it accidentally slips into a subroutine without being sent there by a GOSUB statement.

It is important to keep track of the difference between GOSUB and GOTO. With GOTO *sn*, the computer jumps to statement number *sn*, but it completely loses its memory about where it came from. With GOSUB *sn*, the computer remembers where it came from so it can jump back there once it reaches the RETURN command. The general form of the GOSUB command, written as follows, causes the computer to jump to statement number *sn* and start executing the subroutine that begins there:

GOSUB *sn*

The computer will keep executing the subroutine until it reaches the command RETURN. Then it knows that the subroutine is finished, and it will jump back to where it came from and start executing the statement immediately following the original GOSUB command.

There are two reasons why subroutines are very important. We have seen the first reason. There will often be times when you would like to have the same set of instructions executed at more than one point in a program. It saves computer memory and reduces the amount of typing you must do it you write that set of instructions as a subroutine, which only needs to be included in the program once.

There is another even more important reason for writing programs that include subroutines. Later in the book we will be writing very long, complicated programs. It is difficult for people to write long programs unless they break the program into little pieces. The use of subroutines makes it possible to write programs consisting of a collection of well-understood modules instead of an unintelligible stream of computer statements. As a general rule, the first line of a subroutine should be a REM statement that briefly explains what the subroutine does. Labeling subroutines helps make programs much more readable for humans. It also is a good idea to include a comment on the same line as the GOSUB statement, and it can help to include blank lines to separate subroutines, such as we have done with line 399.

There will often be times when we would like a particular variable to have a certain value the first time the subroutine is executed and a different value the next time the subroutine is executed. In these cases, we must assign the desired value to that variable before the subroutine call. The variable T$ in our program is a string variable that determines what type of report we are printing (current report or cumulative report). The appropriate value is assigned to the variable in statements 200 and 300. Statement 430 in the subroutine will cause the computer to print out the value of T$ that has been assigned for that case.

In the last chapter, we wrote a program that reads in a yeardate (a number from 1 to 365 that represents the number of days that have elapsed since the beginning of the year) and calculates the month and day associated with that date. We will need to perform that same calculation in many different types of programs. Therefore, it will save us a lot of work if we can write a subroutine that performs that function. Actually we will need to write two subroutines. One subroutine will use READ and DATA statements to read in the initial values needed for the calendar array. It will only be called once, at the beginning of the program. The other subroutine will perform the actual calculations. Here is an example:

```
1   REM   THIS PROGRAM READS IN A DATE AND THEN
2   REM      CALCULATES THE DATES 50 AND 100 DAYS AHEAD
10  GOSUB 500 'INITIALIZE CALENDAR ARRAY
20  INPUT "MONTH,DAY:";M,D
```

```
30    Y0=M1(M)+D  'YO IS THE YEARDATE FOR THE INITIAL DAY
40    YD=Y0+50
50    IF YD>365 THEN YD=YD–365 'YD IS THE DATE 50 DAYS AHEAD
60    GOSUB 600 'CALENDAR SUBROUTINE
70    PRINT "MONTH:";M;  " DAY:";D
80    YD=Y0+100
90    IF YD>365 THEN YD=YD-365 'YD IS NOW THE DATE 100 DAYS AHEAD
100   GOSUB 600
110   PRINT "MONTH:";M;"  DAY";D
120   END
499   '
500   REM   SUBROUTINE TO INITIALIZE ARRAY
501   REM      NEEDED BY CALENDAR SUBROUTINE
510   DIM M1(13)
520   FOR I2=1 TO 13:READ M1(I2):NEXT I2
530   DATA 0,31,59,90,120,151,181
540   DATA 212,243,273,304,334,365
550   RETURN
599   '
600   REM   SUBROUTINE THAT CALCULATES THE
601   REM      MONTH AND DAY FOR A GIVEN YEARDATE
610   FOR M=1 TO 12
620      IF YD<=M1(M+1) THEN GOTO 640
630   NEXT M
640   D= YD – M1(M)
650   RETURN
```

Subroutine 500 is executed at the beginning of the program. After it has been executed, the appropriate values have been read into the array M1. Before subroutine 600 is executed you must set the variable YD equal to the yeardate you need to convert to month/day form. After the subroutine has been executed M is the value of the month and D is the value of the day for that date.

SUBROUTINES THAT CALL SUBROUTINES

If you examine this program, you will find some duplication. Lines 40–70 are almost the same as lines 80–110. Let's write a subroutine that contains those lines. It is possible for one subroutine to call another subroutine. Here is the new version:

```
  1   REM    THIS PROGRAM READS IN A DATE AND THEN
  2   REM        CALCULATES THE DATES 50 AND 100 DAYS AHEAD
 10   GOSUB 500  'INITIALIZE CALANDER ARRAY
 20   INPUT "MONTH,DAY:";M,D
 30   Y0=M1(M)+D  'Y0 IS THE YEARDATE FOR THE INITIAL DAY
 40   AD=50 'AD IS THE NUMBER OF DAYS AHEAD
 50   GOSUB 700  'CALCULATE AND PRINT MONTH AND DAY
 60   AD=100
 70   GOSUB 700
 80   END
499   '
500   REM   SUBROUTINE TO INITIALIZE ARRAY NEEDED
501   REM    BY CALENDAR SUBROUTINE
510   DIM M1(13)
520   FOR I2=1 TO 13:READ M1(I2):NEXT 12
530   DATA 0,31,59,90,120,151,181
540   DATA 212,243,273,304,334,365
550   RETURN
599   '
600   REM    SUBROUTINE THAT CALCULATES THE MONTH
601   REM     AND DAY FOR A GIVEN YEARDATE
610   FOR M=1 TO 12
620     IF YD<=M1(M+1) THEN GOTO 640
630   NEXT M
640   D= YD – M1(M)
650   RETURN
699   '
700   REM    SUBROUTINE TO CALCULATE A GIVEN NUMBER
701   REM     OF DAYS IN ADVANCE
710   YD=Y0+AD
720   IF YD>365 THEN YD=YD – 365
730   GOSUB 600
740   PRINT "MONTH";M;" DAY:";D
750   RETURN
```

Carefully trace the pattern of the computer's execution of this program, which does exactly the same thing as the previous program. In line 50, the computer will be sent to subroutine 700. When it reaches line 730, it will then be sent to subroutine 600. Upon reaching line 650, the RETURN command tells the computer that it has reached the end of subroutine 600. It returns to line 730, since this was the line that sent it to subroutine 600 in the first place. However, the computer still remembers that it is in the middle of subroutine 700, so when it reaches the RETURN command in line 750, it knows to return to statement 50, which is the statement that originally sent it to subroutine 700.

THE FACTORIAL SUBROUTINE

If you're at a crucial point in a card game, it helps to know what the probability is that a particular hand will arise. One way to calculate this probability is to deal out millions of hands and count how many times the hand you're interested in turns up. A faster method is to learn a little probability theory. You'll need to know how many different possible hands there are if you deal from a deck of 52 cards.

The answer is given by the formula

$$n = \frac{52!}{j!(52-j)!}$$

where n is the number of possible hands containing j cards that can be dealt from a deck of 52 cards. (The exclamation mark stands for *factorial*; m factorial is equal to the product of all the numbers from 1 up to m. For example, $5! = 5 \times 4 \times 3 \times 2 \times 1 = 120$. See Chapter 4, exercise 15.

This sounds like a problem for the computer. It's easy to write a little program that calculates $m!$, since all it needs to do is multiply together all the numbers from 1 to m.

```
 1   REM   PROGRAM TO CALCULATE M!(M FACTORIAL)
10   INPUT M
20   Z = 1
30   FOR I = 1 TO M
40      Z = Z * I
50   NEXT I
60   PRINT "M FACTORIAL IS";Z
70   END
```

Now we can easily write the program to calculate the number of hands. All we need to do is write the factorial program as a subroutine and call the subroutine three times.

```
1   REM    PROGRAM TO CALCULATE NUMBER OF HANDS
10   INPUT "NUMBER OF CARDS IN HAND:";J
20   REM    CALCULATE 52 FACTORIAL—STORE THE RESULT AS A
30   M = 52
40   GOSUB 200
50   A = Z
51                  REM
60   REM    CALCULATE (5–J)FACTORIAL—STORE THE RESULT AS B
70   M = 52 – J
80   GOSUB  200
90   B = Z
91                  REM
100   REM    CALCULATE J FACTORIAL — STORE THE RESULT AS C
110   M = J
120   GOSUB 200
130   C = Z
131                  REM
140   H = A/(B * C)
150   PRINT "THERE ARE";H;"POSSIBLE HANDS."
160   END
200   REM    SUBROUTINE TO CALCULATE M FACTORIAL
210   Z = 1
220   FOR 1 = 1 TO M
230       Z = Z * I
240   NEXT I
250   RETURN
```

(Note that we need to set M equal to the number whose factorial we want to calculate before we call the subroutine. After we call the subroutine, the variable Z will have the value M!.)

We can run this program a few times to calculate the number of possible hands:

RUN

NUMBER OF CARDS IN HAND: 2

THERE ARE 1326 POSSIBLE HANDS

RUN

NUMBER OF CARDS IN HAND: 3

THERE ARE 22100 POSSIBLE HANDS

   RUN

NUMBER OF CARDS IN HAND: 4

THERE ARE 270725 POSSIBLE HANDS

   RUN

NUMBER OF CARDS IN HAND: 5

THERE ARE 2598960 POSSIBLE HANDS

(Note: This program will not work on some computers because the numbers are too big. In these cases, try the program again, but make the number of cards in the deck smaller.)

CREATING YOUR OWN FUNCTIONS

The GOSUB command is too cumbersome if we just want to read in one independent variable and then calculate the value of a function of that value, so we'll invent a special kind of subroutine called a *function subroutine*.

For example, suppose we need to convert a given temperature from degrees Fahrenheit into degrees Celsius, using the formula $C = \frac{5}{9}(F - 32)$.

We can do that with the GOSUB command like this:

500   REM SUBROUTINE TO CONVERT F DEGREES FAHRENHEIT

501   REM INTO C DEGREES CELSIUS

501   C = 5 ∗ (F − 32)/9

520   RETURN

Then suppose that in the middle of the program we have a variable X representing a temperature measured in degrees F, and we want to convert it into degrees C and store the result under the letter T. We can use these statements:

60   F = X

70   GOSUB 500

80   T = C

These statements will work, but they take too many lines. Here's an easier way. In algebra, we let $f(x)$ stand for a function of x, so why don't we think of a command whereby we can define a function (call it FNA, short for FUNCTION A) so that the expression FNA(X) stands for the expression $(5/9)(X - 32)$?

We already have some built-in functions such as SQR(X). We need some way to define our own optional functions. We can think of the built-in functions as being the standard equipment, and the functions we define can be thought of as our own custom-designed options.

We'll let the functions we define have the form FN*varname*(*x*), where *varname* is any variable name and *x* is the argument of the function. We'll use a definition statement, with the keyword DEF, to tell the computer that we want FNA(*F*) to stand for (5/9)(F − 32) and not something else.

For example,

100 DEF FNA(F) = 5 ∗ (F − 32)/9

means that, whenever the computer comes to the expression FNA(*q*), it will pretend that it has really come across the expression 5 ∗ (*q* − 32)/9.

Let's define FNB to be the opposite of FNA—that is, FNB will convert degrees Celsius into degrees Fahrenheit:

110 DEF FNB(C) = 9 ∗ C/5 + 32

Even if degrees Celsius are more useful for scientific purposes, it's nice to have the results converted into degrees Fahrenheit so we have more of an intuitive feel for what they mean.

Below is an example of a program that will calculate the temperature of an ideal gas and then print the result in both degrees Kelvin and degrees Fahrenheit. (One degree Kelvin is the same as one degree Celsius. Zero degrees Kelvin is at absolute zero, which is −273.2° C.)

```
1    REM   THIS PROGRAM USES THE IDEAL GAS LAW TO

2    REM       CALCULATE THE TEMPERATURE OF A GAS

5    DEF FNB(C) = 9 ∗ C/5 + 32

10   INPUT "PRESSURE:";P

20   INPUT "VOLUME:";V

30   INPUT "NUMBER OF MOLES:";N

31   REM   1 MOLE IS 6.02 TIMES 10 ↑ 23 MOLECULES

40   R = 8.314

41   REM   R IS THE IDEAL GAS CONSTANT

50   T = P ∗ V/(N ∗ R)

51   REM   T IS THE TEMPERATURE IN DEGREES K

60   PRINT T;"DEGREES K"

70   T1 = FNB (T − 273.2)

71   REM   T1 IS THE TEMPERATURE IN DEGREES F
```

80   PRINT T1;"DEGREES F"

90   END

We can also write some other common conversions using the DEF function command (see the exercises). A function is defined with the general DEF statement as follows:

DEFINED FUNCTION

$$\boxed{\text{DEF FN}varname(x) = expression}$$

The name of the function is hereafter FN*varname*. Here *x* can be any variable name and is called the argument of the function. (It is also called a dummy argument because exactly the same function can be defined by using a different letter in place of *x*. For example, the two DEF statements

100 DEF FNF(X) = 5 * X ↑ 2 + 10 * X + 6

and

100 DEF FNF(Y) = 5 * Y ↑ 2 + 10 * Y + 6

will both have exactly the same effect.)

The *expression* can be any arithmetic expression. (Normally, it will depend on *x*.) The DEF statements should be placed at the beginning of the program.

To execute the function, just type

FN*varname* (*n*)

and the computer will automatically calculate the value of *expression* with the value of the actual argument (*n*) substituted in the place of the dummy argument (*x*).

Functions can also be used to round numbers off to a specified number of decimal places. (This feature is particularly valuable if your version does not contain the USING command to specify the format of numeric output.) For example:

DEF FNR2(X) = (INT(100 * X+.5))/100

The INT function is a built-in function that automatically chops off all digits to the right of the decimal part. INT is short for *integer*, which is the mathematical term for a number that does not include a fractional part. For example, INT(6.5) is 6, INT(134.999) is 134, and INT(236) is 236. Our user-defined function FNR2 will first multiply the argument by 100, then add 0.5, chop off the fractional part, and divide by 100. The final result will be the original number rounded to two decimal places. For example, if A is 234.5678 and B is 234.5646, then FNR2(A) will be 234.57 and FNR2(B) will be 234.56.

Microsoft BASIC makes it possible to include more than one argument in a user-defined function. For example, we can write a rounding function that specifies the number of decimal places as well as the number to be rounded:

$$\text{DEF FNR(X,N)} = (\text{INT}(10^N * X+.5))/10^N$$

If A is 234.5678, then FNR(A,0) is 235; FNR(A,1) is 234.6; FNR(A,2) is 234.57; FNR(A,3) is 234.568.

EXERCISES

Write functions that perform the following transformations, along with the reverse transformations:

1. inches to meters
2. gallons to liters
3. acres to hectares
4. miles to kilometers
5. miles to light years
6. pounds to kilograms
7. parallax to distance in parsecs
8. volts RMS to volts peak to peak
9. degrees to radians

10. Write a subroutine that initially reads in the exchange rate between two currencies and then automatically converts prices in one currency into prices in the other currency.

11. Write a function that converts a monthly inflation rate into an annual inflation rate.

Are the programs in exercises 12–16 valid BASIC programs? If not, tell what is wrong.

12.
```
10   INPUT A
20   GOSUB 50
30   B=A^2
40   PRINT A,B
50   A=1/A
60   RETURN
```

13.
```
10   INPUT A
20   GOSUB 100
30   PRINT A,B
40   END
100  IF A<0 THEN GOTO 130
110  B=SQR(A)
120  RETURN
130  B=0
```

```
        140    RETURN
14.  10    INPUT A
     20    GOSUB 100
     30    PRINT A,B
     40    GOSUB 200
     50    PRINT A,C
     60    END
    100    B=10 * A^2+30
    110    RETURN
    200    C=100-2 * A^2
    210    RETURN
15.  10    INPUT A
     20    GOSUB 100
     30    PRINT A
     40    END
    100    A=2 * A
    110    PRINT A
    120    GOSUB 200
    130    RETURN
    200    A=A/2
    210    PRINT A
    220    GOSUB 100
    230    RETURN
16.  10    INPUT X
     15    Z=1
     20    GOSUB 100
     30    PRINT X,Z
     40    END
    100    IF X=1 THEN RETURN
    110    X=X-1
    120    GOSUB 100
    130    Z=X * Z
    140    RETURN
```

17. What will be the output from the following program? (Trace the order of execution by hand.)

```
10    A=100
20    GOSUB 100
30    GOSUB 200
40    GOSUB 300
50    PRINT A
60    END
100   A=A/2
110   GOSUB 200
120   A=2 * A
130   RETURN
200   A=A^2
210   GOSUB 300
220   A=SQR(A)
230   RETURN
300   A=A+1
310   RETURN
```

18. Use the calendar subroutine in a program that prints the dates of full moons from 1990 to 1998. (Full moons occur every 29.53 days; start with the full moon that occurred on December 12, 1989.

19. Write a program that reads in a year and date during the 1990s and then tells what day of the week that date is.

20. Write a program that reads in the date and the stock market average for every day for a year and then calculates the average and the standard deviation of the averages. Then have the computer print how many days the market went up and how many days the market went down.

21. Write a program that reads in two dates and then calculates the number of days that have elapsed between them.

22. Write a program that reads in a date and a number n and then calculates the date of the day that comes n days after the original date.

23. The quantity

$$\frac{n!}{j! \, (n-j)!}$$

is called the *binomial coefficient*. It is often symbolized by

$$\binom{n}{j}$$

The program in the chapter calculates $\binom{n}{j}$ by calling the factorial subroutine three times. This method is not very efficient. Write a subroutine that calculates $\binom{n}{j}$ in a more efficient manner.

24. Suppose you need to conduct an opinion poll from a population of n people. Of these people, r approve the President's performance and the rest disapprove. If you question a total of b people and x number of people in the poll approve of the President's performance, the probability that x will equal a particular number j is given by the expression

$$\Pr(x = j) = \frac{\binom{r}{j} \binom{n-r}{b-j}}{\binom{n}{b}}$$

where x is said to be a random variable with the *hypergeometric distribution*. Write a program that reads in the values for n, r, and b and then prints $\Pr(x = j)$ for $j = 0$ to $j = b$. You will have a good poll if the probability is high that x will be about equal to rb/n. You will have a very poor poll if the probability is high that x will equal 0 or b.)

25. Write a more efficient version of the program in exercise 24. (The program's longest loop should contain no more than either j or $b - j$ iterations.)

26. Suppose you are going to roll a pair of dice n times, and the probability of rolling doubles is p ($p = 1/6$). The probability that you will roll k doubles in the n rolls is

$$\binom{n}{k} p^k \, (1-p)^{n-k}$$

(This is an example of a random variable with a *binomial distribution*.) Suppose you roll the dice 20 times. Use the subroutine from exercise 23 in a program that calculates the probability that you will roll k doubles for $k = 0, 1, 2, 3, 4, ..., 20$.

27. If you're with a group of s people, the probability that no two people in the group will have the same birthday is given by

$$\frac{\dfrac{365!}{(365 - s)!}}{365^s}$$

Write a program that calculates this probability for $s = 2, 5, 10, 15, 20, ..., 50$.

28. Write a subroutine that calculates the determinant of a 4-by-4 matrix. (See Chapter 5, exercise 18.)

29. Use the subroutine from exercise 28 in a program that calculates the solution to a system of simultaneous linear equations using *Cramer's rule*. (Refer to a book on algebra if necessary.)

CHAPTER 7

CHARACTER STRINGS

We have learned two basic features of character strings: how to assign values to string variables, and how to join two strings together with the + sign. (See Chapter 1.) Many computer applications require extensive manipulations of character strings, so we will add several new string operations.

THE LEN FUNCTION

Suppose a program reads a name into a string variable N$. However, suppose there isn't enough room to print any name longer than 12 letters. If the name is too long, we will have to chop off all but the first 12 characters. We will need two string functions: one to test the length of the string and one to perform the chopping operation. The function LEN calculates the length of a string. Here are some examples:

```
PRINT  LEN("A")
```
1
```
PRINT  LEN("GEORGE")
```
6
```
X$="Hi there!"
PRINT LEN(X$)
```
9

(Note that the blank and the exclamation point each count as one character.)

```
PRINT  LEN(X$+" How are you?")
```
22
```
PRINT  LEN(" ")
```
1
```
PRINT  LEN("")
```
0

Two adjacent quotation marks stand for an empty string that has length 0. Note the difference between the empty string and the string that consists of one blank.

LEFT$
RIGHT$
AND MID$

Now we need a function that cuts some characters out of a string. There are three ways of cutting a string: from the left, from the right, or from the middle. Therefore, we will need three different functions: LEFT$, RIGHT$, and MID$. To use the LEFT$ function, we must specify two things: the name of the string to be chopped and the number of characters to be kept. For example, if N$ = "George Washington", then:

PRINT LEFT$(N$,1)

G

PRINT LEFT$(N$,6)

George

PRINT LEFT$(N$,8)

George W

PRINT LEFT$("TUTANKHAMON",3)

TUT

PRINT LEFT$("ABCDEF",2)

AB

M=3
PRINT LEFT$(N$,M)

Geo

You must include the $ in the function name. The two items in the parentheses are called the *arguments* to the function, just as the parenthesized numbers for a numeric function were called the arguments to that function. The string being chopped must always be the first argument, followed by a comma and then the number of characters to be kept.

The original string is not affected by the LEFT$ operation. For example, if we try:

N$ = "George Washington"

PRINT LEFT$(N$,4)

Geor

PRINT N$

George Washington

we can see that N$ remains unchanged. We can, of course, use the LEFT$ function in an assignment statement:

G$ = LEFT$(N$,6)

PRINT G$

George

We could even do this:

N$ = LEFT$(N$,6)

PRINT N$

George

Now we have lost the original value of N$.

The RIGHT$ function works exactly the same as LEFT$, except that the characters are taken from the right edge of the string:

T$ = "Walla Walla Washington"

PRINT RIGHT$(T$,10)

Washington

PRINT RIGHT$(T$,16)

Walla Washington

The MID$ function is used to take some characters from the middle of a string. To use MID$ we need to specify three things: the name of the string, the location where the cutting is to begin, and the number of characters to be taken.
For example:

A$ = "ABCDEFGHIJK"

PRINT MID$(A$,4,2)

DE

The 4 means to start at the fourth character in the string (which is D), and the 2 means to take two characters from the string. Here are some more examples:

PRINT MID$("Computer",4,3)

put

PRINT MID$("OHIO",2,2)

HI

PRINT MID$("AAAAAAA",3,2)

Continued

AA

PRINT MID$("DISK",2,2)

IS

Now we can write a program that checks the length of a string and chops it off if necesssary:

```
10   INPUT N$
20   IF LEN(N$) > 12 THEN N$=LEFT$(N$,12)
30   PRINT N$
```

Here are some examples:

RUN

? WASHINGTON

WASHINGTON

RUN

? CONSTANTINOPLE

CONSTANTINOP

RUN

? NORTH CAROLINA

NORTH CAROLI

Sometimes a string will contain some blank characters that we want to remove. Here is a program to do this:

```
10   REM  PROGRAM TO REMOVE BLANKS FROM STRING
20   INPUT X$
30    Z$=""
40   FOR I=1 TO LEN(X$)
50    X2$=MID$(X$,I,1)
60   IF X2$<>" " THEN Z$=Z$+X2$
70   NEXT I
80   PRINT Z$
90   END
```

The program uses both the LEN and MID$ functions. The loop in lines 40–70 causes the computer to read through the string X$, one character at a time. Two character strings can be compared to see if they are equal (using =) or if they are not equal (using <>). If the character X2$ is not a blank, then that character is added to the string Z$, using the concatenation operation "+". (Note that Z$ is initialized as an empty string in line 30.)

We can write a program that reads in a string and then prints it out, putting the characters in the reverse order:

```
10    REM  PROGRAM TO REVERSE A CHARACTER STRING
20    INPUT X$
30    Z$=""
40    N=LEN(X$)+1
50    FOR I=1 TO LEN(X$)
60       Z$=Z$+MID$(X$,(N–I),1)
70    NEXT I
80    PRINT Z$
90    END
   RUN
? ABCDEF
FEDCBA
   RUN
? NOWHERE
EREHWON
   RUN
? ABLE WAS I ERE I SAW ELBA
ABLE WAS I ERE I SAW ELBA
```

PALINDROMES

A *palindrome* is an unusual type of character string that reads exactly the same in reverse as it does in the original order. Here is a program that reads in a string and then checks to see if it is a palindrome:

```
10    REM   PROGRAM TO TEST FOR PALINDROMES
20    INPUT X$
30    RESULT$="THIS IS A PALINDROME."
40    FOR I = 1 TO INT(LEN(X$)/2)
50       IF MID$(X$,I,1)<>MID$(X$,(LEN(X$)+1–I),1) THEN GOTO 80
60    NEXT I
70    GOTO 100  'THIS IS A PALINDROME
```

Continued

```
80    RESULT$="THIS IS NOT A PALINDROME."
100   PRINT RESULT$
110   END

   RUN
 ? HANNAH
THIS IS A PALINDROME
   RUN
 ? ABBA
THIS IS A PALINDROME
   RUN
 ? ABLE WAS I ERE I SAW ELBA
THIS IS A PALINDROME
   RUN
 ? ABCDEF
THIS IS NOT A PALINDROME
   RUN
 ? A MAN A PLAN A CANAL PANAMA
THIS IS NOT A PALINDROME
   RUN
AMANAPLANACANALPANAMA
THIS IS A PALINDROME
```

The string "A MAN A PLAN A CANAL PANAMA" would have been judged a palindrome if we first had the program remove the blanks. We'll add a subroutine based on the blank-removal program we wrote earlier.

```
10   REM   PROGRAM TO TEST FOR PALINDROMES
11   REM      THIS PROGRAM REMOVES THE BLANKS
12   REM      BEFORE IT TESTS  THE STRING
20   INPUT X$
25   GOSUB 500 'BLANK REMOVAL SUBROUTINE
30   RESULT$="THIS IS A PALINDROME"
40   FOR I=1 TO INT(LEN(X$)/2)
50      IF MID$(X$,I,1)<>MID$(X$,(LEN(X$)+1-I),1) THEN GOTO 80
60   NEXT I
70   GOTO 100 'THIS IS A PALINDROME
```

```
80    RESULT$="THIS IS NOT A PALINDROME"
100   PRINT RESULT$
110   END
500   REM   SUBROUTINE TO REMOVE BLANKS FROM STRING
520   Z$=""
530   FOR I=1 TO LEN(X$)
540   X2$=MID$(X$,I,1)
550   IF X2$<>" " THEN Z$=Z$+X2$
560   NEXT I
570   X$=Z$
580   RETURN
      RUN
? A MAN A PLAN A CANAL PANAMA
THIS IS A PALINDROME
```

ARRAYS OF STRINGS

In most practical character string problems we will need to use arrays of strings. We can use a string array containing abbreviations for the months to improve the output from our calendar program from Chapter 5. We will create a 12-element array called MNAME$ containing the abbreviations for the months. Here is the new version of the program:

```
1     REM   CALENDAR PROGRAM
2     REM   THIS PROGRAM READS IN A YEAR DATE AND CALCULATES
3     REM   THE MONTH AND DAY FOR THAT DATE
10    DIM M1(13),MNAME$(12)
20    FOR I=1 TO 13:READ M1(I):NEXT I
30    DATA 0,31,59,90,120,151,181
35    DATA 212,243,273,304,334,365
40    FOR I=1 TO 12:READ MNAME$(I):NEXT I
50    DATA "Jan","Feb","Mar","Apr","May","Jun"
55    DATA "Jul","Aug","Sep","Oct","Nov","Dec"
60    INPUT "Year date:";YD
70    FOR M=1 TO 12
80       IF YD<=M1(M+1) THEN GOTO 100
90    NEXT M
100   D=YD-M1(M)
```

Continued

110   PRINT MNAME$(M);D

120   END

We will often need to keep track of lists of names, and lists of names are much easier to deal with if they are in alphabetical order. In Chapter 5, we wrote a program that used the bubble sort method to read in a list of numbers and arrange them in order. We can use the same method to sort a list of character strings. You can compare two character strings using symbols for greater than, >, or less than, <. The string that occurs first in alphabetical order will be regarded as being less than the other string. For example, "A" is less than "B", "CAT" is less than "DOG", and "XRAY" is less than "ZENITH". On many computers, lower-case letters are regarded as coming after upper-case letters. For example, "A" is less than "a", and "Z" is less than "b". Other characters, such as numeric digits and punctuation marks, will be placed in order according to the computer's code-numbering system for characters. We will say more about that later in this chapter.

Here is the program to read in a list of names and print the list out in alphabetical order:

```
1     REM This program reads in a list of names and then
2     REM alphabetizes them
10    DIM A$(100)      'Assume that less than 100 names will be read
20    GOSUB 100        'Read in names
30    GOSUB 200        'Alphabetize names
40    GOSUB 300        'Print names
50    END
100   REM  Read in names
110     INPUT "How many names";N
120     FOR I=1 TO N
130       PRINT I;
140       INPUT A$(I)
150     NEXT I
160   RETURN
200   REM  Bubble sort procedure
210     FOR I=1 TO N
220       FOR J=1 TO N-I
230         IF A$(J)>A$(J+1) THEN T$=A$(J+1):A$(J+1)=A$(J):A$(J)=T$
240       NEXT J
250     NEXT I
260   RETURN
300   REM  Display output
310     PRINT "Here is the list in alphabetical order:"
320     FOR I=1 TO N
330       PRINT USING "####";I;
340       PRINT ".   ";A$(I)
350     NEXT I
360   RETURN

RUN
How many names? 41
```

```
 1   ?  Washington
 2   ?  Adams
 3   ?  Jefferson
 4   ?  Madison
 5   ?  Monroe
 6   ?  Adams
 7   ?  Jackson
 8   ?  Van Buren
 9   ?  Harrison
10   ?  Tyler
11   ?  Polk
12   ?  Taylor
13   ?  Fillmore
14   ?  Pierce
15   ?  Buchanan
16   ?  Lincoln
17   ?  Johnson
18   ?  Grant
19   ?  Hayes
20   ?  Garfield
21   ?  Arthur
22   ?  Cleveland
23   ?  Harrison
24   ?  Cleveland
25   ?  McKinley
26   ?  Roosevelt
27   ?  Taft
28   ?  Wilson
29   ?  Harding
30   ?  Coolidge
31   ?  Hoover
32   ?  Roosevelt
33   ?  Truman
34   ?  Eisenhower
35   ?  Kennedy
36   ?  Johnson
37   ?  Nixon
38   ?  Ford
39   ?  Carter
40   ?  Reagan
41   ?  Bush
Here is the list in alphabetical order:
    1.   Adams
    2.   Adams
    3.   Arthur
    4.   Buchanan
    5.   Bush
    6.   Carter
    7.   Cleveland
    8.   Cleveland
    9.   Coolidge
   10.   Eisenhower
   11.   Fillmore
   12.   Ford
   13.   Garfield
   14.   Grant
```

Continued

15. Harding
16. Harrison
17. Harrison
18. Hayes
19. Hoover
20. Jackson
21. Jefferson
22. Johnson
23. Johnson
24. Kennedy
25. Lincoln
26. Madison
27. McKinley
28. Monroe
29. Nixon
30. Pierce
31. Polk
32. Reagan
33. Roosevelt
34. Roosevelt
35. Taft
36. Taylor
37. Truman
38. Tyler
39. Van Buren
40. Washington
41. Wilson

THE INSTR FUNCTION

Now we would like a program that allows us to type in a date using natural notation, such as "January 1," and then calculates the yeardate for that date. We will need two new string functions to calculate this task. First, we need to split the string "January 1" into two strings: "January" and "1". Second, we need to convert the string "1" into the number 1.

We could split the string like this:

X$="January 1"

M$=LEFT$(X$,7)

PRINT M$

January

D$=RIGHT$(X$,1)

PRINT D$

1

However, we also need the program to work for date strings such as "March 4" and "January 20". We are using a blank to separate the month and the date, so we need to tell the computer that the characters to the left of the blank are the month and the characters to the right of the blank are the day number. Microsoft BASIC provides a new function called INSTR (short for in-string) to find out where the blank is. For example:

```
X$="January 1"
PRINT INSTR(X$," ")
```

8

```
X$="March 4"
PRINT INSTR(X$," ")
```

6

```
X$="January 20"
PRINT INSTR(X$," ")
```

8

To use the INSTR function, you must specify two strings. The computer will search through the first string to see if it can find the second string. If it does find the second string, the result of the function will be the number of the character position where the second string starts. In our first example above, the first string is X$ (which is "January 1") and the second string is " " (one blank). The computer searches through "January 1" until it finds one blank character. Since the blank is the eighth character in the string, the result of the function is 8.

Here are some more examples of the INSTR functions:

```
PRINT INSTR("ABCDEFGHIJ","A")
```

1

```
PRINT INSTR("ABCDEFGHIJ","J")
```

10

The second string can be longer than one character:

```
PRINT INSTR("ABCDEFGHIJ","CDE")
```

3

```
N$="Tom, Dick, and Harry"
PRINT INSTR(N$,"Dick")
```

6

The INSTR function only reports the first time that the second string occurs in the first string, no matter how many times the second string does occur.

```
P$="Puuanahulu"
PRINT INSTR(P$,"u")
```

Continued

2

PRINT INSTR(P$,"a")

4

If the second string does not occur in the first string, then the value of the INSTR function is zero:

PRINT INSTR("THE QUICK BROWN FOX JUMPED OVER THE LAZY DOG","S")

0

PRINT INSTR("ABCDEFGHIJKLMOPQRSTUVWXYZ","N")

0

PRINT INSTR("JUDGMENT","JUDGE")

0

In case your version does not include the INSTR function, here is a subroutine that does the same thing:

```
1000   REM  SUBROUTINE TO SEARCH STRING X1$ FOR
1001   REM      THE FIRST OCCURRENCE OF THE STRING X2$
1002   REM  THIS SUBROUTINE DUPLICATES THE FUNCTION OF
1003   REM      THE INSTR FUNCTION WHICH IS PROVIDED BY
1004   REM      SOME VERSIONS OF BASIC
1010   L2=LEN(X2$)
1020   FOR I=1 TO LEN(X1$)-L2+1
1030     IF MID$(X1$,I,L2)=X2$  THEN GOTO 1060
1040   NEXT I
1050   Z=0:RETURN
1060   Z=I:RETURN
1061   REM  AFTER THE SUBROUTINE HAS BEEN CALLED THE VARIABLE
1062   REM  Z   WILL BE THE LOCATION WHERE X2$ FIRST OCCURS
1063   REM  IF X2$ DOES NOT OCCUR IN X1$ THEN Z WILL BE ZERO
```

Now we can write a program that reads in a date and then separates the month and the day:

```
10   INPUT X$
20   B=INSTR(X$,"")
30   M$=LEFT$(X$,B-1)
40   D$=RIGHT$(X$,LEN(X$)-B)
50   PRINT "M$:";M$
```

```
60   PRINT "D$:";D$
70   END
RUN
? January 1
M$:January
D$:1
RUN
? December 25
M$:December
D$:25
```

VAL AND STR$

We still have the second problem: the character string "1" is not the same as the number 1, and the string "25" is not the same as the number 25. For example, if we try this program:

10 IF "1" = 1 THEN PRINT "They are equal"

the result is a "Type Mismatch" error. It is perfectly obvious to us how to convert a numerical character string into a number, but we must add a special function that tells the computer to do that. The VAL function (short for "value") turns a character string into its numerical value. For example, VAL("1") is the number 1, VAL("236") is the number 236, VAL("–26") is the number –26, and VAL("116.235") is the number 116.235. What happens to the VAL function if it is applied to a string that is not a number? In such cases the result is zero. For example, VAL("q") is 0, VAL("ABC") is 0, VAL("ABRACADABRA") is 0. If the string starts with some numerical characters, the VAL function will calculate the value of the initial numeric characters but ignore everything past the first non-numeric character. For example, VAL("3/20/82") is 3. If you attempt to apply the VAL function to a number, such as VAL(2), then the result is a "Type mismatch" error.

There will be times when we will want to reverse the VAL function: that is, turn a number into a string. The STR$ function does this. For example, STR$(1) is the string "1", STR$(236) is the string "236", STR$(–265) is the string "–265", and STR$(16.23) is the string "16.23". In many versions (other than Applesoft BASIC), one blank is put in front of the number if it is a positive number. If the STR$ function is applied to a string (for example, STR$("25"), the result is a "Type mismatch" error.

We can now write our new calendar program:

```
1    REM  CALENDAR PROGRAM
2    REM  This program allows you to type in a date using normal
3    REM      notation, such as January 1, and then it calculates
```

Continued

```
 4   REM      the yeardate for that date.
15   DIM M1(13)
16   DIM MNAME$(12)
20   FOR I=1 TO 13:READ M1(I):NEXT I
30   DATA 0,31,59,90,120,151,181
35   DATA 212,243,273,304,334,365
37   FOR I=1 TO 12:READ MNAME$(I):NEXT I
38   DATA "Jan","Feb","Mar","Apr","May","Jun"
39   DATA "Jul","Aug","Sep","Oct","Nov","Dec"
50   INPUT "Date:";X$
60   M$=LEFT$(X$,3)      'MONTH NAME
65   L1=INSTR(X$,"")
70   D=VAL(RIGHT$(X$,LEN(X$)–L1))  'DAY NUMBER
90   FOR MON=1 TO 12:IF M$=MNAME$(MON) THEN GOTO 120
100  NEXT MON
110  PRINT "INVALID EXPRESSION": GOTO 50
120  YEARDATE=D+M1(MON)
130  PRINT YEARDATE
140  END
```

COMPUTER CONVERSATIONS

The use of strings makes it possible to simulate conversations between you and the computer. Here is a simple example:

```
 10   INPUT X$

 20   IF X$="Hello" THEN PRINT "How are you?":GOTO 10

 30   IF X$="How are you?" THEN PRINT "I'm fine, How are you?":GOTO 10

 40   IF X$="What are you?" THEN PRINT "I'm a computer":GOTO 10

 50   IF X$="What languages do you know?" THEN PRINT "BASIC":GOTO 10

 60   IF X$="Have a nice day" THEN PRINT "You too.":GOTO 10

 70   IF X$="Thank you" THEN PRINT "You're welcome.":GOTO 10

 80   IF X$="Goodbye" THEN PRINT "Goodbye.":END

 90   PRINT "I haven't learned that phrase yet."

100   GOTO 10
```

This particular conversation would get boring very quickly, but you could add more phrases to the program to make it more interesting.

A problem arises if you wish to enter a string that contains a comma. For example, if the computer reaches the command

INPUT X$

and you type

Hello, how are you?

the computer will think that the comma is serving as a separator between two strings, instead of being one of the characters in the middle of a long string. In order to get around this problem, Microsoft BASIC provides an additional input command called LINE INPUT, which will read all characters on the line and assign them to a string variable. For example, if the computer reaches the command

LINE INPUT X$

and you type

Hello, how are you?

the computer will assign the string "Hello, how are you?" to the string variable X$.

It would be more useful to write a conversational program that performs an educational function. We can write a program that quizzes us on state capitals. The program will store the name of each state and its capital in an array. You may choose whether you would like to be given the state and asked for its capital or vice versa. The computer will select a state at random and ask you for the capital. If your answer is correct, it will print a congratulatory message. If not, it will ask you for one more guess before it tells you the answer. The computer will count how many questions you answered correctly so it can tell you your score at the end of the program.

The computer will select a random number using a new function called the RND function. If you type PRINT RND (in Microsoft BASIC) or PRINT RND(1) (in Commodore BASIC and Applesoft BASIC), the computer will respond with a number randomly selected between 0 and 1. If you try PRINT RND again, the result will be a completely different number with no relation to the first number. If you use the RND function several times, you will get a sequence of numbers that do not follow any apparent pattern. It may seem rather frivolous to include this function, but it turns out to have many uses in game, simulation, and quiz programs.

The computer cannot generate truly unpredictable numbers. The numbers it generates are governed by a rule, but the rule is so complicated that they appear to be random numbers. The exact workings of the RND function vary with different versions. In Microsoft BASIC, we need to include the command RANDOM-IZE in the first section of the program so that we don't get the same sequence of numbers each time.

In our program we need a random number that will be a whole number between 1 and 50, which we can create with the expression INT(50 * RND+1). Here is the program:

```
10 REM STATE CAPITAL EXAM PROGRAM
20 DIM STATE$(50),CAP$(50)
25 DIM ASKED(50):FOR I=1 TO 50:ASKED(I)=0:NEXT I
30 FOR I=1 TO 50:READ STATE$(I),CAP$(I):NEXT I
40 DATA "Alabama","Montgomery","Alaska","Juneau"
42 DATA "Arizona","Phoenix","Arkansas","Little Rock"
44 DATA "California","Sacramento","Colorado","Denver"
46 DATA "Connecticut","Hartford","Delaware","Dover"
48 DATA "Florida","Tallahassee","Georgia","Atlanta"
50 DATA "Hawaii","Honolulu","Idaho","Boise"
52 DATA "Illinois","Springfield","Indiana","Indianapolis"
54 DATA "Iowa","Des Moines","Kansas","Topeka"
56 DATA "Kentucky","Frankfort","Louisiana","Baton Rouge"
58 DATA "Maine","Augusta","Maryland","Annapolis"
60 DATA "Massachusetts","Boston","Michigan","Lansing"
62 DATA "Minnesota","St. Paul","Mississippi","Jackson"
64 DATA "Missouri","Jefferson City","Montana","Helena"
66 DATA "Nebraska","Lincoln","Nevada","Carson City"
68 DATA "New Hampshire","Concord","New Jersey","Trenton"
70 DATA "New Mexico","Santa Fe","New York","Albany"
72 DATA "North Carolina","Raleigh","North Dakota","Bismarck"
74 DATA "Ohio","Columbus","Oklahoma","Oklahoma City"
76 DATA "Oregon","Salem","Pennsylvania","Harrisburg"
78 DATA "Rhode Island","Providence","South Carolina","Columbia"
80 DATA "South Dakota","Pierre","Tennessee","Nashville"
82 DATA "Texas","Austin","Utah","Salt Lake City"
84 DATA "Vermont","Montpelier","Virginia","Richmond"
86 DATA "Washington","Olympia","West Virginia","Charleston"
88 DATA "Wisconsin","Madison","Wyoming","Cheyenne"
100 PRINT "Type 1 if you want to be asked for state names."
105 PRINT "Type 2 if you want to be asked for capital city names."
110 INPUT Q
120 PRINT "How many questions do you want to be asked?"
130 INPUT N
140 SCORE=0
150 SCORE2=0
155 RANDOMIZE
160 FOR J=1 TO N  :PRINT USING "####";J;:PRINT". ";
170   K=INT(50*RND+1)'  K IS A RANDOM NUMBER FROM 1 TO 50
```

```
175    IF ASKED(K)=1 THEN GOTO 170   'DON'T ASK THIS ONE AGAIN
176    ASKED(K)=1  'RECORD THAT THIS ONE HAS ALREADY BEEN ASKED
180    IF Q=1 THEN QUEST$=CAP$(K):ANS$=STATE$(K)
190    IF Q=2 THEN QUEST$=STATE$(K):ANS$=CAP$(K)
200    IF Q=1 THEN PRINT "What state is ";QUEST$;" capital of?"
210    IF Q=2 THEN PRINT "What is the capital of ";QUEST$;"?"
220    INPUT RESPONSE$
225    X$=RESPONSE$:GOSUB 1000:RESPONSE$=X$ 'CONVERT TO ALL CAPS
227    X$=ANS$:GOSUB 1000:ANS2$=X$
230    IF RESPONSE$=ANS2$ THEN SCORE=SCORE+1:PRINT "CORRECT!":GOTO 290
240    PRINT "Sorry, wrong answer. Guess Again."
250    INPUT RESPONSE$
260    X$=RESPONSE$:GOSUB 1000:RESPONSE$=X$
270    IF RESPONSE$=ANS2$ THEN SCORE2=SCORE2+1:PRINT "Correct.":GOTO 290
280    PRINT "The correct answer is:";ANS$
290 NEXT J
300 REM -- PRINT SCORE
310 PRINT SCORE;" OUT OF ";N;" WERE CORRECT ON THE FIRST GUESS."
320 PRINT "That is ";:PRINT USING "######.#";100*SCORE/N;:PRINT " percent"
330 PRINT SCORE2; "WERE ANSWERED ON THE SECOND TRY"
340 END
1000 REM  PROGRAM TO CONVERT ALL LOWER CASE LETTERS TO CAPS
1020 FOR I=1 TO LEN(X$)
1030    A1=ASC(MID$(X$,I,1))
1040    IF (A1<97) OR (A1>122) THEN GOTO 1060
1041    REM  DON'T DO ANYTHING UNLESS CHARACTER IS A LOWER CASE LETTER
1050    MID$(X$,I,1)=CHR$(A1-32)
1051    REM NOTE USE OF MID$ ON LEFT SIDE OF ASSIGNMENT STATEMENT
1060 NEXT I
1080 RETURN
```

Note that this program contains a subroutine to convert lower-case letters to upper-case letters. Now we will explain how to do that.

ASC AND CHR$

You do not need to know very much about the inner workings of the computer to write computer programs, but it helps to know a bit about the way the computer deals with characters. Each character stored in the computer memory is represented by a code number, according to a system called the ASCII code. ASCII stands for American Standard Code for Information Interchange. The computer actually stores the codes using the binary (base-2) number system, but we can write the code numbers as ordinary decimal numbers. The ASCII code of character for "A" is 65; the ASCII code of "B" is 66, and so on for the capital letters. We also need ASCII codes for the lower-case letters and for special symbols.

The BASIC function ASC calculates the ASCII code of a character. For example:

PRINT ASC("A")

65

PRINT ASC("Z")

90

Suppose we know the ASCII code number for a character, but we need to know what the character itself is. The CHR$ function does the opposite of the ASC function: it calculates the character associated with a given code number. For example:

PRINT CHR$(65)

A

PRINT CHR$(68)

D

We can now write a program that prints a table of ASCII codes:

```
1   PRINT "TABLE OF ASCII CODES"
10  FOR C=32 TO 122 STEP 3
20  PRINT C;CHR$(C),C+1;CHR$(C+1),C+2;CHR$(C+2)
30  NEXT C:END
RUN
TABLE OF ASCII CODES
 32            33 !          34 "
 35 #          36 $          37 %
 38 &          39 '          40 (
 41 )          42 *          43 +
 44 ,          45 -          46 .
 47 /          48 0          49 1
 50 2          51 3          52 4
 53 5          54 6          55 7
 56 8          57 9          58 :
 59 ;          60 <          61 =
 62 >          63 ?          64 @
 65 A          66 B          67 C
 68 D          69 E          70 F
 71 G          72 H          73 I
 74 J          75 K          76 L
 77 M          78 N          79 O
 80 P          81 Q          82 R
 83 S          84 T          85 U
 86 V          87 W          88 X
 89 Y          90 Z          91 [
 92 \          93 ]          94 ^
 95 _          96 `          97 a
 98 b          99 c         100 d
```

101 e	102 f	103 g
104 h	105 i	106 j
107 k	108 l	109 m
110 n	111 o	112 p
113 q	114 r	115 s
116 t	117 u	118 v
119 w	120 x	121 y
122 z	123 {	124 |

Here is one use of the ASC and CHR$ functions. Suppose we have read in a string and we would like to convert all of the lower-case letters to upper-case letters. We will need to read through the string one character at a time and first determine if the character is a lower-case letter (ASCII code 97 to 122). If it is not, then we leave the character unchanged. If it is a lower-case letter, then we need to convert it. Since ASC("a") is 97 and ASC("A") is 65, we can see that we have to subtract 32 from the ASCII code of "a" to get the ASCII code of "A". The same rule works for every letter. Here is the program:

```
1000   REM   PROGRAM TO CONVERT ALL LOWER CASE LETTER TO CAPS
1010   INPUT X$
1015   Z$=""
1020   FOR I=1 TO LEN(X$)
1030      A1=ASC(MID$(X$,I,1))
1040      IF (A1>=97) AND (A1<=122) THEN A1=A1-32
1050      Z$=Z$+CHR$(A1)
1060   NEXT I
1065   X$=Z$
1070   PRINT X$
1080   END
```

This program will work in Microsoft BASIC or on an Apple IIe. If you have an older Apple that does not provide for lower-case letters, then you won't have any use for this program. The situation with the Commodore 64 is different. Commodore computers provide two different character sets, but you can only use one set at a time. Press the SHIFT key and the COMMODORE key together to switch to the other character set. One of the sets contains lower-case letters; the other set contains a much wider set of graphics characters. In the set with the graphics characters, the capital letters have ASCII codes from 65 to 90. In the other set, the lower-case letters have codes from 65 to 90 and the upper-case letters have codes from 193 to 218. Here is a Commodore version of the conversion program:

```
10   rem   commodore program to convert lower case letters
```

Continued

```
11   rem     to upper case letters.
12   rem   note that the computer must be shifted to the
13   rem     character set mode that contains lower case letters
14   rem     to use this program.
20   inputx$
30   z$=""
40   for i=1 to len(x$)
50   x2=asc(mid$(x$,i,1))
60   if (x2>=65) and (x2<=90) then x2=x2+128
70   z$=z$+chr$(x2)
80   next i
90   print z$
100  end
```

In Microsoft BASIC, the program can be written in a shorter fashion, since that version allows you to use the MID$ function on the left side of an assignment statement. For example, if X$ is "Hello. How are you?" and the computer is given the command

MID$(X$,6,1)="!"

then the computer will find the sixth character in X$ and change it to an exclamation point. The result will be:

Hello! How are you?

Here is the Microsoft BASIC version of the letter-conversion program:

```
1000   REM  PROGRAM TO CONVERT ALL LOWER CASE LETTERS TO CAPS
1001   REM  THIS PROGRAM RUNS IN MICROSOFT BASIC
1010   INPUT X$
1020   FOR I=1 TO LEN(X$)
1030     A1=ASC(MID$(X$,I,1))
1040     IF (A1>=97) AND (A1<=122) THEN A1=A1-32
1050     MID$(X$,I,1)=CHR$(A1)
1051   REM  NOTE THE USE OF THE MID$ FUNCTION ON THE LEFT SIDE
1052   REM  OF THE ASSIGNMENT COMMAND
1060 NEXT I
1070 PRINT X$
1080 END
```

Here is a summary of the BASIC character string functions:

LEN(*string*)
    is the number of characters in *string*.

LEFT$(*string,numchar*)
    will take the first *numchar* characters in *string*.

RIGHT$(*string,numchar*)
    will take the last *numchar* characters in *string*.

MID$(*string,startpos,numchar*)
    will take *numchar* characters from *string*, starting at the character position given by *startpos*.

    (In the above descriptions, *string* can be any string, expressed either as a string variable or as a literal string enclosed in quotation marks, and *numchar* and *startpos* can be any whole number, expressed either as a numeric variable or as an explicit number.)

INSTR$(*string1,string2*)
    will cause the computer to look through *string1* to see if it can find the characters given by *string2*. If *string2* is found, the result of the function will be the number of the character position in *string1* where *string2* starts. If *string2* is not found, the result of the function will be 0.

VAL(*numericstring*)
    will be the numerical value of *numericstring*. If the first character in the string is not a numeric character, the result of the function will be 0.

STR$(*number*)
    will be the string whose characters are the digits of *number*.

ASC(*character*)
    will be the ASCII code of *character*.

CHR$(*codenumber*)
    will be the character whose ASCII code is *codenumber*.

NOTES   • The SPC function generates a character string consisting of all blanks. For example, SPC(5) will be a string of five blanks.

• Many versions of BASIC provide a quick way to read in one character as input. In Applesoft BASIC, the command GET X$ will cause the computer to assign the character represented by the next key typed to the variable X$. When you use this command, you do not need to type the <RETURN> key. In Commodore BASIC, the command GET X$ will represent the character value of the key being pressed at the instant the computer reaches the GET command. If no character is being pressed at that instant, then X$ will be assigned as an empty string. In order to tell the computer to wait for you to type in a character, we must use a loop like this:

10 GET X$:IF X$="" THEN GOTO 10

The computer will remain stuck at line 10 until you press a key. Then it will assign the character associated with that key to X$ and move on. In Microsoft BASIC, the function INKEY$ works the same as GET in Commodore BASIC. Here is an example of a Microsoft BASIC program that uses the INKEY$ function to insert a pause in a program:

```
10    FOR K=1 TO 10:PRINT "********":NEXT K
20    PRINT "Press any key to continue"
30    GOSUB 100   'INKEY$ function subroutine
40    GOTO 10
41    REM    This program runs in an infinite loop so
42    REM       you will need to press Control-C to interrupt it.
100   REM    INKEY$ subroutine
101   REM       When this subroutine is called the computer
102   REM    will pause until a key is pressed.
103   REM    After a key hs been pressed the variable
104   REM       K$ will have the value of that key.
110   K$=INKEY$:IF K$="" THEN GOTO 110
120   RETURN
```

• You may be wondering what characters are represented by the other ASCII codes. Many of these codes represent special characters that vary from computer to computer. On many computers, PRINT CHR$(7) will cause a bell to sound. The <RETURN> key is represented by ASCII code number 13. Many of these special characters can be generated by using the control key. For example, if you hold the control key down and press G, the result will be the character with ASCII code 7 (the bell character). Here is a short program that will allow you to find the ASCII code for any key on your keyboard:

```
1  REM    MICROSOFT BASIC VERSION
10 K$=INKEY$:IF K$="" THEN GOTO 10
20 PRINT ASC(K$)
30 GOTO 10
31 REM    PRESS CONTROL-C TO BREAK OUT OF THIS PROGRAM

1  REM    COMMODORE VERSION
10 GET K$:IF K$="" THEN GOTO 10
20 PRINT ASC(K$)
30 GOTO 10
31 REM    PRESS RUN/STOP TO BREAK OUT OF THIS PROGRAM

1  REM    APPLE VERSION
10 GET K$
20 PRINT ASC(K$)
30 GOTO 10
31 REM    PRESS CONTROL-RESET TO BREAK OUT OF THIS PROGRAM
```

After you type RUN, you can type any key and the screen will display the ASCII code for that key. You do not need to type <RETURN> after you type the key. In fact, if you do press the <RETURN> key, the computer will respond by telling you that its ASCII code is 13. You can also find the codes for key combinations such as control-A. All of these programs are written as endless loops, so you will need to use a special key to break out of the program.

• Some ASCII codes do not represent printable characters; instead, they represent commands that cause the computer to perform a particular action. You should check with your specific computer to see the codes that perform actions such as:

— clear the screen

— move the cursor to the upper left-hand corner of the screen

— move the cursor up one row

— move the cursor down one row

— move the cursor one column to the left

— move the cursor one column to the right

— move the cursor to a specified location on the screen

EXERCISES

1. Write a program that reads in a character string and drops the last *n* characters from that string.

2. Write a program that reads in a character string and drops the first *n* characters from that string.

3. Write a program that reads in a character string and then prints the string several times, each time dropping the last character, until the string has been reduced to nothing.

4. Write a program that reads in a specific character and then deletes all occurrences of that character in another string.

5. Write a program that reads in a character and a number *n* and then creates a string consisting of that character repeated *n* times.

6. Write a subroutine that prints out a number with a dollar sign in front of it.

7. Write a subroutine that reads in a number and then prints out the number with commas inserted between every three digits. For example, if the subroutine is given 164329186, it will print out 164,329,186.

8. When you type in a number in response to the INPUT command, you may not include commas in that number. Write a subroutine that allows you to include commas when you type in a number.

9. Write a program that reads in a letter and then prints 1 if the letter is A, 2 if it is B, 3 if it is C, and so on.

10. Write a program that reads in a sentence and then counts how many vowels and how many consonants it contains. (Treat *y* as a consonant.)

11. Write a program that reads in a sentence and checks to make sure that every *q* is followed by a *u*.

12. Write as program that reads in a sentence and checks to make sure that the rule "*i* before *e* except after *c*" is followed.

13. Write a program that reads in a sentence, then clears the screen, and then displays the sentence one word at a time, pausing for about five seconds between each word.

14. Write a program that splits a seven-character string into a seven-element array of one-character strings.

15. Write a program that reads in a paragraph. Have each line

of the paragraph stored as a character string in a string array. For example, if A$ is the name of the array, then A$(1) will be the first line of the paragraph, A$(2) will be the second line of the paragraph, and so on. Assume that there is one blank space separating each word from the neighboring words. Write a program that reads through the paragraph and creates an array such that each element of the array stores one of the words found in the paragraph.

16. Write a program that performs the same function as the program in exercise 15, and then have the program count how many times each word occurred in the paragraph.

17. Write a program that performs the same function as the program in exercise 16, except have it print the list of words contained in the paragraph in alphabetical order.

18. Write a coder/decoder program. Decide on a coding system so that each letter can be represented by another letter.

19. Write a Fake Personalized Form Letter program. The program should read in some relevant information, such as the name of the person to whom you are sending the letter, the age, school, or hobbies of the person, and the address of the person. Then have the program print out a letter that sounds as if it is a personal letter because it inserts personal information in the middle of the letter.

20. Write a program that acts as a full-screen editor. (A full-screen editor allows you to type characters at any location on the screen.) You may go back and change characters that you have already typed. Use an array that contains as many rows and columns as there are rows and columns on your screen. Whenever you type a character, have that character appear both on the screen and in the corresponding location in the array. Use cursor movement controls to make it possible to move the cursor up or down or right or left. For example, if you notice that you made a mistake at the upper-left-hand corner of the screen, you will need to move the cursor to that location so you can fix the error. When you have finished typing, have the computer print the array containing the characters you typed.

A full-screen editor is one important component of a word-processing system, so the program you have written for this exercise can serve as a very simple word processor. If you will be doing a lot of word processing, you will want to obtain a word processing program that contains a full-screen editor and many other features.

CHAPTER 8

MATHEMATICAL OPERATIONS

In the old days (before computers), mathematical subjects such as algebra and trigonometry were difficult to learn partly because the calculations were so tedious. Math concepts are still difficult, but we can ease the burden considerably by using the computer to perform the calculations. Thus, we will add several mathematical functions to our computer. If you are not mathematically inclined, you may skip this chapter. In this case, it is true that what you don't know can't hurt you.

We have used one mathematical function already: the square root function SQR. For example, SQR(9) is 3, SQR(25) is 5, SQR(2) is 1.41421356.

SQR, INT, AND ABS

Suppose we need to know the diagonal distance across a field that is 100 yards long and 30 yards wide. (See Figure 8–1.) From the Pythagorean theorem, the distance will be

$$\sqrt{100^2 + 30^2}$$

In BASIC this can be written:

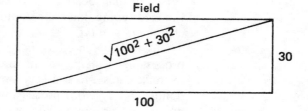

Field

PRINT SQR(100^2 + 30^2)

104.403065

The number of digits that appears in the result depends on the type of computer being used.

We can use the INT function if we would like to simplify the result by only considering the whole-number part:

PRINT INT(SQR(100 ↑ 2 + 30 ↑ 2))

104

(Note that one function can occur inside another function. Whenever a computer comes to an expression with one set of parentheses inside another set of parentheses, it will always evaluate the expression inside the innermost set first.)

Try some more examples of square roots. However, if you try

PRINT SQR(4 ↑ 2 – 5 ↑ 2)

the computer will give you another error message. If you look closely at the expression, you will see that you're asking the computer to calculate the square root of a negative number, and it can't do that. You will always get an error message if you try to use a function on a number that is not an allowable argument for that function. (The argument of a function is the number to which you're applying the function. For example, in the expression SQR(25), the number 25 is the argument of the function SQR.)

Another simple function we can include is the absolute value function, symbolized by ABS. The absolute value of a positive number is equal to itself; the absolute value of a negative number is equal to the negative of that number. For example:

ABS(16)

16

ABS(–10)

10

ABS(–165.42354)

165.42354

ABS(0)

0

Now we can calculate:

SQR(ABS(4 ↑2 – 5 ↑ 2))

3

TRIGONOMETRIC FUNCTIONS

If you are familiar with trigonometry, you may want the computer to be able to do some trigonometric functions. That will be much easier than having to look up the values of the trigonometric functions in a table. We can use SIN, COS, and TAN to stand for sine, cosine, and tangent, respectively, and we can use ATN to stand for the inverse trigonometric function arctan.

Suppose you need to measure the distance to a rock that is located in the middle of a river. You can't very well swim across the river with a tape measure, but you can calculate the distance if you know some trigonometry. First, stand along the river bank directly opposite the rock (point *A* in Figure 8–2). Then go to a point 10 yards away (point *B* in Figure 8–2), and observe the rock from there. Next, measure the angle between the rock and point *A*.

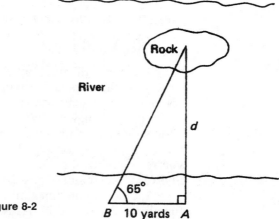

Figure 8-2

Suppose this angle turns out to be 65°, which is the same as 1.13446 radians. (Many computers require that the input numbers for trigonometric functions be expressed in radians.) Then the distance (*d*) to the rock can be found from the formula

$$d = 10 \tan 1.13446$$

We can calculate this on the computer:

PRINT 10 * TAN(1.13446)

21.445

Therefore, the rock is 21.445 yards away from the shore. Here are some other examples of trigonometric functions:

PRINT SIN(1)

0.84147

PRINT SIN(0)

0

PRINT COS(0)

1

R = 3.14159265/180

PRINT SIN(R ∗ 30)

0.500000

PRINT COS(R ∗ 30)

0.866025

PRINT SIN(R ∗ 90)

1

For many purposes it is more convenient to deal with angles expressed in degree measure, so it will help to create a user-defined function that calculates the sine of an angle expressed in degrees. If X_d is the measure of an angle expressed in degrees and X_r is the measure of the same angle when expressed in radians, then $X_d = 180 X_r/\pi$, where π (pi) is a special number approximately equal to 3.14159. Here is our function:

10 REM   THIS FUNCTION CALCULATES THE SINE OF X WHEN

11 REM   X IS MEASURED IN DEGREES

12 DEF FNSD(X)=SIN(3.14159 ∗ X/180)

Examples:

FNSD(0) IS 0

FNSD(30) IS .5

FNSD(60) IS .866025

FNSD(90) IS 1

Suppose we know that tan X is 1.5, but we don't know what X itself is? This problem calls for the use of the inverse tangent function, called the *arctangent* function, abbreviated ATN in BASIC. If $A = \tan X$, then $X = ATN\ A$. For example:

PRINT ATN(1.5)

.982794

Therefore, we know that the tangent of 0.982794 is 1.5:

PRINT TAN(.982794)

1.5

Here are some more examples:

PRINT TAN(.785398)

1

                       PRINT ATN(1)

.785398

                       PRINT TAN(.5)

.546302

                       PRINT ATN(.546302)

.5

The result of the ATN function is expressed in radians, but we can create our own user-defined function that will calculate the arctangent of X with the result expressed in degrees:

```
20   REM   THIS FUNCTION CALCULATES THE ARCTANGENT OF
21   REM      X AND EXPRESSES THE RESULT IN DEGREES
22   DEF FNATD(X)=180 * ATN(X)/3.14159
```

Examples:

        FNATD(1) IS 45

        FNATD(1.73205) IS 60.0001

        FNATD(–1) IS –45

Most versions of BASIC do not include any inverse trigonometric functions other than the ATN function. However, we can use the ATN function to find the other inverse functions, such as the arcsine function:

```
30   REM   THIS FUNCTION CALCULATES THE ARCSINE OF X
31   REM      THE RESULT IS EXPRESSED IN DEGREES
32   REM      X MUST BE A NUMBER BETWEEN –1 AND 1
33   DEF FNAS(X)=180 * ATN(X/SQR(1–X * X))/3.14159
```

FNAS(0) IS 0

FNAS(.5) IS 30

FNAS(.7071) IS 44.9995

FNAS(.866025) IS 60

Trigonometric functions are essential tools for solving many problems in science and engineering. We will use trigonometric functions again in Chapter 15 when we write some scientific application programs.

EXP AND LOG

There are two more mathematical functions we will need: a logarithm function and an exponential function. (If you are unfamiliar with these functions, you can read Appendix 2 at the back of the book.)

Here is an application of these functions. If we start with some radioactive atoms, then the fraction (f) of our original sample that will be remaining at time t is:

$$f = \left(\tfrac{1}{2}\right)^{t/t2}$$

where t_2 is the *half-life* of the element. For example, at the end of one half-life, only half of the original sample will be left. (The rest of the sample will have undergone radioactive decay and turned into something else.) At the end of two half-lives, one-quarter of the original sample will be remaining; at the end of three half-lives, one-eighth of the original sample will be remaining, and so on. The half-life of radium is 1,600 years, so we can use these statements to calculate the fraction of radium that will be remaining at the end of 10,000 years:

T2 = 1600

PRINT (1/2)^(10000/T2)

.013139

Suppose we want to know how many years will pass until only one-tenth of the original sample remains. We need to reverse our original formula, using logarithms:

$$t = \frac{t_2 \log f}{\log \tfrac{1}{2}}$$

Here, f represents the fraction of the original sample that will be remaining at time t.

In BASIC, the word LOG represents the *natural logarithm* function, which uses the number e as its base; e is a special number approximately equal to 2.71828. (You won't appreciate why this number is special unless you have studied calculus.) The natural logarithm of x tells you to what power e must be raised in order to get x. In other words, if $e^a = x$, then $\log x = a$. Now we can solve the radium problem:

T2 = 1600

PRINT T2 * LOG(.1)/LOG(.5)

5315.08

Therefore, after 5315 years there will only be one-tenth of the original sample of radium remaining.

Here are some more examples of the LOG function:

PRINT LOG(1)

0

PRINT LOG(2)

.693147

PRINT LOG(3)

1.09861

PRINT LOG(1000000)

13.8155

If we want to calculate e^x, then we can use the BASIC function EXP (short for exponential.) For example:

PRINT EXP(1)

2.71828183

PRINT LOG(2.71828)

1

PRINT EXP(.693147181)

2

PRINT LOG(2)

.693147181

Note that the EXP function does the opposite of the LOG function. If EXP(A) = X, then LOG(X) = A. Here are two more examples:

PRINT EXP(0)

1

PRINT EXP(10)

22026.466

One interesting property of the exponential function is that it can generate very large numbers. For example, suppose you try

PRINT EXP(50)

5.1874E+21

At first what the computer printed looks confusing because it slipped a letter E into the middle of the number. But the E has a meaning: it stands for exponent. That means that the computer is now using exponential notation (which is the same as *scientific notation*). For example, the number 5E+21 means 5×10^{21}, which is the same as a 5 followed by 21 zeros. Very long numbers are difficult to read, so the computer will automatically convert numbers into exponential notation when they become too large.

You can also enter numbers using exponential notation:

PRINT 6 E 34 / 2 E 15

3E+19

PRINT 2.5 E 6 * **3 E 8**

7.5E+14

PRINT 3 E 16 + 2 E 12

3.0002E+16

PRINT 1 E 20 – 1 E 17

9.99E+19

There are many times when it is useful to calculate logarithms to the base 10 (called *common logarithms*.) On some computers, the expression LOG(X) represents the common logarithm of X and LN(X) represents the natural logarithm. However, most versions of BASIC do not include a built-in common logarithm function, so we will need to create one. A mathematical formula called the *change of base* rule states that

$$\log_{10} x = \log_e x / \log_e 10$$

where $\log_{10} x$ is the logarithm to the base 10 of x, $\log_e x$ is the logarithm to the base e of x, and $\log_e 10$ is the logarithm to the base e of 10 (which is 2.30259). Here is our function:

40   REM   THIS FUNCTION CALCULATES THE COMMON LOGARITHM

41   DEF FNL10(X)=LOG(X)/LOG(10)

For example:

FNL10(10) IS 1

FNL10(100) IS 2

FNL10(1000) IS 3

FNL10(2) IS .30103

The magnitude system used to measure the brightness of stars is based on common logarithms. The faintest stars visible to the eye have magnitude 6. If a star is b times as bright as a sixth magnitude star, the its magnitude is

$$m = 6 - 2.5 \log b$$

Here is a program that reads in the relative brightness of a star and calculates its magnitude:

```
10    DEF FNL10(X) = LOG(X)/LOG(10)
20    INPUT B
30    M = 6 – 2.5 * FNL10(B)
40    PRINT "IF A STAR IS ";B;" TIMES BRIGHTER THAN A 6TH"
50    PRINT "MAGNITUDE STAR THEN ITS MAGNITUDE IS";M
60    END
  RUN
? 100
IF A STAR IS 100 TIMES BRIGHTER THAN A 6TH
MAGNITUDE STAR THEN ITS MAGNITUDE IS 1
  RUN
? 10
IF A STAR IS 10 TIMES BRIGHTER THAN A 6TH
MAGNITUDE STAR THEN ITS MAGNITUDE IS 3.5
  RUN
? 2
IF A STAR IS 2 TIMES BRIGHTER THAN A 6TH
MAGNITUDE STAR THEN ITS MAGNITUDE IS 5.24743
```

Note that brighter stars have smaller magnitudes.

CALCULATING AREAS

If you have studied calculus, then you have learned how to calculate the area under a curve. However, there are many important curves whose area cannot be found by a simple formula, and then the only possible method to find the area is a technique called

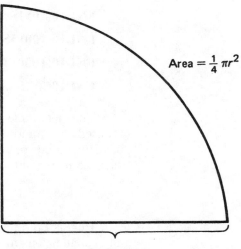

Area $= \frac{1}{4}\pi r^2$

Figure 8-3

Radius $= 1$

numerical integration. Numerical integration requires a lot of tedious calculation, so it is the type of work perfectly suited for a computer.

For example, suppose we want to calculate the area of a quarter of a circle (see Figure 8–3). We know that the area is $\frac{1}{4}\pi r^2$. With the computer we can find the area even if we don't know the value of π. We'll approximate the area by dividing the circle into a series of small rectangles, as shown in Figure 8–4. The more rectangles we draw, the more accurate the approximation will be.

Consider a circle of radius 1. If there are *n* rectangles and the *x* coordinate of the midpoint of a particular rectangle is *x*, then the height of each rectangle is $y = \sqrt{1-x^2}$ and the width of each rectangle is $1/n$. The program to find the area looks like this:

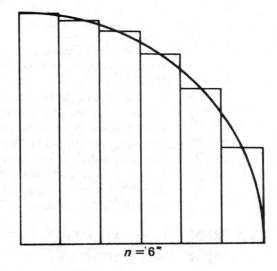

$n = 6$

Figure 8-4

```
1    REM  PROGRAM TO FIND THE AREA OF A QUARTER CIRCLE
2    REM     OF RADIUS 1
10   INPUT "NUMBER OF RECTANGLES:";N
20   A = 0
30   FOR I = 1 TO N
40     X = I/N – 1/(2 * N)
50     Y = SQR(1 – X ↑ 2)
60       A = A + Y * (1/N)
70   NEXT I
```

Continued

```
80   PRINT "AREA OF QUARTER CIRCLE IS:";A
90   PRINT "AREA OF WHOLE CIRCLE IS:";4 * A
100  END
```

This program allows us to vary the number of rectangles, so we run the program for different values of *n*.

n	*A*	$4 * A$
4	0.7960	3.1839
10	0.7881	3.1524
50	0.7856	3.1426
100	0.7855	3.1419
500	0.7854	3.1416

Normally, as soon as we type the instructions, the computer comes right back with the results. With this program, though, there is a delay from the time we type RUN until the answer appears on the screen. The delay is longer for larger values of *n*.

We're having the computer multiply by $1/n$ (the width of each rectangle) during every single pass through the loop. It will save the computer a lot of multiplications if we add together the heights of all the rectangles first, and then multiply by the width of each rectangle after the loop is finished. It will save the computer a lot of work if it has to multiply by $1/n$ only once, instead of *n* times. Here is the new version of the program:

```
1    REM   PROGRAM TO FIND THE AREA OF A QUARTER CIRCLE
2    REM        OF RADIUS 1
10   INPUT "NUMBER OF RECTANGLES:";N
20   A = 0
30   FOR I = 1 TO N
40   X = I/N – 1/(2 * N)
50   Y = SQR(1 – X ↑ 2)
60   A = A + Y
70   NEXT I
80   A = A * (1/N)
90   PRINT "AREA OF QUARTER CIRCLE IS";A
100  PRINT "AREA OF WHOLE CIRCLE IS:";4 * A
110  END
```

NOTES

• If a particular variable will always have integer values, then it can be declared to be an integer variable by putting a % after the name. For example, I%, COUNT%, and N1% are integer variables. Integer variables do not require as much memory space as ordinary numeric variables, which is particularly important in programs with large arrays. For example, if your program contains an array A:

10 DIM A (200)

then you can save a lot of memory by using an integer array instead:

10 DIM A%(200)

Of course, this only works if the values of A% will always be integers. You must include the % every time you refer to A% in the program, just as you must always include the $ when you refer to a string variable.

• If the INT function is applied to a negative number, the result will be the greatest integer that is smaller than that number. For example:

PRINT INT(–0.5)

 – 1

PRINT INT(–10.7)

–11

PRINT INT(–18)

–18

EXERCISES

Translate each of the following algebraic expressions into BASIC:

1. $\sqrt{x^2 + y^2 + z^2}$

2. $\sqrt{(x - h)^2 + (y - k)^2}$

3. $\dfrac{-b + \sqrt{b^2 - 4ac}}{2a}$

4. $r \sin A \cos B$

5. $\sin A \sin B + \cos A \cos B$

6. $\frac{1}{2}(1 - \cos 2A)$

7. $\cos^2 A - \sin^2 A$

8. $a^2 + b^2 - 2ab \cos C$

9. $b_1 \sin A/\sin B$

10. $\frac{1}{2}(e^x + e^{-x})$

11. $\ln(a + b + c)$

12. Write a program that reads in the distance to a star (d) in parsecs and the absolute magnitude of the star (M), then calculates the apparent magnitude (that is, the brightness of the star as seen from earth). Use the formula

$$\text{Magnitude} = M + 5 \log \frac{d}{10}$$

13. Write a program that reads in an angle in radians and converts it into an angle in degrees.

14. Write a program that reads in the two coordinates (x,y) of a point and an angle T and then calculates the new coordinates (x_2,y_2) of the same point when measured in the coordinate system formed by rotating the original x and y axes by T degrees. Use the formulas

$$x_2 = x \cos T + y \sin T$$

$$y_2 = y \cos T - x \sin T$$

15. Write a program that reads in a number x and then calculates the *hyperbolic cosine* of x, using the formula:

$$\cosh x = \frac{1}{2}(e^x + e^{-x})$$

16. Suppose that one day you bought what you thought was a very large triangle of land. It had dimensions of 200 miles, 101 miles, and 100 miles. It turned out that this triangle did not have as much area as you thought. Write a program that reads in the three lengths of the sides of a triangle and then calculates the area of the triangle.

17. Write a program that reads in two sides (a and b) of a triangle as well as the angle between those two sides (C), then calculates the length of the third side (c) from the law of cosines:

$$c^2 = a^2 + b^2 - 2ab \cos C$$

18. Write a program that reads in three numbers a, b, and c

(where a is not zero) and then calculates the value(s) of x that solve the quadratic equation

$$ax^2 + bx + c = 0$$

19. An error message will be printed if a computer is asked to find tan 90°. Write a program that prints out a table of sin, cos, and tan for the angles 0°, 10°, 20°, ..., 90° without generating any error messages. Have the computer print "INFINITY" as the value for tan 90°.

20. Write a program that reads in the x coordinate of a point on the ellipse $x^2/a^2 + y^2/b^2 = 1$ and then prints the two possible values for the y coordinate of that point.

21. Write a program that reads in a number N and then prints the rightmost b digits of N.

22. Write a program that reads in a number less than 64 and then prints the five digits of the binary representation of that number.

23. Write a program that reads in a, b, c, d, and e and then calculates

$$ax^4 + bx^3 + cx^2 + dx = e$$

(Can you write this program without using the ↑ exponentiation operator? Don't type x more than four times in the program.)

24. Write a program that reads in the two coordinates of a point (x,y) and then calculates the angle between the x axis and the ray passing through that point. Express the result as an angle between 0° and 360°. (Hint: Use the arctangent function, but remember that the result needs to be placed in the correct quadrant.)

25. Write a program that uses Newton's method to solve the third-degree equation

$$ax^3 + bx^2 + cx + d = 0$$

First, have the computer read in values for a, b, c, and d. Next have the computer read in an initial guess for the solution (x_1). Then calculate a closer guess from the formula

$$x_2 = x_1 - \frac{ax_1^3 + bx_1^2 + cx_1 + d}{3ax_1^2 + 2bx_1 + c}$$

Keep repeating the process. Each time you will have a closer approximation to the true solution. Continue until the solution you find for x satisfies

$$|ax^3 + bx^2 + cx + d| < 0.01$$

Use rectangles to find approximations for the areas of the regions in exercises 26 to 28.

26. The area under the curve $y = \sin x$ from $x = 0$ to $x = \pi/2$.

27. The area of the ellipse $x^2/9 + y^2/16 = 1$.

28. The area under the curve $y = e^{-x^2}$ from $x = 0$ to $x = 2$.

29. Make a table that gives the area under the curve $y = (2\pi)^{-1/2}e^{-1/2\hat{x}}$, to the right of the line $x = 0$, and to the left of the line $x = x_1$ for these 300 values of x_1: 0.01, 0.02, 0.03, 0.04,....3. (This area is very important because this curve is the standard normal probability curve.)

30. Find the approximate volume of the ellipsoid formed by rotating the ellipse $x^2/25 + y^2/9$ about the x axis. (Use nested loops.)

31. Approximate the curve $y = \sin x$ from $x = 0$ to $x = \pi/2$ by a series of small straight segments. Then add up the lengths of all the straight segments to find an approximation for the total length of the curve.

32. Write a program that reads in a number x and then calculates an approximation for e^x, using the formula

$$e^x = 1 + x + \frac{x^2}{2!} + \frac{x^3}{3!} + \frac{x^4}{4!} + \dots$$

(The exclamation point stands for *factorial*.)

33. Write a program that reads in a number x and then calculates an approximation for $\sin x$, using the formula

$$\sin x = x - \frac{x^3}{3!} + \frac{x^5}{5!} - \frac{x^7}{7!} + \frac{x^9}{9!} - \dots$$

34. Write a program that reads in a number x and then calculates an approximation for $\cos x$, using the formula

$$\cos x = 1 - \frac{x^2}{2!} + \frac{x^4}{4!} - \frac{x^6}{6!} + \dots$$

35. Write a program that calculates an approximate value for π, using the formula

$$\frac{\pi}{4} = 1 - \frac{1}{3} + \frac{1}{5} - \frac{1}{7} + \frac{1}{9} - \frac{1}{11} + \ldots$$

(Warning: It takes a long time for this series to come up with a close approximation for π.)

Suppose your computer had no built-in functions and no exponentiation (↑) operation. Write subroutines that perform the following tasks:

36. Raise a number to a positive integer power.

37. Calculate the square root of a number.

38. Calculate the sine of a number. (See exercise 33.)

CHAPTER 9

FILES

Suppose we decide to use our computer to keep track of the mailing list for our organization. We can store the names and addresses as arrays of character strings, and we have seen how to put the names in alphabetical order and how to print them out. However, the computer will not help very much if we need to retype the names every time we turn the machine on. We have seen how much work is saved because the computer can remember its instructions. It will also save a lot of work to have the computer remember data. So far all data used by our programs has been either written into the program itself or read in from the keyboard. The output has gone either to the screen or the printer. What we need now is a way for the output from the program to be sent someplace where that same information can be used as input at a later time. Fortunately, we can store data on disks or tapes just as we can store programs on disks or tapes.

If you tried to store information by randomly throwing it in your desk drawer, you would have a very difficult time ever finding it again. It is much better to put related sheets of paper together in a file folder and to put a label on the folder so that you know what information it contains. When a computer stores information, it puts it in a *file*. Of course, a computer disk file does not have any physical resemblance to a file folder. (The computer file actually consists of a series of coded magnetic marks on the disk.) But the disk file does have a name or label, which you will use when you want to get information from the file. Each version handles disk files differently, so you will need to check your manual. Here is the way files work in Microsoft BASIC, Commodore BASIC, and Applesoft BASIC:

FILES IN MICROSOFT BASIC

Before you can use a disk file you must open it, using the OPEN command. By analogy, a person cannot put anything in or take anything out of a file folder without first opening it. When you open a file, you must specify three things:

1. Whether you will be sending information to the file (then it is designated as an output file) or whether you will be taking information from the file (then it is designated as an input file); note that the terms "input" and "output" are always used from the computer's point of view, not the point of view of the file. When you open a file folder, you may use it for either input or output, but

a computer disk file cannot be used for both input and output at the same time.

2. The *file number*, which will be used by the computer in all subsequent references to this file.

3. The name of the file.

Here is an example of an OPEN command:

10   OPEN "O",#1,"HELLO"

It also can be written:

10   OPEN "O",1,"HELLO"

The "O" means that this file will be an output file. (If we want to read from a file, we would open it as an input file, using "I".) The name of the file we are opening is "HELLO". The name of the file must be written in quotation marks, or else the name can be specified as a string variable. The #1 means that this file will be referred to as file number 1. Whenever you open a file, you must specify a file number. If you only use one file at a time, you can always use 1 as the file number. If you will be opening more than one file at a time, you must give each file a different file number. You will need to check with your manual to see how many files you may have open at a time and what are the permissible values for file numbers.

Once the file has been open as an output file, we can write information to it:

20   A$ = "Hello. How are you?"

30   PRINT #1,A$

The command PRINT#1,A$ tells the computer that the string variable A$ is to be written to file number 1. We can also write a numeric variable to the file:

40   N = 100

50   PRINT#1,N

After we have finished writing output to the file, we must use the CLOSE command:

60   CLOSE#1

which can also be written: 60 CLOSE 1

In order to read information from the file we must first open it again, but this time we will specify that we are opening it for input instead of output:

70   OPEN "I",#2,"HELLO"

This time we are opening the file HELLO as file number 2. Now we can read from the file:

80   INPUT#2,X$

90   INPUT#2,Z

The command INPUT#2,X$ tells the computer to read the next item from file number 2 and store that item under the name X$. Then it will read the next item from the file and store it under the variable name Z. Note that the name of the variable used in the INPUT command does not have to be the same as the name that the variable had when it was originally saved on the disk file.

We can cause the computer to print the new values of these variables:

100 PRINT X$,Z

and the screen will display:

Hello. How are you?   100

Now we are done with the file, we can close it:

110 CLOSE#2

Here is the general form of the Microsoft BASIC commands for file input and output:

To open an input file:

OPEN "I",#*filenum,name*

To open an output file:

OPEN "O",#*filenum,name*

where *filenum* is the file number and *name* is the name of the file, expressed either as a string within quotation marks or as a string variable. Remember that a computer reads information *from* an input file and it writes information *to* an output file.
To write information to a file:

PRINT#*filenum,item*

where *filenum* is the file number and *item* is the information to be written to the file (either a number, numeric variable, string, or string variable.) If a variable name is used, then only the value of that variable is saved. The variable name itself is not saved, so you do not need to use the same name when you read the data back from the file.

To read information from an input file:

INPUT#*filenum,varname*

where *filenum* is the file number and *varname* is the variable name that will take its value from the next item in the file. If the next item in the file is a string, *varname* must be a string variable.

To close a file:

CLOSE#*filenum*

where *filenum* is the file number.

* * * * *

FILES IN COMMODORE BASIC

Before you can use a disk file, you must open it, using the OPEN command. By analogy, a person cannot put anything in or take anything out of a file folder without first opening it. When you open a file, you must specify a file number, a device number, a channel number, and a file name. You also need to specify that the file will be a sequential data file, and you must say whether you will be writing information to the file or reading information from the file. Here is an example of an OPEN command:

10   OPEN 2,8,2,"HELLO,S,W"

The first 2 means that this file will be referred to as file number 2. You must specify a file number whenever you open a file. If you will be opening more than one file at a time, you must give each file a different number. Check your manual to see how many files you may have open at one time and what are the permissible values for file numbers. The 8 is the device number for the disk drive. The second 2 is called the channel number, which can conveniently be the same as the file number. (See your manual for more information about the channel number.)

The name of the file we are opening is "HELLO". The name of the file must be written in quotation marks, or else the name can be specified as a string variable. The S means that this file will be a sequential data file. In the file directory, the file will have the file type SEQ. (Remember that program files have type PRG.) The W means that we will be writing information to the file, so this file is an output file. (The terms "input" and "output" are always used from the computer's point of view, not the point of view of the file.)

Once the file has been open as an output file, we can write information to it:

20   A\$ = "HELLO HOW ARE YOU?"

30   PRINT#2,A\$

The command PRINT#2,A\$ tells the computer that the string variable A\$ is to be written to file number 2. We can also write a numeric variable to the file:

40   N = 100

50   PRINT#2,N

After we have finished writing output to the file, we use the CLOSE command:

60 CLOSE 2

We must open the file again if we would like to read some information from it:

70   OPEN 3,8,3,"HELLO,S,R"

This time we are opening the file HELLO as file number 3. Once again, 8 is the device number, the channel number (3) is the same as the file number, and the S means that this is a sequential data file. The R means that we will be reading information from the file.

Now we can have the computer perform the read operation:

80   INPUT#3,X\$

90   INPUT#3,Z

The command INPUT#3,X\$ tells the computer to read the next item from file number 3 and store that item under the name X\$. Then it will read the next item from the file and store it under the variable name Z. Note that the name of the variable used in the INPUT command does not have to be the same as the name that the variable had when it was originally saved on the disk file.

We can cause the computer to print the new values of these variables:

100 PRINT X\$,Z

and the screen will display:

HELLO HOW ARE YOU?   100

Now we are done with the file, we can close it:

110 CLOSE 3

Here is the general form of the commands for file input and

and output on the Commodore 64:

To open a file:

OPEN *filenum,devicenum,channum,idstring*
where *filenum* is the file number, *devicenum* is the device number (which will be 8 for disk files), *channum* is the channel number (which can be the same as the file number), and *idstring* is a string that identifies the file; *idstring* can be expressed either as a string written in quotation marks or it can be a string variable. It must consist of three parts: the name of the file followed by a comma, the letter S followed by a comma to indicate that this is a sequential file, and the letter W (if information is to be written to this file) or the letter R (if information is to be read from this file.)
To write information to a file:

PRINT#*filenum,item*

where *filenum* is the file number and *item* is the information to be written to the file (either a number, numeric variable, string, or string variable.) If a variable name is used, then only the value of that variable is saved. The variable name itself is not saved, so you do not need to use the same name when you read the data back from the file.
To read information from a file:

INPUT#*filenum,varname*

where *filenum* is the file number and *varname* is the variable name that will take its value from the next item in the file. If the next item in the file is a string, *varname* must be a string variable.
To close a file:

CLOSE*filenum*

where *filenum* is the file number

---

* * * * *

FILES IN APPLESOFT BASIC

Before you can use a disk file you must open it, using the OPEN command. By analogy, a person cannot put anything in or take anything out of a file folder without first opening it. The OPEN command is a special type of PRINT statement. The first character in the PRINT statement is the character with ASCII code 4. This character is represented by typing Control-D at the keyboard. We will assign this value to a character string variable called D$.

10 D$ = CHR$(4)

You will find it convenient to include this statement at the beginning of every program that uses files. Now we can open a file:

20 PRINT D$;"OPEN HI"

The D$ character signals the computer that this PRINT statement deals with files. HI is the name of the file that is being opened. Note carefully the position of the semicolon and the quotation marks.

Now we need to include a command to tell the computer to write information to this file:

30 PRINT D$;"WRITE HI"

Once this command has been executed, the output from all subsequent PRINT statements will be directed to the file named HI. For example, the statements

40 A$ = "HELLO HOW ARE YOU?"

50 PRINT A$

will cause the characters HELLO HOW ARE YOU? to be stored on the disk. We can also write numerical values to the disk:

60 N = 100

70 PRINT N

After we are finished writing data to the file, we need to include this command:

80 PRINT D$

and then we need to close the file:

90 PRINT D$;"CLOSE HI"

A program must always close a file after writing to it in order to prevent information from being lost. In normal circumstances you would not reopen the file immediately after closing it, but that is what we will do next in this example program:

100 PRINT D$;"OPEN HI"

Now we need a command to tell the computer to take data for all subsequent input statements from the file HI instead of from the keyboard:

110 PRINT D$;"READ HI"

Here are two input statements:

120 INPUT X$

130 INPUT Z

The command INPUT X$ causes the computer to look for the first item in the file HI and assign that item to X$. Then it will look for the next item in the file and assign that item to Z. After we are finished reading from the file, we once again use a PRINT D$ command.

140 PRINT D$

Now we can display the values of X$ and Z:

150 PRINT X$,Z

The result is:

HELLO HOW ARE YOU?   100

Note that the variable names for the items read from the file (lines 120–130) do not need to be the same as the variable names that the items had before they were written to the file (lines 50–70).
Now we must close the file:

160 PRINT D$;"CLOSE HI"

Here is the general form of the commands for file input and output for Apple computers:

Include the assignment statement D$ = CHR$(4) at the beginning of your program.

To open a file, write:

PRINT D$;"OPEN *filename*"

or

PRINT D$;"OPEN" *stringvar*

where *filename* is the name of the file being opened or *stringvar* is a string variable whose value is the name of the file.
To write information to the file, include the command

PRINT D$;"WRITE *filename*"

or the command

PRINT D$;"WRITE" *stringvar*

The output from all subsequent PRINT statements will be directed to the file until the command

PRINT D$

occurs.

To read information from the file, include the command

PRINT D$;"READ *filename*"

or the command

PRINT D$;"READ" *stringvar*

The input for all subsequent INPUT statements will be read from the file until the command

PRINT D$

occurs.

When the program is done with the file, it must be closed with the command

PRINT D$;"CLOSE *filename*"

or the command

PRINT D$;"CLOSE" *stringvar*

* * * * *

ALPHABETIZING NAMES

Here are some examples of programs that use data files. In Chapter 7, we wrote a program that read in a list of names and then printed them out in alphabetical order. Now we can have the program store the names on a disk file. The next time we use the program, we can have it read in the names from the disk file. At this time we can also add new names to the list, once again storing the list when we are done. Here is the program, written in Microsoft BASIC:

```
1 REM  This program reads in a list of names from a disk file,
2 REM   allows you to add more names, alphabetizes the names,
3 REM   prints them out, and then stores them on a disk file.
4 REM  This is Microsoft BASIC
5 S=1
10  DIM A$(100)   'Assume that less than 100 names will be read
15 PRINT "Enter file name or press <RETURN> to start new file"
16 INPUT F$
```

```
17 IF F$<> "" THEN GOSUB 400   'Read file from disk
20    GOSUB 100    'Read in names
30    GOSUB 200    'Alphabetize names
40    GOSUB 300    'Print names
50    GOSUB 500    'Store names on disk
60    END
100 REM   Read in names
110   INPUT "Number of names to add?";N
115     N=N+S-1   'N is now the total number of names
120   FOR I=S TO N
130     PRINT I;
140     INPUT A$(I)
150   NEXT I
160 RETURN
200 REM   Bubble sort procedure
210   FOR I=1 TO N
220     FOR J=1 TO N-I
230         IF A$(J)>A$(J+1) THEN T$=A$(J+1):A$(J+1)=A$(J):A$(J)=T$
240     NEXT J
250   NEXT I
260   RETURN
300   REM PRINT OUTPUT
305   PRINT "Here is the list in alphabetical order:"
310   FOR I=1 TO N
320     PRINT USING "####";I;
330     PRINT ".   ";A$(I)
340   NEXT I
350   RETURN
400 REM Read file from disk
410 OPEN"I",#1,F$
420   I=0
430   REM - START LOOP
440     I=I+1
450     INPUT#1,A$(I)
460     IF A$(I)<>"END" THEN GOTO 430
470     CLOSE#1
475     S=I
480     PRINT S-1;" names were read in."
490     PRINT "NOW YOU MAY ADD MORE NAMES"
495   RETURN
500 REM Store names on disk
510 INPUT "Name of file:";F$
511 REM   Note that the file where we store the names does not
512 REM   have to be the same as the file where we first read them.
520 OPEN"O",#1,F$
530 FOR I=1 TO N
540     PRINT#1,A$(I)
550   NEXT I
560   PRINT #1,"END"
570   CLOSE#1
580 RETURN
```

Note that we use F$ as a string variable that will hold the name of the file. The use of a string variable to specify the file name makes the program much more flexible, since we can use the same program for several different files. In Chapter 12, we will write a much more detailed program that stores information in a disk file.

BASKETBALL STATISTICS

In Chapter 5, we wrote a program that calculates the statistics for a basketball team, but that program could only process the statistics for one game at a time. It will be much more helpful to write a program that can also calculate the cumulative season statistics. After each game, such a program stores the season totals in a file so that they will be available to calculate the new season totals after the next game. Here is the program, written in Commodore BASIC:

```
1   REM   BASKETBALL STATISTICS PROGRAM
2   REM   THIS PROGRAM RUNS ON A
3   REM   COMMODORE 64 COMPUTER WITH
4   REM   A COMMODORE 1541 DISK DRIVE
50  DIM N$(12):REM ASSUME 11 PLAYER MAX
51  REM ONE LINE WILL BE THE TEAM TOTALS
60  DIM S(2,12,8)
61  REM   S IS THE ARRAY HOLDING STATISTICS
62  REM   THE FIRST SUBSCRIPT IDENTIFIES
63  REM   WHETHER THESE ARE INDIVIDUAL
64  REM   GAME STATISTICS (1) OR
65  REM   CUMULATIVE SEASON STATISTICS (2)
66  REM   THE SECOND SUBSCRIPT IS THE
67  REM   PLAYER NUMBER.  THE THIRD
68  REM   SUBSCRIPT IS THE STATISTIC NUMBER
70  DIM   SL$(8)
75  FOR J = 1 TO 8 : READ SL$(J) : NEXT J
80  DATA "   FG","  FGA","   FT","  FTA"
82  DATA " REB"," PTS"," FG%"," FT%"
90  H$(1) = "THIS GAME"
92  H$(2) = "CUMULATIVE SEASON TOTALS"
100 PRINT "HOW MANY GAMES HAVE BEEN"
105 PRINT "PLAYED SO FAR ";NG
110 IF NG = 0 THEN GOSUB 1000:GOTO 135
120 GOSUB 200 : REM READ IN NAMES
130 GOSUB 300 : REM READ IN PAST STATS
135 GOSUB 370 : REM READ IN CURRENT STATS
140 GOSUB 400 : REM PROCESS STATS
150 GOSUB 500 : REM OUTPUT
160 GOSUB 600 : REM SAVE STATS
170 END
199 REM *********************
200 REM READ IN NAMES
210 OPEN 2,8,2,"NLIST,S,R"
220 INPUT#2,N : REM NUMBER OF PLAYERS
230 FOR I = 1 TO N
240 INPUT#2,N$(I)
250 NEXT I
260 CLOSE 2
```

```
265 N2 = N + 1 : N$(N2) = "TOTAL"
270 RETURN
299 REM **********************
300 REM   READ IN STATS
310 F1$ = STR$(NG-1)
320 F2$ = "ST"+RIGHT$(F1$,LEN(F1$)-1)
321 REM   F2$ IS THE NAME OF THE FILE
322 REM   THAT HOLDS THE PAST STATISTICS
330 F3$ = F2$ + ",S,R"
340 OPEN 3,8,3,F3$
350 FOR I = 1 TO N : FOR J = 1 TO 5
355 INPUT#3,S(2,I,J)
360 NEXT J : NEXT I
362 CLOSE 3
365 RETURN
369 REM *********************
370 REM READ IN CURRENT STATS
372 FOR I = 1 TO N
375 PRINT "INPUT STATS FOR ";N$(I)
380 FOR J = 1 TO 5 : PRINT SL$(J),
385 INPUT S(1,I,J)
390 NEXT J : NEXT I
395 RETURN
399 REM *********************
400 REM   PROCESS STATS
405 FOR I = 1 TO N : FOR J = 1 TO 5
410 S(2,I,J)=S(2,I,J)+S(1,I,J)
415 NEXT J : NEXT I
420 FOR K = 1 TO 2
424 REM CALCULATE TEAM TOTALS
425 FOR J = 1 TO 5 : T = 0
430 FOR I = 1 TO N : T = T + S(K,I,J): NEXT I
435 S(K,N2,J) = T : NEXT J
439 REM CALCULATE POINTS AND PERCENTS
440 FOR I = 1 TO N2
445 S(K,I,6) = 2 * S(K,I,1) + S(K,I,3)
450 IF S(K,I,2)<>0 THEN S(K,I,7)=INT(100*S(K,I,1)/S(K,I,2))
455 IF S(K,I,4)<>0 THEN S(K,I,8)=INT(100*S(K,I,3)/S(K,I,4))
460 NEXT I
465 NEXT K
470 RETURN
499 REM ***************************
500 REM   OUTPUT
505 FOR K = 1 TO 2
510 PRINT : PRINT H$(K)
515 PRINT "        ";
520 FOR J = 1 TO 8:PRINT SL$(J);:NEXT J
530 FOR I = 1 TO N2
535 PRINT
540 N1$=N$(I):IF LEN(N1$)>=7 THEN PRINT LEFT$(N1$,7);:GOTO 555
545 PRINT N1$;
550 PRINT SPC(7-LEN(N1$));
555 FOR J = 1 TO 8
560 S1$=STR$(S(K,I,J))
565 PRINT SPC(4-LEN(S1$));S1$;
570 NEXT J
575 NEXT I
```

Continued

```
580 NEXT K
590 RETURN
599 REM ****************************
600 REM   SAVE STATS
605 F1$ = STR$(NG)
610 F2$ = "ST"+RIGHT$(F1$,LEN(F1$)-1)
615 REM F2$ IS THE NAME OF THE NEW
616 REM DATA FILE
620 F3$ = F2$ + ",S,W"
625 OPEN 4,8,4,F3$
630 FOR I = 1 TO N
635 FOR J = 1 TO 5
640 PRINT#4,S(2,I,J)
645 NEXT J
650 NEXT I
660 CLOSE 4
670 RETURN
999 REM ****************************
1000 REM START OF NEW  SEASON
1001 REM  0 GAMES HAVE BEEN PLAYED SO FAR
1010 INPUT "HOW MANY PLAYERS ";N
1015 PRINT "TYPE IN NAMES OF PLAYERS:"
1020 FOR I = 1 TO N
1025 PRINT I;
1030 INPUT N$(I)
1035 NEXT I
1037 N2=N+1:N$(N2)="TOTAL"
1040 OPEN 2,8,2,"NLIST,S,W"
1050 PRINT#2,N
1060 FOR I = 1 TO N
1070 PRINT#2,N$(I)
1080 NEXT I
1090 CLOSE 2
1100 RETURN
```

The program initially asks the question, "How many games have been played so far?" If the answer is 0, the computer knows it is the beginning of the season so it executes the subroutine that reads in the names of the players and stores the names in a disk file called NLIST. (See lines 1000–1100.)

If it is not the beginning of the season, the computer will first read the players' names from the disk file (lines 200–270). Then it will read in the past cumulative statistics (lines 300–365). The name of the file that stores the statistics consists of the letters ST followed by the number of games that have been played previously. For example, the file name is ST2 if two games have been played previously. Note how the string variable F3$ is used in the OPEN command (line 330). The remaining steps are: read in the statistics for the current game (lines 370–395), calculate the new cumulative totals (lines 405–415), calculate the total statistics for the team (lines 420–435), calculate total points, field goal percent, and free throw percent (lines 440–465), display the output on the screen (lines 500–580), and store the new cumulative totals on the disk (lines 600–670).

There are many types of problems where it helps to calculate the total for each row and each column in a table of numbers. For example, a teacher who gives five exams during a quarter needs to calculate the total score on all five exams for each student. In order to calculate the class average, it is also necessary to find the total score for the entire class on each exam. After the scores for one of the exams have been entered, the computer will need to store those scores on a disk file so they will be available when it is time to enter the scores for the next exam.

Here is a general program to calculate row totals and column totals, written for an Apple IIe computer:

```
1    REM   THIS PROGRAM CALCULATES THE
2    REM   ROW TOTAL AND COLUMN TOTAL
3    REM   FOR AN ARRAY OF NUMBERS
4    REM   THE USER ENTERS THE NUMBERS
5    REM   ONE COLUMN AT A TIME.
6    REM   THE ARRAY IS STORED ON A
7    REM   DISK FILE SO MORE COLUMNS
8    REM   CAN BE ADDED LATER
9    REM   THIS IS APPLE BASIC
10   REM   ASSUME THE ARRAY HAS LESS
11   REM   THAN 30 ROWS AND 8 COLUMNS
12   DIM A(30,8)
13   FW = 5 : D$ = CHR$(4)
14   INPUT "NAME OF TABLE:";F$
15   PRINT "TYPE NEW IF THIS IS A"
16   PRINT "NEW TABLE. ELSE TYPE OLD"
20   INPUT Q$
25   IF Q$="OLD" THEN GOTO 70
30   INPUT "NUMBER OF ROWS:";NR
40   INPUT "NUMBER OF COLUMNS:";NC
60   GOTO 80
70   GOSUB 200 : REM READ IN DATA
80   GOSUB 300 : REM PRINT TABLE
85   PRINT
90   PRINT "ENTER NUMBER OF COLUMN YOU"
100  PRINT "WANT TO ENTER. TYPE 0 IF"
110  PRINT "YOU ARE DONE"
120  INPUT C
125  IF C > NC THEN NC = C
130  IF C=0 THEN GOSUB 400 : END
140  FOR I = 1 TO NR
150  PRINT I;":";
160  INPUT A(I,C)
170  NEXT I
180  GOSUB 300 : REM PRINT TABLE
190  GOTO 85
200  REM   READ IN DATA
220  PRINT D$;"OPEN"F$
225  PRINT D$;"READ"F$
227  INPUT NR
```

Continued

```
228    INPUT NC
230    FOR I = 1 TO NR
240    FOR J = 1 TO NC
250    INPUT Z
252    A(I,J)=Z
260    NEXT J : NEXT I
270    PRINT D$
280    PRINT D$;"CLOSE"F$
290    RETURN
300    REM  PRINT TABLE
302    FOR J = 1 TO NC : T = 0
303    FOR I = 1 TO NR : T = T + A(I,J)
304    NEXT I : A(NR+1,J)=T : NEXT J
305    FOR I = 1 TO NR + 1
307    PRINT
310    T = 0
315    FOR J = 1 TO NC
320    T = T + A(I,J)
330    N = A(I,J) : GOSUB 500 : REM PRINT NUM
340    NEXT J
345    N = T : GOSUB 500
350    NEXT I
360    RETURN
400    REM  SAVE DATA
410    PRINT D$;"OPEN"F$
420    PRINT D$;"WRITE"F$
425    PRINT NR
426    PRINT NC
430    FOR I = 1 TO NR
440    FOR J = 1 TO NC
450    PRINT A(I,J)
460    NEXT J
470    NEXT I
480    PRINT D$
490    PRINT D$;"CLOSE"F$
495    RETURN
500    REM  PRINT OUTPUT
510    N1$ = STR$(N)
520    L1 = LEN(N1$)
530    PRINT SPC(FW-L1);N1$;
540    RETURN
```

Note the assignment statement D$ = CHR(4) in line 13. The variable FW stands for field width, which is the maximum number of characters the program will show when it displays the output numbers. If you will be using big numbers, you will need to increase this value, but then you will not be able to fit as many columns on the screen.

The string variable F$ holds the name of the file that will store the table. In lines 15–20 the program asks the user whether this is a new table or an old table. If it is a new table, the program asks the user for the number of rows (NR) and the number of columns (NC). If it is an old table, the computer reads NC and NR from the disk file and then reads in the values for the numbers in the table. When you are done with the program, the new numbers in the table will be stored in the file. If you use this program regularly, you will most likely want to have the computer print labels for the rows and columns. (Note how the basketball program stored the names of the players in a file so that they could be read in each time.)

You will frequently use data files in programs that solve practical problems. We will use data files again in Chapter 11, when we write a financial record keeping program, and in Chapter 12, when we write a general data processing program.

By now we have covered the important features of the BASIC programming language. However, that doesn't mean we're finished with the subject of computer programming.

We still have a difficult lesson to learn. All the programs that we have done up to now have been reasonably simple. They have been so simple, in fact, that we have been able to keep track of everything that the computer has done. But we will soon come to programs that are so long that they're too confusing for us to remember how they work or even what they do. If we make the slightest mistake in such a program, it can take hours to find the error.

We have learned the BASIC programming language, but we have yet to learn the essence of programming. We have yet to learn a strategic way to develop an *algorithm* to solve a particular problem.

NOTE

• The files that we have been using in this chapter are called *sequential files*. In order to reach a particular item in a sequential file the computer must read through all of the preceding items in the file. If you have a program that frequently needs to access items in the middle of a file, you can use a different type of file called a *random file*. The use of random files requires more complicated commands, so we will only use sequential files in this book.

EXERCISES

1.   Write a program to copy the contents of one file to another file with a new name. The program should ask the user for the name of the file to copy from and the name of the new file.

For exercises 2, 3, and 4, consider files that contain a list of names in alphabetical order, such as were discussed in the chapter.

2.   Write a program that deletes a specific name from the file.

3.   Write a program that inserts a new name in the file.

4.   Write a program that merges two files into one file. Make sure that the names in the resulting file are in alphabetical order.

5. Write a program that reads in values for a two-dimensional array and then stores those values in a disk file. Write another program that reads the values from the file and puts them back in the two-dimensional array.

6.   Suppose you have several files that store values for two-dimensional arrays, as discussed in exercise 5. All of the arrays have the same dimensions. Write a program that calculates the sum of the elements in row 1, column 1 for all of the arrays; then calculates the sum of the elements in row 1, column 2 for all of the arrays; and so on for all of the elements.

7.   In Microsoft BASIC, program files are normally stored in a special coded format. However, if you include the "A" option in the SAVE command, then files are stored in ASCII format. For example, the command

SAVE "CIRCLE",A

will store the program in ASCII format with the file name CIRCLE.BAS.   When a program file has been stored in ASCII format, it is possible to read the program file as if it were a data file. Write a program that reads in a BASIC program stored in an ASCII file and displays that program on the screen. (The output from this program will look very similar to the LIST command.) Here are two useful Microsoft BASIC commands that will help you:

LINE INPUT#1,X$

The LINE INPUT#1 command is similar to the INPUT#1 command, except that the computer will read an entire line of text from the file. It will not treat commas as separators.

EOF(1)

EOF stands for *end-of-file*. You can use EOF in an IF statement. The expression EOF(1) will be true if you have reached the end of file number 1.

8.   It often would be helpful to have a list of all variables and keywords used in a program. It also would help to have a list for each variable that shows all of the line numbers that contain that variable. Write a Microsoft BASIC program that creates a variable list. See exercise 7 to learn how to store a BASIC program as an ASCII file and how that file can be used as data by another program. (A program that accomplishes this job is included in the answer section [Appendix 3].)

CHAPTER 10

PROGRAMMING TECHNIQUES

EXAMPLES OF ALGORITHMS

"What's an algorithm?" An *algorithm* is a set of instructions that specifies exactly how to solve a particular problem in a finite number of steps. For example, here is an algorithm to determine the denomination of the largest bill you currently have in your wallet.

1. Take the first bill out of your wallet and hold it in your hand.
2. Look at the next bill in your wallet.
3. If the value of the next bill in your wallet is greater than that of the bill in your hand, put down the bill in your hand and put the next bill in your hand.
4. Otherwise, take the next bill out of your wallet and put it down.
5. If there are any more bills in your wallet, go back to step 2.
6. The denomination of the bill in your hand is now the highest denomination you had in your wallet.

This algorithm can be expressed in many different languages besides English. In order for a computer to execute an algorithm, however, it needs to be translated into a computer programming language such as BASIC. Thus there are two distinct jobs involved in writing a computer program: the problem-solving part, which involves developing the algorithm, and the coding part, which involves writing that algorithm in a computer language.

Imagine that we have just been given a very complicated computer programming problem. How do we go about solving it? In this chapter we'll develop some general rules that can be helpful in developing algorithms for computers to solve. The first rule follows:

STRATEGY RULE 1

> As far as possible, try to write the program so that people can understand it.

WRITE PROGRAMS PEOPLE UNDERSTAND

A computer program needs to be understood by two quite different types of creatures—computers and people. The computer will be able to understand the program just fine if the program is boring, if it contains no REM statements, and if it has variable names that have no particular meanings. The computer doesn't care whether the variable you use to represent height has the name H or Q7. The computer will be satisfied with any method that works, even if it is very difficult to know why the method works.

However, there are several reasons why an effort should be made to write programs that are understandable by people. The process of writing the program will be much easier if you try to understand what you're doing while you're doing it. It will be much easier to make changes in a program or correct errors in it if the program is written so as to be people oriented. And other people will be able to use your program if you specify very clearly what is going on. Drawing a general strategy flowchart, using the flowchart symbols we discussed earlier, is often a good idea. A general strategy flowchart specifies the broad outline of what steps are to be taken in a program. A detailed program flowchart, which specifies each step of the program, also helps sometimes. You will have to decide for yourself whether a detailed program flowchart will help you.

The rest of the rules include suggestions for how to write programs that people understand.

STRATEGY RULE 2

> Break a major problem into smaller problems and, if necessary, break the smaller problems into still smaller problems.

BREAK PROBLEMS INTO BITE-SIZED PIECES

After you have specified exactly what each part should do, go ahead and write the parts.

If you face a very large unmanageable problem, there is no general way to tackle it. However, if you break the problem down into bite-sized pieces, they become much easier to handle. The final program then becomes a group of modules, that is, different parts with different purposes that fit together. This type of approach to programming is sometimes called the *top-down* approach because you start at the top and look at the whole problem first before you look at the details. While you're working at the top level, you decide exactly what each part is supposed to do, but you don't have to worry about how the subparts work until later. Each subpart is small enough that it is possible for you to understand how it works.

Here is a non-computer-programming example of the top-down approach, which illustrates Strategy Rule 2. Suppose you need to plan a driving trip across the country from New York to Los Angeles. The wrong way to plan the trip would be first to pull out the street map of New York and figure out what streets you need to drive on to get out of New York. It would be even worse to pull out a map of Kansas City and plan your route through that city since you won't even know for sure whether you'll go through Kansas City. What you should do first is look at a map of the entire United States and then figure out what your general course will be without worrying about the specific details. Then you should make a list of all the states you will go through and look at maps of those states. Finally, after you know what road you will be on when you go into a city and what road you will be on when you leave it, you can look at a detailed street map for that city to plot your course through it.

Next are two important rules to follow to keep track of variable names.

STRATEGY RULE 3

> Whenever possible, a variable name should give some indication of what that variable represents.

MAKE VARIABLE NAMES MEANINGFUL

A mnemonic device is a way to help us remember something, so we can say that a variable name should be a mnemonic variable name.

It is easier to use mnemonic variable names if your version of BASIC allows you to use whole words as variable names. For example, a variable that represents the height of something could be called H, but it would be even better to call it HEIGHT. Check your manual to see how many characters are allowed in variable names in your version. Microsoft BASIC allows very long variable names, but you probably want to avoid names longer than eight or nine characters. After all, somebody (probably you) needs to type the variable name at every location it appears in the program. In Commodore BASIC and Applesoft BASIC, variable names can be as long as you want, but only the first two characters are significant. That means that two variable names with the same first two letters will be treated as the same variable. You must be careful if you use variable names longer than two letters, since two variables that look different (such as HEIGHT and HEAT) will be considered the same by the computer.

STRATEGY RULE 4

> Keep a list of variable names and their meanings handy as you write the program.

REMEMBER WHAT EACH VARIABLE MEANS

You must be especially careful that you don't use a variable name to mean one thing in one place in a large program, and then use the same variable name to mean something totally different in another place in the program.

STRATEY RULE 5

> Use a REM statement to explain in English what each important BASIC statement does.

USE REM STATEMENTS

The beginning of a program should contain a REM statement that explains what the program itself does. (You may also like to include your name and the date that the program was written in a REM statement.) A REM statement should contain some useful information and not just repeat what is obvious by looking at the program. For example, in the program segment:

```
100   REM  IF A < 0 OR B < 0, GO TO LINE 200
110   IF A < 0 GOTO 200
120   IF B < 0 GOTO 200
130   REM  C IS THE SQUARE ROOT OF
131   REM     A SQUARED PLUS B SQUARED
140   C = SQR(A ↑ 2 + B ↑ 2)
```

the REM statements do not convey any useful information at all. This example is much better:

```
100   REM  A AND B ARE THE TWO SHORT SIDES
101   REM     OF A RIGHT TRIANGLE
102   REM  IF EITHER A OR B IS NEGATIVE
103   REM     WE NEED TO PRINT AN ERROR
104   REM     MESSAGE
110   IF A < 0 GOTO 200
120   IF B < 0 GOTO 200
130   REM  C IS THE LENGTH OF THE HYPOTENUSE
140   C = SQR(A ↑ 2 + B ↑ 2)
```

In this segment the REM statements are more helpful.

STRATEGY RULE 6

> The appearance of a program listing is important.

MAKE THE PROGRAM LOOK GOOD

A program will be easier to read if it looks neat. Statements that are in loops and subroutines should be indented, and all other statements should be aligned evenly. It is especially important to make sure that the major sections of a program are clearly separated. This can be done by inserting blank REM statements or REM statements consisting of a row of stars. Each subroutine should have a REM statement that clearly labels its beginning. Working on the appearance of the program listing can often be a nice break from the rigors of actual programming.

STRATEGY RULE 7

> Spend time to make the program output look nice.

MAKE THE OUTPUT LOOK GOOD

Make sure that everything is labeled with explanatory messsages, and arrange lists of numbers in neat rows and columns. Decide on the correct number of decimal places that need to be displayed for each numerical result, and make sure that each number is rounded off by the appropriate amount. The effort spent on maintaining neat program output will be well worth it.

However, it is important *not* to spend time worrying about how the output will look while you're working on the main problem. The development of the main program algorithm requires a lot of creative thinking, whereas writing the section of the program that directs the computer to print the output is a tedious and often boring task. You shouldn't let the creative algorithm development task be interrupted by worrying about petty details such as whether to use PRINT USING "####.###" or PRINT USING "###.###". Develop the main part of the program first. Then, after you've rested up from that arduous creative task, spend some time to get the output format right.

Another cause for concern is the proliferation of GOTOs in programs. A program that has too many GOTOs can be as disorderly as a bowl of spaghetti.

STRATEGY RULE 8

> Avoid having too many GOTOs in programs.

DON'T CONFUSE YOURSELF WITH TOO MANY GOTOS

This is one of the important rules for writing *structured programs*.

First we need to look at some common reasons why GOTO statements are used. One situation that occurs frequently is an IF statement, where there is one instruction to execute if the condition is true and another one to execute if the condition is false. (See Figure 10–1 for a flowchart of this kind of situation.) This situation can be programmed by using crisscrossed GOTOs. However, since the second half of an IF statement does not have to be a GOTO statement, we can rewrite the program as follows to avoid the crisscrossed GOTOs:

IF H > 40 LET P = 40 ∗ 7 + 1.5 ∗ 7 ∗ (H − 40): REM   OVERTIME

IF H < = 40 LET P = 7 ∗ H   : REM   REGULAR

If we have more than one statement that needs to be executed in each case, we can take advantage of the fact that the computer will ignore that entire rest of the line if the initial IF condition is false. For example:

10   IF X < 5 PRINT "X < 5" : A = 5 : B = X – 5

20   IF X > = 5 PRINT "X > = 5" : A = X : B = 5

However, there will be some cases where the blocks of statements we need to execute are too long to fit on one line. In that case there is no way (in BASIC) to avoid crisscrossed GOTOs.

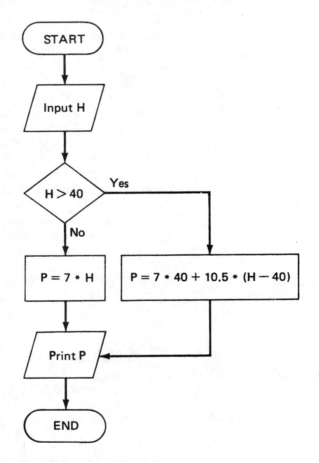

Figure 10-1

The best thing to do then is to make sure that there are enough comments to make clear what is happening.

100   IF *condition* **GOTO 200**

110   REM

111   REM ***

120   REM ----------- **DO THIS SECTION IF THE** ------

```
121   REM   CONDITION IS FALSE
            .
            .
            .
180   GOTO 300
185   REM -------------------------------------------------
186   REM ************************************************
187   REM
188   REM
200   REM ----------- DO THIS SECTION IF THE ------
201   REM   CONDITION IS TRUE
            .
            .
            .
299   REM -------------------------------------------------
300 etc.
```

In general, GOTO statements are understandable if they crisscross around two well-marked alternative paths or if they are part of a well-marked iteration. If you have to use a GOTO in a situation other than the two mentioned, mark the destination of the GOTO clearly and make sure that the destination is at the beginning of a major program segment rather than in the middle of one.

STRATEGY RULE 9

> Whenever possible, be as general as you can.

BE GENERAL

This rule means that it is a good idea to use variable names instead of numbers as much as possible in the middle of a program. For example, suppose you need to find the average of seven numbers. You can use this program:

```
100   T = 0
110   FOR I = 1 TO 7
120      INPUT X
130      T = T + X
140   NEXT I
150   A = T/7
```

Suppose that some other day you want to find the average of eight numbers. It would have been much easier if you had originally written this program:

```
100    T = 0
110    N = 7
120    FOR I = 1 TO N
130       INPUT X
140       T = T + X
150    NEXT I
160    A = T/N
```

Now, to make the program work for eight numbers, all you need to do is change the second line to N = 8. (If you expect a lot of variation in the number of items you will need to average, it would be a good idea to change the second line to INPUT "N = ";N.)

For another example, suppose you wrote a program in 1977 to calculate the average per-game statistics for National Football League (NFL) teams. The wrong way to do it would have been to fill your program with statements such as A = T/14. These statements would have worked if the NFL schedule had always stayed 14 games long. But if you wanted to run the program in 1978, you would have found that the NFL schedule contained 16 games for each team, so you would have had to go through the entire program and change each 14 to a 16.

It is often a good idea to make a list of the items that will remain constant during a particular run of the program but may change during some future run. Then the assignment statements for these values should be grouped together near the start of the program.

IS IT RIGHT?

After you have followed all these procedures, there still remains one nagging problem: How do you know that the program you have written is correct? In other words, how do you know that the program does what you want it to?

With a simple program you should be able to tell just by looking at it whether it is correct. The task is more difficult with complicated programs. The easiest way is to check the output of the program to see whether the program gave the correct answer. Of course, this is often impossible since if you had known the correct answer in advance you wouldn't have needed to write the program. However, there are some cases where you can tell just by looking whether the output is correct. For example, if you have a program to sort a list of numbers, you can scan through the output list to make sure that the numbers really have been put in the correct order. There will also be cases in which the program answer is obviously wrong, for example, if the program prints a negative result for a variable that you know must be positive, such as a person's weight. In those cases you know that you have to go back to the program to make changes.

There will be other programs for which you won't know in general what the correct answer will be, but you will know what the answers will be for some values of the input data. Then you can test the program by running those data through the program.

STRATEY RULE 9

> Before a program is used in normal operation, it should be checked using test data, that is, data for which the correct results have already been determined.

TEST THE PROGRAM

It will be necesssary to run several tests of a program to see if it really works, since it is possible that the program might give the correct answer for some values just by accident. The test data used should be varied enough so that several of the possible conditional paths through the program are followed.

Now we come to an even more difficult problem. What if you test run the program and find that, horror of horrors, it doesn't work? Then what? That means that the program is infested with an error, or, as computer people say, it has a bug. (There is a slight possibility that an error might be caused by hardware failure, that is, the computer failing to execute correctly the instructions it has been given. However, such errors are relatively rare on most computers.)

GETTING THE BUGS OUT

The process of correcting a program to remove bugs is called *debugging*. If you have thought carefully about the program before running it, then it should not take too long to debug. However, sometimes debugging can be one of the longest and most frustrating parts of programming.

There are several different types of bugs for which you should be on the lookout. The first type is the typographical error or simple syntax error. Examples of these include mismatched parentheses or misspelled key words. They can occur because you were careless in translating your program idea into BASIC or because you hit the wrong key on the typewriter. These types of errors are the easiest to correct since the computer will print an informative message to tell you what kind of error has occurred. Then you just have to examine the statement with the error and rewrite it. One helpful technique in examining complicated expressions is to draw lines connecting each opening parenthesis with its closing parenthesis. For example:

$$Y = B * SQR(1 - (((X + E * A)/A) \uparrow 2))$$

This procedure allows you to make sure that the parentheses match up correctly and that the operations will be executed in the order that you intend.

There are several other types of errors that the computer itself will catch. For example, the computer will make sure that each FOR statement has a corresponding NEXT statement and that every statement referred to in a GOTO or GOSUB statement really exists in the program.

The nature of the error messages you receive depends on the way your system translates BASIC programs. There are two distinct ways of translating programs into the computer's native machine language: *interpreters* and *compilers*. In an interpreter system, the computer reads one BASIC instruction at a time and then executes it immediately. Then it proceeds to translate the next instruction. In a compiler system, the entire program is translated into a machine language program (called an *object program*). For many compilers you must give a separate command to tell the computer to execute the program it has just compiled.

Most BASIC systems are interpreters, although there are some compiler versions of BASIC available, such as Quick Basic from Microsoft. Many other programming languages, such as Pascal, use compiler systems. In this book we have been assuming you are working with an interpreter system. Each system has its advantages and disadvantages. The main advantage of an interpreter is that it is easier to use. To execute our programs all we need to do is type RUN, and the program starts running right away. In a compiler system, you cannot run the program for the first time until after it has been compiled. Every subsequent time you run the program, however, it will be executed faster than it would in an interpreter system because it is no longer necessary to interpret each line again.

When the computer reaches an error in an interpreter system, the program stops immediately and an error message is displayed. You must fix that error before you run the program again. In some compiler systems, the computer checks the entire program for syntax errors and prints a list of any errors that need to be fixed before compiling the program again.

Even if the syntax of the program is entirely correct, there are other types of errors that the computer might uncover. For example, suppose the computer is running the program and it comes across the instruction $A = 1/B$, where B has the value 0. Since the computer cannot divide by 0, it will have to print an error message. This type of error is called an *execution time error*. An execution time error can also occur if the result of a calculation is a number too big for the computer to handle (this is called an *overflow error*) or if an array subscript is used that is not permissible for that array.

There are several possible reasons for these types of errors. They could be the result of a simple mistake; for example, you might have typed 1/B when you meant 1/V. Or they could result because the computer is being asked to calculate a special case for which the formula you are using doesn't work. For example, a simple program using the quadratic formula will not work if $a = 0$, even if the program will work in all other cases. When this situation arises, you will need to add some modification to your program to take care of the special case. In the case of an overflow error it is also possible that the problem you are attempting is simply beyond the capability of the computer; for example, the computer cannot calculate 100000 factorial.

Computer error messages can be very annoying. However, all the preceding types of errors are easier to correct than a program logic error. With the preceding types of errors the computer will give you some clue as to what kind of error has been made and where it occurred. However, suppose the computer generates no error messages at all and happily prints results. You still need to make sure that those results are right, using test data to check the program. But suppose you do that and find that the program gives the wrong results for the test data.

Here are two possible ways to locate program logic errors. The first is to have the computer display the changes in a particular variable; the second is to execute the program by hand yourself. To display the changes in a variable, insert several auxiliary PRINT statements in strategic locations in the middle of the program. For example, if your program has the statement

100 X1 = X2 * COS(L) + Y2 * SIN(L)

you can insert the statement

110   PRINT "X1 = " ;X1;"X2 = ";X2; "Y2 = ";Y2; "L = ";L

after statement number 100. Then you can check to make sure that the values of the variables change in the way that you want them to. This method often allows you to catch errors since you can pinpoint which variables are not taking on the values they're supposed to. After you've corrected all the errors and the program is ready to run, you can remove all the auxiliary PRINT statements.

Some computers allow you to include the command STOP at key places in the middle of the program. The computer will temporarily halt execution when it comes to the STOP command. This allows you to peek inside and see what is going on in the middle of the program. You can make sure that all variables have the proper values at that point. After you're finished checking the situation, you can type the command CONT (for CONTINUE), and the computer will resume execution at the place where it stopped.

You might ask: How do I know what the correct values of the variables are? You will have to do some calculations on your own. It will help to have the description of each variable available, and often the process of writing that description can help with debugging the program.

Another useful command on some computers is the TRACE (or TRON) command. If you put the command TRACE at the beginning of the program, the computer will display the number of each line as it executes the line. This allows you to observe whether the computer is executing the lines in the order that you intended.

The first method—checking the values of key variables at strategic points in the program—is the best way to detect the errors if you have a hunch about what variables are ending up with wrong values or if you think you can localize an error to a specific region of the program. But if you have no idea about where the error is, you may have to use the second method—the hand-check method. Take a piece of paper, a small calculator, and a printed listing of your program. Then, starting at the top, pretend that you are the computer and do everything that the program tells you to do. Every time you come to an assignment statement, calculate the new value for that variable and write it down. Eventually you will find the error. The hand-check method will probably work, but it is very tedious since it requires you to do all the work that you wanted the computer to do for you.

One advantage of the hand-check method is that you will quickly catch an error that arises when a variable is given a wrong initial value. Many program errors result because of a failure to initialize variables properly. On some computers, all numerical variables will automatically be given the initial value 0. However, it is still a good idea to assign the initial values explicitly for all variables.

Now we're ready to write some long programs. The rest of the book contains several examples of programs that perform a variety of different functions: maintain financial records, keep track of information on filing cards, play games, draw pictures, and perform scientific calculations. You will quickly learn to appreciate how versatile computers can be.

CHAPTER 11

FINANCIAL RECORD PROGRAM

PROGRAM GOALS

Now we are ready to write a complete program for personal financial record keeping. Here are the goals we would like the program to accomplish:

1. Print a report of income and expenditures in different categories at the end of each month.
2. Store the totals for each month on a disk, so that we can also print a report showing year-to-date totals at the end of each month.
3. Have the reports show the balance in each asset account. Examples of asset accounts include bank checking and savings accounts and the amount of cash you currently hold. Since we should have a record of all transactions into or out of each account, we can calculate the account balance by starting with the balance at the end of the previous month and then adding or subtracting the amount of each transaction affecting that account. We can double-check the accuracy of the transaction information by making sure that the balance calculated in this manner equals the actual balance for the account reported by the bank.

To use the program you will need to keep records of three different types of transactions:

1. Expenditure transactions (from an asset account to an expenditure category).
2. Income transactions (from an income category to an asset account).
3. Transfer transactions (from one asset account to another; an example of a transfer transaction would be when you withdraw some cash out of your checking account).

175

During the month you will need to keep a record of each transaction in a notebook. You already should have been keeping a record of each transaction in your checking account. Now you will also need to keep a record of cash transactions. However, you are not likely to find it worthwhile to keep track of every single penny that you spend. Therefore, the program will have some flexibility. There will be a category called "unrecorded cash expenditure" that will represent the total amount of nickels and dimes you spent without bothering to record them.

We will need three different types of code numbers: for expenditure categories, for income categories, and for asset accounts. Code numbers from 1 to 99 will represent expenditure categories; code numbers from 101 to 199 will represent income categories; and code numbers from 201 to 299 will represent asset accounts. We will not use every possible code number, since we will not have 99 different categories of each type. Here is one possible list of codes:

EXPENDITURE CATEGORIES

Code Number	Category
1	Housing
2	Groceries
3	Restaurant meals
4	Medical expenses
5	Charity
6	Car payments
7	Gasoline
8	Travel
9	Parking
10	Heating fuel
11	Computer supplies
12	Insurance
13	Entertainment
14	Gifts
15	Electricity
16	Other utilities
17	Phone
18	Books
19	Magazines
20	Newspapers
21	Clothes
22	Furniture
23	Shoes
24	Cleaning
25	Health supplies
26	Recreation
27	Car maintenance
28	Hotel
29	Electronic goods

Code Number	Category
30	Education
31	Office supplies
32	Donations
33	Memberships
34	Postage
35	Photography supplies
36	Special events
37	Bank service charges
38	Interest payments
39	Records/tapes
40	Hair care
41	Yard care/gardening
42	Appliances
43	Kitchen supplies
44	Taxes
54	Other
55	Unrecorded cash expenditures

INCOME CATEGORIES

Code Number	Category
101	Paycheck (list your regular employer here)
102	Interest earned
103	Gift income
108	Other

ASSET ACCOUNTS

Code Number	Category
201	Cash
202	Checking account
203	Savings account
204	IRA
205	Credit Union account

You will want to develop your own list of code numbers using the categories that are most convenient for you.

You may study accounting and double-entry bookkeeping if you would like to learn the formal way to keep track of financial data. We will apply the same principles in a slightly more informal manner. In our system, each transaction record will contain the amount of the transaction and two codes: the *from* code and the *to* code. The *from* code states where the money comes from (either an income category or an asset account). The *to* code states where the money went (either an expenditure category or an asset account).

The computer can tell which type of transaction it is by the nature of the code numbers:

Type of transaction	*from* code	*to* code
expenditure	asset account	expenditure category
income	income category	asset account
transfer	asset account	asset account

Here is a sample of the notebook you would use to keep track of cash expenditures in this system:

Date	Category	Amount	Description
1/3	2	42.35	groceries
1/5	13	4.50	movie
1/7	9	2.00	parking
1/7	7	12.54	gas
1/8	20	.25	newspaper

PROGRAM SECTIONS

Now we can develop the general structure of the program. Here are the tasks it must perform along with references to the line numbers in the program:

1. Dimension the arrays and initialize the category list (lines 20–410).
2. Read in the past cumulative totals from the disk file (lines 15000–15190).
3. Read in the transaction data (lines 1000–1099). After each transaction is entered, the computer will display a listing of the transaction so that you can check to make sure it was entered correctly. It will also display the balance of the affected asset accounts. After all transaction records have been entered, the computer will store a list of the transactions on a disk file in case it becomes necessary to make corrections later.
4. Provide a means to fix any errors that may have occurred while the transactions were entered (lines 4000–4210).
5. Calculate the totals for each category (lines 3000–3690).
6. Read in the actual cash balance (line 3550). This balance can be compared with the computed cash balance, which is figured by starting with the previous month's cash balance and then subtracting or adding the amount of each recorded cash transaction for this month. Any discrepancy between the actual balance and the computed balance must have arisen because of unrecorded cash expenditures.
7. Print the reports (lines 2000–2580). Note there are four types of reports (current expenditures, current income, year-to-date expenditures, and year-to-date income), but

we can use the same subroutines to sort and print each report (lines 2100–2580).

8. Store the cumulative totals on a disk file so that they will be ready to read in for next month's report (lines 16000–16190). In order for this section to work, it is essential that the information be written to the disk in the same order that it is read from the disk by the disk input routine.

PROGRAM LISTING

This program is much longer than any program we have done previously, but don't panic. It consists of many small sections. Here is the program:

```
1 REM      EXPENDITURE AND INCOME RECORD PROGRAM
2 REM       WRITTEN IN MICROSOFT BASIC
3 REM       THIS PROGRAM READS IN INFORMATION ON THREE TYPES
4 REM       OF TRANSACTIONS:
5 REM       EXPENDITURE TRANSACTIONS -  FROM AN ASSET ACCOUNT
6 REM            TO AN EXPENDITURE CATEGORY
7 REM       INCOME TRANSACTIONS - FROM AN INCOME CATEGORY
8 REM            TO AN ASSET ACCOUNT
9 REM       TRANSFER TRANSACTIONS - FROM ONE ASSET ACCOUNT
10 REM           TO ANOTHER ASSET ACCOUNT
11 REM       EXPENDITURE CATEGORIES HAVE CODE NUMBERS FROM 1 TO 99
12 REM       INCOME CATEGORIES HAVE CODE NUMBERS FROM 101 TO 199
13 REM       ACCOUNTS HAVE CODE NUMBERS FROM 201 TO 299
14 REM       AFTER THE INFORMATION HAS BEEN ENTERED THE COMPUTER
15 REM       PRINTS CURRENT AND CUMULATIVE REPORTS FOR INCOME
16 REM       AND EXPENDITURES AND THEN SAVES THE CUMULATIVE TOTALS
17 REM       AND ACCOUNT BALANCES ON A DISK FILE WITH THE FILE
18 REM       EXTENSIN .FRP SO THIS INFORMATION CAN BE USED IN
19 REM       NEXT MONTH'S REPORT.
20 INPUT "DATE:",DT$
30 ON ERROR GOTO 18000    ' THIS STATEMENT IS INCLUDED TO PROTECT
31 REM                     THE PROGRAM FROM A FILE NOT FOUND ERROR
50 DIM FRLIST(300), TOLIST(300)  ' FRLIST=FROM CODE FOR EACH TRANSACTION
51  REM                            TOLIST=TO CODE FOR EACH TRANSACTION
52 DIM AMLIST(300)      'THE ARRAY THAT HOLDS THE AMOUNT
53 REM                  FOR EACH TRANSACTION
54 DIM EXPEND(55)       'EXPEND IS THE ARRAY THAT HOLDS THE
55 REM                  TOTAL EXPENDITURE IN EACH CATEGORY.
56 NUMEXP=55            'NUMBER OF EXPENDITURE CATEGORIES
57 DIM CAT$(230)        'CAT$ IS THE ARRAY HOLDING THE LABELS FOR
58 REM                  THE CATEGORIES
59 DIM A(55),A2(55),ORDER(55)   'THESE ARRAYS ARE USED IN THE SORT PROCESS
60  NUMINC=8            'NUMBER OF INCOME CATEGORIES
61  NUMACTS=10          'NUMBER OF ACCOUNTS  (CASH,BANK ACCTS)
65 DIM CUMEXP(55),CUMINC(10) 'ARRAYS THAT STORE CUMULATIVE TOTALS
70 DIM BALANCE(10),INCOME(10),BAL2(10)
71 REM  BALANCE HOLDS THE BALANCE IN EACH ACCOUNT
72 REM  BAL2 HOLDS THE WORKING BALANCES
```

Continued

```
73 REM   INCOME HOLDS THE INCOME AMOUNT FOR EACH CATEGORY
100 FOR J=1 TO NUMEXP: READ CAT$(J) : NEXT J   'EXPENDITURE CATEGORIES
110 DATA "   HOUSING"," GROCERIES","RESTAURANT","  MEDICINE"
111 DATA "   CHARITY","       CAR","       GAS","    TRAVEL"
112 DATA "   PARKING","   HEATING","COMP. SUPP"," INSURANCE"
113 DATA "ENTERTAIN."," 	 GIFTS","ELECTRICIT","OTHER UTIL"
114 DATA "     PHONE","     BOOKS"," MAGAZINES","NEWSPAPERS"
115 DATA "   CLOTHES"," FURNITURE","     SHOES","  CLEANING"
116 DATA "    HEALTH","RECREATION","CAR MAINT.","     HOTEL"
117 DATA "ELECTRONIC"," EDUCATION","    OFFICE","  DONATION"
118 DATA "MEMBERSHIP","   POSTAGE","     PHOTO","SPEC EVENT"
119 DATA "      BANK","  INTEREST","   RECORDS"," HAIR CARE"
120 DATA "YARD  CARE","APPLIANCES","   KITCHEN","     TAXES"
121 DATA "          ","          ","          ","          "
122 DATA "          ","          ","          ","          "
123 DATA "          ","     OTHER","      CASH"
200  FOR J=101 TO (100+NUMINC): READ CAT$(J): NEXT J   'INCOME CATEGORIES
210  DATA " PAYCHECK","  INTEREST","      GIFT","          "
211  DATA "          ","          ","          ","     OTHER"
300  FOR J=201 TO (200+NUMACTS) : READ CAT$(J):NEXT J 'ACCOUNT NAMES
310  DATA "      CASH","  CHECKING","   SAVINGS","       IRA"
311  DATA "  CR UNION","          ","          ","          "
312  DATA "          ","          "
395 PRINT "TYPE YES IF YOU WOULD LIKE A LISTING OF THE CATEGORIES"
396 INPUT "PRINTED:";Q$
397 IF Q$<>"YES" THEN GOTO 500
400 FOR I=1 TO NUMEXP:LPRINT USING "###";I;
402   LPRINT ".";CAT$(I):NEXT I
404 FOR I=1 TO NUMINC:LPRINT USING "###";(100+I);
406   LPRINT ".";CAT$(100+I):NEXT I
408 FOR I=1 TO NUMACTS:LPRINT USING "###";(200+I);
410   LPRINT ".";CAT$(200+I):NEXT I
497 '
498 '
499  REM ********************************************
500  REM *** MAIN PROGRAM BLOCK                  ***
501  REM ********************************************
505   GOSUB 15000    'READ IN CUMULATIVE TOTALS
510   GOSUB 1000     'READ IN DATA
520   GOSUB 4000     'MAKE CHANGES IF NECESSARY
530   GOSUB 3000     'PROCESS DATA
540   GOSUB 2000     'OUTPUT
550   GOSUB 16000    'STORE CUMULATIVE TOTALS ON DISK
590   END
997 '
998 '
999  REM ********************************************
1000 REM *** READ IN FIGURES FOR CATEGORY/AMOUNT  ***
1001 REM ********************************************
1002  CONTINUE=1
1003  PRINT: FOR I=1 TO NUMACTS:BAL2(I)=BALANCE(I)
1004  PRINT CAT$(200+I);:PRINT USING "#########.##";BAL2(I):NEXT I
1005  F=201    'THE FIRST TRANSACTION IS ASSUMED TO COME
1006  REM        FROM THE CASH CATEGORY UNLESS TOLD OTHERWISE
1009  PRINT "TYPE S WHEN YOU ARE DONE ENTERING TRANSACTION DATA."
```

```
1010   INPUT "CODES, AMNT:   ";X$
1020     GOSUB 20000   ' SEPARATE OUT CATEGORY/AMOUNT FIGURES
1025     IF CONTINUE=0 THEN GOTO 1070
1030     NUM=NUM+1
1040     FRLIST(NUM)=F
1045     TOLIST(NUM)=T
1050     AMLIST(NUM)=AMNT
1055     PRINT NUM;"   ";CAT$(F);"    ";CAT$(T);"    ";
1057     PRINT USING "#########.##";AMNT
1058     GOSUB 17000    'PRINT NEW ACCOUNT BALANCE
1060     GOTO 1010    'ENTER NEXT VALUE
1070     INPUT "FILE NAME TO SAVE TRANSACTION LIST:",F2$
1072     F2$=F2$+".TRN"
1075     OPEN"O",#1,F2$
1076     FOR I=1 TO NUM:PRINT#1,FRLIST(I),TOLIST(I),AMLIST(I):NEXT I
1077     PRINT #1,-1,-1,-1   '-1 IS A MARKER FOR THE END OF THE FILE
1080     CLOSE#1
1085     FOR I=1 TO NUMACTS:PRINT CAT$(200+I);
1086     PRINT USING "#########.##";BAL2(I):NEXT I
1099 RETURN
1997 '
1998 '
1999   REM *****************************************
2000   REM ***    OUTPUT REPORT                  ***
2001   REM *****************************************
2005   HD$= "CURRENT EXPENDITURE REPORT"
2008     TYPE=0   '  TYPE = 0 FOR EXPENDITURE CATEGORIES
2010     NUM=NUMEXP:FOR I=1 TO NUM:A(I)=EXPEND(I):NEXT I
2015     GOSUB 2100  : GOSUB 2500    'SORT/PRINT
2017     TOTEXP=TOT
2020   HD$= "CURRENT INCOME REPORT"
2022     TYPE=100   'TYPE = 100 FOR INCOME CATEGORIES
2025     NUM=NUMINC:FOR I=1 TO NUM:A(I)=INCOME(I):NEXT I
2030     GOSUB 2100  : GOSUB 2500    'SORT/PRINT
2032     TOTINC=TOT
2035   HD$= "YEAR TO DATE EXPENDITURE REPORT"
2037     TYPE=0
2040     NUM=NUMEXP:FOR I=1 TO NUM:A(I)=CUMEXP(I):NEXT I
2045     GOSUB 2100  : GOSUB 2500    'SORT/PRINT
2055   HD$= "YEAR TO DATE INCOME REPORT"
2057     TYPE=100
2060     NUM=NUMINC:FOR I=1 TO NUM:A(I)=CUMINC(I):NEXT I
2065     GOSUB 2100  : GOSUB 2500    'SORT/PRINT
2070   LPRINT:LPRINT:LPRINT "BALANCES:"
2072     TOT=0
2075     FOR I=1 TO NUMACTS: LPRINT CAT$(200+I);
2077     TOT=TOT+BALANCE(I)
2080     LPRINT USING "#########.##";BALANCE(I)   : NEXT I
2085     LPRINT "      TOTAL";
2086     LPRINT USING "#########.##";TOT
2090   LPRINT:LPRINT:LPRINT "OLD BALANCE   ";
2091     LPRINT USING "#########.##";OLDBAL
2092     LPRINT "+TOTAL INCOME";:LPRINT USING "#########.##";TOTINC
2093     LPRINT "-TOTAL EXPEND";:LPRINT USING "#########.##";TOTEXP
2094     LPRINT "=NEW BALANCE ";
2095     LPRINT USING "#########.##";(OLDBAL+TOTINC-TOTEXP)    Continued
```

```
2097 RETURN
2098 '
2099 REM ********************************************
2100 REM *** SORT ENTRIES                       ***
2101 REM ********************************************
2102  REM  THIS SUBROUTINE USES THE BUBBLE SORT PROCEDURE
2105  FOR I=1 TO NUM:ORDER(I)=I:A2(I)=A(I):NEXT I
2110  FOR I=1 TO NUM
2115     PRINT "*";
2120     FOR J=1 TO (NUM-I)
2130        IF A2(J)>A2(J+1) THEN GOTO 2140
2133        TEMP=ORDER(J+1):ORDER(J+1)=ORDER(J):ORDER(J)=TEMP
2137        TEMP=A2(J+1):A2(J+1)=A2(J):A2(J)=TEMP
2140     NEXT J
2150   NEXT I
2155 PRINT
2160 RETURN
2497 '
2498 '
2499 REM ********************************************
2500 REM *** PRINT OUTPUT                       ***
2501 REM ********************************************
2502 PRINT "TYPE P TO PRINT":GOSUB 20200   'INKEY SUBROUTINE
2503 LPRINT DT$;"     ";HD$
2505 TOT=0:TOT2=0:FOR I=1 TO NUM:TOT=TOT+A(I)
2506    IF A(I)>0 THEN TOT2=TOT2+A(I)
2507    NEXT I
2510 LPRINT "          CATEGORY    AMOUNT   FRACTION"
2520 FOR J1=1 TO NUM:  J=ORDER(J1)+TYPE      'TYPE=0 FOR EXPEND.  CAT.S
2521                  J2=ORDER(J1)           ' TYPE=100 FOR INCOME CAT.S
2523     IF A(J2)=0 THEN GOTO 2550  'DON'T PRINT IF AMOUNT IS ZERO
2525    LPRINT USING "####";J1;
2526    LPRINT ". ";
2530    LPRINT CAT$(J);
2540    LPRINT USING "#######.##";A(J2);
2545    LPRINT USING "######.###";(A(J2)/TOT2)
2550  NEXT J1
2560  LPRINT "          TOTAL";
2570  LPRINT USING "#######.##";TOT
2580 RETURN
2999 REM ********************************************
3000 REM *** PROCESS TRANSACTIONS DATA          ***
3001 REM ********************************************
3030   FOR I=1 TO NUM    'NUM IS THE NUMBER OF TRANSACTIONS
3040     F = FRLIST(I):   T = TOLIST(I) :  AMNT = AMLIST(I)
3050     IF (F>100) AND (F<200) THEN GOTO 3200  'INCOME TRANSACTION
3060     IF T>200 THEN GOTO 3300  'TRANSFER TRANSACTION
3070     REM ----  EXPENDITURE TRANSACTION
3080       EXPEND(T)=EXPEND(T)+AMNT
3090       ACTNUM=F-200
3100       BALANCE(ACTNUM)=BALANCE(ACTNUM)-AMNT
3110       GOTO 3490  'NEXT I
3200     REM ---- INCOME TRANSACTION
3210       CATEG=F-100
3220       INCOME(CATEG)=INCOME(CATEG)+AMNT
```

```
3230        ACTNUM=T-200
3240        BALANCE(ACTNUM)=BALANCE(ACTNUM)+AMNT
3250        GOTO 3490   'NEXT I
3300     REM ----   TRANSFER TRANSACTION
3310       BALANCE(F-200)=BALANCE(F-200)-AMNT
3320       BALANCE(T-200)=BALANCE(T-200)+AMNT
3490      NEXT I
3500 REM -- LIST BALANCES
3510    FOR I=1 TO NUMACTS
3520       PRINT CAT$(200+I);
3525       PRINT USING"#########.##";BALANCE(I)
3530     NEXT I
3550    INPUT "NEW CASH BALANCE:";CB
3560    CASHEXP=BALANCE(1)-CB
3565    PRINT "CASH EXPEND:";CASHEXP
3570    EXPEND(NUMEXP)=CASHEXP
3580    BALANCE(1)=CB
3600 REM --   ADD CURRENT TOTALS TO CUMULATIVE TOTALS
3610   FOR I=1 TO NUMEXP
3620       CUMEXP(I)=CUMEXP(I)+EXPEND(I)
3630   NEXT I
3640   FOR I=1 TO NUMINC
3650       CUMINC(I)=CUMINC(I)+INCOME(I)
3660   NEXT I
3690 RETURN
3999  REM *******************************************
4000  REM *** LIST OR CORRECT TRANSACTIONS RECORD   ***
4001  REM *******************************************
4005  FOR I=1 TO NUMACTS:BAL2(I)=BALANCE(I):NEXT I
4010   PRINT "TO LIST TRANSACTIONS, TYPE L FOLLOWED BY A"
4011   PRINT "NUMBER, SUCH AS L 5  OR L 1-100"
4012   PRINT "TO CORRECT A TRANSACTION, TYPE C FOLLOWED BY"
4013   PRINT "THE TRANSACTION NUMBER"
4014   PRINT "TYPE S TO LEAVE THIS SECTION"
4020   INPUT X$
4030   IF LEFT$(X$,1)="L" THEN GOTO 4060
4035   IF LEFT$(X$,1)="S" THEN GOTO 4590
4040   IF LEFT$(X$,1)="C" THEN GOTO 4300
4050   PRINT "THE FIRST CHARACTER MUST BE L, S, OR C" :GOTO 4010
4060   REM --   LIST TRANSACTIONS
4070     X$=RIGHT$(X$,LEN(X$)-1)
4080     N4=INSTR(X$,"-")
4090     IF N4>0 THEN GOTO 4100
4095     REM -- ONLY ONE TRANSACTION WILL BE DISPLAYED
4096     STARTT=VAL(X$):STOPP=STARTT:GOTO 4150
4100     REM -- A RANGE OF TRANSACTIONS WILL BE DISPLAYED
4110     STARTT=VAL(LEFT$(X$,N4-1))
4120     STOPP=VAL(RIGHT$(X$,LEN(X$)-N4))
4150     REM -- LIST THE TRANSACTIONS
4155     PRINT  "            FROM        TO      AMOUNT"
4160     FOR I=STARTT TO STOPP
4170       F=FRLIST(I) : T= TOLIST(I) : AMNT=AMLIST(I)
4175     IF F=0 THEN GOTO 4200   'DON'T PRINT IF ZERO
4180     PRINT I;"  ";CAT$(F);"  ";CAT$(T);"  ";
4190     PRINT USING "#######.##";AMNT
4195     IF STARTT=1 THEN GOSUB 17000   'PRINT ACCOUNT BALANCES
```

Continued

```
4200      NEXT I
4210   GOTO 4005
4297   '
4298   '
4299   REM *****************************************
4300   REM *** CORRECT TRANSACTION               ***
4301   REM *****************************************
4310      TNUM=VAL(RIGHT$(X$,LEN(X$)-1))
4315      PRINT "OLD VERSION:"
4320      PRINT "          FROM        TO        AMOUNT"
4330      F=FRLIST(TNUM)  :  T=TOLIST(TNUM)  :  AMNT=AMLIST(TNUM)
4335      PRINT CAT$(F);"   ";CAT$(T);"   ";
4340      PRINT USING "#######.##";AMNT
4345      INPUT "NEW FROM CODE:";F : FRLIST(TNUM)=F
4350      INPUT "NEW TO CODE:";T   :TOLIST(TNUM)=T
4355      INPUT "NEW AMOUNT:";AMNT :AMLIST(TNUM)=AMNT
4357      IF TNUM>NUM THEN NUM=TNUM
4360     GOTO 4010
4590   RETURN
14997  '
14999  REM *****************************************
15000  REM *** INPUT CUMULATIVE TOTALS/BALANCES   ***
15001  REM *****************************************
15002   OLDBAL=0
15003  FILES "*.TRN":FILES "*.FRP":PRINT
15005  PRINT "TYPE NEW IF YOU ARE STARTING A NEW TRANSACTION"
15006  PRINT "LIST. ELSE TYPE TRANSACTION CODE"
15007  INPUT F1$
15008  IF F1$<>"NEW" THEN GOSUB 15300 ELSE NUM=0 '# TRANS. PREV. READ IN
15010   PRINT "TYPE NEW IF YOU ARE STARTING A NEW YEAR"
15015   PRINT "ELSE TYPE 3-LETTER ABBREVIATION FOR PREVIOUS MONTH"
15020   INPUT F$
15025     IF F$="NEW" THEN GOSUB 15200 : RETURN
15030   F$=F$+".FRP"
15040   OPEN "I",#1,F$
15050   INPUT#1,NUMACTS      'NUMBER OF ACCOUNTS
15060   FOR I=1 TO NUMACTS
15070      INPUT#1,BALANCE(I)      'READ IN BALANCE IN EACH ACCOUNT
15075      OLDBAL=OLDBAL+BALANCE(I)
15080   NEXT I
15090   INPUT#1,NUMINC        ' NUMBER OF INCOME CATEGORIES
15100   FOR I=1 TO NUMINC
15110      INPUT#1,CUMINC(I)      'CUMULATIVE INCOME TOTALS
15120   NEXT I
15130   INPUT#1,NUMEXP        'NUMBER OF EXPENDITURE CATEGORIES
15140   FOR I=1 TO NUMEXP
15150      INPUT#1,CUMEXP(I)      'CUMULATIVE EXPENDITURE TOTALS
15160   NEXT I
15170   CLOSE#1
15190   RETURN
15197  '
15198  '
15199   REM *****************************************
15200   REM *** START NEW YEAR                    ***
```

```
15201   REM *******************************************
15210     FOR I=1 TO NUMEXP:CUMEXP(I)=0:NEXT I
15220     FOR I=1 TO NUMINC:CUMINC(I)=0:NEXT I
15230     FOR I=1 TO NUMACTS
15240       PRINT "ENTER BALANCE FOR ACCOUNT ";(200+I);" ";
15245         PRINT CAT$(200+I)
15250       INPUT BALANCE(I)
15255       OLDBAL=OLDBAL+BALANCE(I)
15260     NEXT I
15270   RETURN
15297  '
15298  '
15299   REM *******************************************
15300   REM *** LOAD IN OLD TRANSACTION FILE        ***
15301   REM *******************************************
15310   F1$=F1$+".TRN"
15320   I=0
15330   OPEN "I",#1,F1$
15340     I=I+1
15350       INPUT#1,FRLIST(I),TOLIST(I),AMLIST(I)
15360     IF FRLIST(I)<>-1 THEN GOTO 15340
15370     NUM=I-1    'NUMBER OF TRANSACTIONS READ IN
15380   CLOSE#1
15390   RETURN
15997  '
15998  '
15999   REM *******************************************
16000   REM ***   STORE CUMULATIVE TOTALS/BALANCES   ***
16001   REM *******************************************
16010   INPUT "NAME OF FILE TO STORE TOTALS:";F$
16030   F$=F$+".FRP"
16040   OPEN "O",#1,F$
16050   PRINT#1,NUMACTS           'NUMBER OF ACCOUNTS
16060   FOR I=1 TO NUMACTS
16070       PRINT#1,BALANCE(I)      'STORE BALANCE IN EACH ACCOUNT
16080   NEXT I
16090   PRINT#1,NUMINC         'NUMBER OF INCOME CATEGORIES
16100   FOR I=1 TO NUMINC
16110         PRINT#1,CUMINC(I)      'CUMULATIVE INCOME TOTALS
16120   NEXT I
16130   PRINT#1,NUMEXP          'NUMBER OF EXPENDITURE CATEGORIES
16140   FOR I=1 TO NUMEXP
16150         PRINT#1,CUMEXP(I)       'CUMULATIVE EXPENDITURE TOTALS
16160   NEXT I
16170   CLOSE#1
16190   RETURN
16997  '
16998  '
16999   REM *******************************************
17000   REM ***   PRINT NEW ACCOUNT BALANCE          ***
17001   REM *******************************************
17010     IF (F>100) AND (F<200) THEN GOTO 17200    'INCOME TRANSACTION
17020     IF T>200 THEN GOTO 17300    'TRANSFER TRANSACTION
17030     REM  EXPENDITURE TRANSACTION
17040       ACTNUM=F-200
```

Continued

```
17050       BAL2(ACTNUM)=BAL2(ACTNUM)-AMNT
17060       PRINT CAT$(F);" BALANCE:";
17070       PRINT USING "#########.##";BAL2(ACTNUM)
17080       GOTO 17399  'RETURN
17200   REM  INCOME TRANSACTION
17210       ACTNUM=T-200
17220       BAL2(ACTNUM)=BAL2(ACTNUM)+AMNT
17230       PRINT CAT$(T);" BALANCE:";
17240       PRINT USING "#########.##";BAL2(ACTNUM)
17250       GOTO 17399  'RETURN
17300   REM TRANSFER TRANSACTION
17310       BAL2(F-200)=BAL2(F-200)-AMNT
17320       BAL2(T-200)=BAL2(T-200)+AMNT
17330       PRINT CAT$(F);" BALANCE:";
17340       PRINT USING "#########.##";BAL2(F-200);
17350       PRINT "    ";CAT$(T);" BALANCE:";
17360       PRINT USING "#########.##";BAL2(T-200)
17399    RETURN
17997 '
17998 '
17999 '
18000 REM IF THERE IS A FILE NOT FOUND ERROR, THE PROGRAM
18001 REM  WILL PROCEED ANYWAY.  IF THERE IS ANY OTHER KIND
18002 REM  OF ERROR THE PROGRAM WILL STOP.
18010 IF ERR<>53 THEN ON ERROR GOTO 0
18020 GOTO 15005
19997 '
19998 '
19999 REM ********************************************
20000 REM *** SEPARATE OUT CATEGORY/AMOUNT FIGURES ***
20001 REM ********************************************
20002 REM     IF THREE ITEMS ARE INCLUDED THEN THE FIRST IS THE
20003 REM     FROM CODE, THE SECOND IS THE TO CODE, AND THE
20004 REM     THIRD IS THE AMOUNT.  IF TWO ITEMS ARE INCLUDED THEN
20005 REM     THE FIRST IS THE TO CODE AND THE SECOND IS THE AMOUNT.
20006 REM     IF AN S IS TYPED THEN IT IS TIME TO LEAVE THE INPUT
20007 REM     SECTION.
20008   IF X$="S" THEN CONTINUE=0: GOTO 20190
20010   N1=INSTR(X$," ")
20020   M1=VAL(LEFT$(X$,N1-1))
20025   X$=RIGHT$(X$,LEN(X$)-N1)
20027   IF LEFT$(X$,1)=" " THEN X$=RIGHT$(X$,LEN(X$)-1):GOTO 20027
20030   N2=INSTR(X$," ")
20035   IF N2=0 THEN GOTO 20100  'ONLY TWO ITEMS ARE INCLUDED
20040 REM -- THREE ITEMS ARE INCLUDED
20045     F=M1   'FROM CODE
20050     T=VAL(LEFT$(X$,N2-1))  'TO CODE
20055     AMNT=VAL(RIGHT$(X$,LEN(X$)-N2))
20060     GOTO 20190
20100 REM  -- TWO ITEMS ARE INCLUDED
20105     T=M1    'TO CODE
20110     AMNT=VAL(X$)
20115  REM  THE FROM CODE STAYS THE SAME AS IT WAS
20190 RETURN
20197 '
```

```
20198 '
20199 REM *******************************************
20200 REM *** INKEY SUBROUTINE                  ***
20201 REM *******************************************
20210   KK$=INKEY$:IF KK$="" THEN 20210
20215   RETURN
```

The major parts of the program are labeled with REM statements and separated from each other by blank lines. Lines 500–590 form the main program block, which consists solely of subroutine calls. The program is written in Microsoft BASIC, which allows the use of a single quote mark, ', to indicate that the rest of the line is to be treated as a comment. To make the program work for other versions, the biggest changes would be in the two sections that deal with disk files. The FILES command in Microsoft BASIC is used to display a directory of the files on a disk, so these statements need to be changed for other versions. The general structure of the commands to open and close files must be changed for other versions (see Chapter 9). The LPRINT command is used to direct output to the printer. The procedure for printing output is different in other versions.

Several of the category labels are left blank, which allows room to add more category labels in the future.

Here is an example of the execution of this program. First, we will show the appearance of the screen while you are entering the transactions data. The circled numbers correspond to the step-by-step description of the program's operation.

```
RUN
DATE:Jan 31        ①
TYPE YES IF YOU WOULD LIKE A LISTING OF THE CATEGORIES    ②
PRINTED:NO
TST1    .TRN TST2    .TRN TST3    .TRN TST4    .TRN TST5    .TRN    ③
TST1    .FRP TST2    .FRP
TYPE NEW IF YOU ARE STARTING A NEW TRANSACTION    ④
LIST. ELSE TYPE TRANSACTION CODE
? NEW
TYPE NEW IF YOU ARE STARTING A NEW YEAR        ⑤
ELSE TYPE 3-LETTER ABBREVIATION FOR PREVIOUS MONTH
? NEW
ENTER BALANCE FOR ACCOUNT  201        CASH        ⑥
?  89.95
ENTER BALANCE FOR ACCOUNT  202     CHECKING
?  545.42
ENTER BALANCE FOR ACCOUNT  203      SAVINGS
?  809.85
ENTER BALANCE FOR ACCOUNT  204          IRA
?  2503.45
ENTER BALANCE FOR ACCOUNT  205     CR UNION
?  405.65
ENTER BALANCE FOR ACCOUNT  206
```

Continued

```
?  0
ENTER BALANCE FOR ACCOUNT  207
?  0
ENTER BALANCE FOR ACCOUNT  208
?  0
ENTER BALANCE FOR ACCOUNT  209
?  0
ENTER BALANCE FOR ACCOUNT  210
?  0
        CASH         89.95
    CHECKING        545.42
     SAVINGS        809.85
         IRA       2503.45
    CR UNION        405.65
                      0.00
                      0.00
                      0.00
                      0.00
                      0.00
TYPE S WHEN YOU ARE DONE ENTERING TRANSACTION DATA. ⑦
CODES, AMNT: ?  202 1 456
  1     CHECKING       HOUSING        456.00
    CHECKING BALANCE:       89.42
CODES, AMNT: ?  201 2 45.23
  2        CASH      GROCERIES        45.23
        CASH BALANCE:       44.72
CODES, AMNT: ?  13 4.5
  3        CASH      ENTERTAIN.        4.50
        CASH BALANCE:       40.22
CODES, AMNT: ?  9 2
  4        CASH      PARKING           2.00
        CASH BALANCE:       38.22
CODES, AMNT: ?  7 12.54
  5        CASH         GAS           12.54
        CASH BALANCE:       25.68
CODES, AMNT: ?  20 .25
  6       CASH    NEWSPAPERS           0.25
        CASH BALANCE:       25.43
CODES, AMNT: ?  5 10
  7       CASH      CHARITY           10.00
        CASH BALANCE:       15.43
CODES, AMNT: ?  202 201 50
  8    CHECKING       CASH           50.00
    CHECKING BALANCE:       39.42          CASH BALANCE:       65.43
CODES, AMNT: ?  201 2 36.89
  9       CASH     GROCERIES         36.89
        CASH BALANCE:       28.54
CODES, AMNT: ?  11 18.45
 10       CASH    COMP. SUPP         18.45
        CASH BALANCE:       10.09
CODES, AMNT: ?  101 202 1200
 11    PAYCHECK     CHECKING       1200.00
    CHECKING BALANCE:     1239.42
CODES, AMNT: ?  202 203 300
 12    CHECKING      SAVINGS        300.00
```

```
    CHECKING BALANCE:      939.42      SAVINGS BALANCE:    1109.85
CODES, AMNT: ?  201 100
  13    CHECKING         CASH        100.00
    CHECKING BALANCE:      839.42        CASH BALANCE:     110.09
CODES, AMNT: ?  17 26
  14    CHECKING         PHONE        26.00
    CHECKING BALANCE:      813.42
CODES, AMNT: ?  5 100
  15    CHECKING         CHARITY     100.00
    CHECKING BALANCE:      713.42
CODES, AMNT: ?  S
FILE NAME TO SAVE TRANSACTION LIST:JAN        ⑧
        CASH      110.09                      ⑨
    CHECKING      713.42
     SAVINGS     1109.85
         IRA     2503.45
    CR UNION      405.65
                    0.00
                    0.00
                    0.00
                    0.00
                    0.00
TO LIST TRANSACTIONS, TYPE L FOLLOWED BY A     ⑩
NUMBER, SUCH AS L 5   OR L 1-100
TO CORRECT A TRANSACTION, TYPE C FOLLOWED BY
THE TRANSACTION NUMBER
TYPE S TO LEAVE THIS SECTION
? L 1-6
          FROM        TO      AMOUNT
  1    CHECKING     HOUSING      456.00
   CHECKING BALANCE:      89.42
  2        CASH    GROCERIES     45.23
     CASH BALANCE:      44.72
  3        CASH   ENTERTAIN.      4.50
     CASH BALANCE:      40.22
  4        CASH     PARKING       2.00
     CASH BALANCE:      38.22
  5        CASH       GAS        12.54
     CASH BALANCE:      25.68
  6        CASH  NEWSPAPERS       0.25
     CASH BALANCE:      25.43
TO LIST TRANSACTIONS, TYPE L FOLLOWED BY A
NUMBER, SUCH AS L 5   OR L 1-100
TO CORRECT A TRANSACTION, TYPE C FOLLOWED BY
THE TRANSACTION NUMBER
TYPE S TO LEAVE THIS SECTION
? C 2
OLD VERSION:
       FROM         TO      AMOUNT
       CASH    GROCERIES      45.23
NEW FROM CODE: 201
NEW TO CODE: 2
NEW AMOUNT: 42.35
TO LIST TRANSACTIONS, TYPE L FOLLOWED BY A
NUMBER, SUCH AS L 5   OR L 1-100
```

Continued

```
TO CORRECT A TRANSACTION, TYPE C FOLLOWED BY
THE TRANSACTION NUMBER
TYPE S TO LEAVE THIS SECTION
? L 2
                FROM        TO      AMOUNT
    2         CASH    GROCERIES      42.35
TO LIST TRANSACTIONS, TYPE L FOLLOWED BY A
NUMBER, SUCH AS L 5  OR L 1-100
TO CORRECT A TRANSACTION, TYPE C FOLLOWED BY
THE TRANSACTION NUMBER
TYPE S TO LEAVE THIS SECTION
? S
        CASH      112.97
    CHECKING      713.42
     SAVINGS     1109.85
         IRA     2503.45
    CR UNION      405.65
                    0.00
                    0.00
                    0.00
                    0.00
                    0.00
NEW CASH BALANCE:? 105.64
CASH EXPEND: 7.33
*************************************************
TYPE P TO PRINT
********
TYPE P TO PRINT
*************************************************
TYPE P TO PRINT
********
TYPE P TO PRINT
NAME OF FILE TO STORE TOTALS:? JAN
Ok
```

(11)

(12)

(13)

STEP-BY-STEP DESCRIPTION

Here is the description of each step:

1. The program first asks for the date so that it can label the output reports. In our example, the date is January 31. This will be the first monthly report for this year.

2. The computer asks if we would like a listing of the categories printed, but we decline this option.

3. The computer displays a listing of the files that are stored on this disk. The program deals with two different types of files: cumulative report files, which have file type FRP, and transaction files, which have file type TRN. The cumulative totals at the end of each month are stored in a file of type FRP. The file name ordinarily should be a three-letter abbreviation for the month. For example, the file that stores the cumulative totals after January would be called JAN.FRP. (The files with names such as TST1 are test files that happened to be on this disk.)

4. The computer asks us if we are starting a new transaction list. In most cases, we will type NEW in reponse to this question. (Suppose that we ran the program yesterday to calculate the report for January. Then the list of all transactions would be stored in a file named JAN.TRN. However, suppose that today we realize that we left out some important transactions from January. Then we could type JAN in response to this question, the computer would load all of the transactions from the file JAN.TRN, and we could proceed as if we had just retyped all of those transactions.)

5. The computer displays the messsage:

TYPE NEW IF YOU ARE STARTING A NEW YEAR

ELSE TYPE 3-LETTER ABBREVIATION FOR PREVIOUS MONTH

Since the January 31 report is the first report of the year, we will type NEW in response to this question. (On February 28, we will type JAN in response to this question, since January will be the previous month. We will show an example of the February report later.)

6. Since we typed NEW to tell the computer that it did not have a previous cumulative report file to read in, we must enter the balance for each of the asset accounts. In our example we have five asset accounts: cash, checking, savings, IRA, and a credit union account. (Accounts 206–210 currently do not represent anything, but you can use those numbers if you have additional accounts.) After we have entered the account balances, the computer responds by displaying the balances for us. Then we are ready to start entering the transaction data.

7. The screen displays

CODES, AMNT: ?

when the computer is ready for us to enter a transaction. There are two ways of entering transaction data. We can enter the *from* code, the *to* code, and the amount. (Use blanks to separate the three numbers.) For example, in our first transaction, the *from* code is 202 (checking) and the *to* code is 1 (housing). Therefore, this transaction represents a check of $456.00 used for a house payment. Since the computer responds by displaying both the transaction information and the new checking account balance, we have the information needed to confirm that we entered the transaction correctly.

We will probably be entering several cash expenditures in a row, and it would be tedious to type the 201 code for cash each time. Therefore, the program allows you to omit the *from* code for a transaction. If the *from* code is omitted, then it is automatically assumed that the *from* code is the same as the *from* code for the previous transaction. For example, transaction 2 is entered as

201 2 45.23

which means a cash expenditure for groceries (201 is the code for the cash asset account, and 2 is the code for the grocery expenditure category). Transaction 3 is entered as

13 4.5

There are only two numbers, so the program knows that the *from* code has been omitted. Therefore, the *from* code is the same as for transaction 2 (which was 201: cash) and the *to* code is 13 (representing entertainment expenditure). The subroutine starting at line 20000 checks the input expression to determine whether two or three numbers have been included.

The computer can tell whether a transaction is an expenditure transaction, an income transaction, or a transfer transaction by checking the nature of the codes. If the *to* code is less than 100, then it is an expenditure transaction. If the *from* code is between 100 and 199, then it is an income transaction. Otherwise it is a transfer transaction. In the program, lines 3050–3060 check this.

Transaction 8 is entered as follows:

202 201 50

Since both the *from* code and the *to* code are asset accounts, this transaction is a transfer, taking $50.00 out of checking (code 202) and putting it in cash (code 201).

Transaction 11 is entered as follows:

101 202 1200

Since the *from* code is an income category, this transaction is an income transaction: depositing a $1200 paycheck from your employer (code 101) into your checking account (code 202).

8.   After we have entered all transactions, we type S. The computer then asks for the file name to use in order to save the transaction list. We will give it the name JAN, since this list records the transactions for January. (The computer will automatically add the file extension TRN when it saves the file.)

9. The computer displays a list of the new account balances. We can compare this list with the actual account balances to see if we omitted any transactions or entered a transaction incorrectly.

10. We enter the correction section. Our first option is to list some transactions. For example, if we type L 1-6, the computer will list transactions from transaction number 1 to transaction number 6. In this case, we discover that transaction 2 contains a mistake. Instead of spending $45.23 on groceries January 3, we find from our notebook that the actual amount was $42.35 (see page 178). Therefore, we type C 2 to tell the computer that we need to correct transaction 2. The computer displays the old version of the transaction, then asks us to enter the *from* code, the *to* code, and the amount for the corrected version of the transaction.

11. We type S when we have completed this section. The computer displays the account balances again, so we can make sure that this time they are correct. However, the cash balance is not likely to agree with the actual cash balance. As we said, in this system we will not try to keep track of every single penny. There will be a difference between the actual cash expenditures and the recorded cash expenditures. This difference is the amount that we call "unrecorded cash expenditure" or just "cash expenditure" for short. We have to enter the current cash balance, and then the computer can calculate the amount of the cash expenditures. (The cash expenditure amount could conceivably be negative if, for example, you found a few extra coins that you did not record as an income transaction.)

12. Now we are finished entering information. The computer will sort the figures so that it can print them out in order. The rows of asterisks slowly appear on the screen during the sorting process to assure us that the computer is still working. When it is ready to print, it displays the message TYPE P TO PRINT. Then the computer will call the subroutine at line 20200 that causes it to wait until you type P (or any other key). This pause is included before each report to give you a chance to position the paper in the printer.

13. After the reports have been printed, the computer will ask you for the name of the file to store the cumulative totals. Normally, it will be best to name this file after the month to which it corresponds. In our case, we will type JAN and the computer will store the information under the file name JAN.FRP. The computer displays OK when it is done with the program.

Here are the reports that the computer printed:

```
Jan 31    CURRENT EXPENDITURE REPORT
          CATEGORY      AMOUNT   FRACTION
      1.    HOUSING     456.00     0.637
      2.    CHARITY     110.00     0.154
      3.  GROCERIES      79.24     0.111
      4.      PHONE      26.00     0.036
      5. COMP. SUPP      18.45     0.026
      6.        GAS      12.54     0.018
      7.       CASH       7.33     0.010
      8. ENTERTAIN.       4.50     0.006
      9.    PARKING       2.00     0.003
     10. NEWSPAPERS       0.25     0.000
          TOTAL        716.31
Jan 31    CURRENT INCOME REPORT
          CATEGORY      AMOUNT   FRACTION
      1.   PAYCHECK    1200.00     1.000
          TOTAL       1200.00
Jan 31    YEAR TO DATE EXPENDITURE REPORT
          CATEGORY      AMOUNT   FRACTION
      1.    HOUSING     456.00     0.637
      2.    CHARITY     110.00     0.154
      3.  GROCERIES      79.24     0.111
      4.      PHONE      26.00     0.036
```

Continued

```
 5.  COMP. SUPP     18.45      0.026
 6.         GAS     12.54      0.018
 7.        CASH      7.33      0.010
 8.  ENTERTAIN.      4.50      0.006
 9.     PARKING      2.00      0.003
10.  NEWSPAPERS      0.25      0.000
          TOTAL    716.31
Jan 31    YEAR TO DATE INCOME REPORT
          CATEGORY     AMOUNT  FRACTION
 1.    PAYCHECK    1200.00     1.000
          TOTAL    1200.00


BALANCES:
        CASH      105.64
    CHECKING      713.42
     SAVINGS     1109.85
         IRA     2503.45
    CR UNION      405.65
                   0.00
                   0.00
                   0.00
                   0.00
                   0.00
       TOTAL     4838.01


OLD BALANCE       4354.32
+TOTAL INCOME     1200.00
-TOTAL EXPEND      716.31
=NEW BALANCE      4838.01
```

Since this is the end of January, the year-to-date report is exactly the same as the current report. The computer also displays the balance in each account and includes a proof total at the end so we can see that the new balance is equal to the old balance plus the total income for January minus the total expenditures for January.

Here is what the screen looks like when we run the program again at the end of February:

```
RUN
DATE:Feb 28
TYPE YES IF YOU WOULD LIKE A LISTING OF THE CATEGORIES
PRINTED:NO
TST1    .TRN TST2    .TRN TST3    .TRN TST4    .TRN TST5    .TRN
JAN     .TRN TST1    .FRP TST2    .FRP JAN     .FRP
TYPE NEW IF YOU ARE STARTING A NEW TRANSACTION
LIST. ELSE TYPE TRANSACTION CODE
? NEW
TYPE NEW IF YOU ARE STARTING A NEW YEAR
ELSE TYPE 3-LETTER ABBREVIATION FOR PREVIOUS MONTH
? JAN
        CASH      105.64
    CHECKING      713.42
     SAVINGS     1109.85
         IRA     2503.45
```

```
          CR  UNION       405.65
                            0.00
                            0.00
                            0.00
                            0.00
                            0.00
       TYPE S WHEN YOU ARE DONE ENTERING TRANSACTION DATA.
       CODES, AMNT: ?   202 1 456
         1     CHECKING      HOUSING        456.00
            CHECKING BALANCE:     257.42
       CODES, AMNT: ?   201 2 12.56
         2         CASH   GROCERIES          12.56
              CASH BALANCE:       93.08
       CODES, AMNT: ?   2 13.45
         3         CASH   GROCERIES          13.45
              CASH BALANCE:       79.63
       CODES, AMNT: ?   2 1.95
         4         CASH   GROCERIES           1.95
              CASH BALANCE:       77.68
       CODES, AMNT: ?   2 15.46
         5         CASH   GROCERIES          15.46
              CASH BALANCE:       62.22
       CODES, AMNT: ?   101 202 1200
         6     PAYCHECK      CHECKING      1200.00
            CHECKING BALANCE:    1457.42
       CODES, AMNT: ?   202 203 400
         7     CHECKING      SAVINGS        400.00
            CHECKING BALANCE:    1057.42        SAVINGS BALANCE:     1509.85
       CODES, AMNT: ?   102 203 6
         8     INTEREST      SAVINGS          6.00
            SAVINGS BALANCE:    1515.85
       CODES, AMNT: ?   S
       FILE NAME TO SAVE TRANSACTION LIST:FEB
              CASH        62.22
          CHECKING      1057.42
           SAVINGS      1515.85
               IRA      2503.45
          CR  UNION      405.65
                           0.00
                           0.00
                           0.00
                           0.00
                           0.00
       TO LIST TRANSACTIONS, TYPE L FOLLOWED BY A
       NUMBER, SUCH AS L 5   OR L 1-100
       TO CORRECT A TRANSACTION, TYPE C FOLLOWED BY
       THE TRANSACTION NUMBER
       TYPE S TO LEAVE THIS SECTION
       ? S
              CASH        62.22
          CHECKING      1057.42
           SAVINGS      1515.85
               IRA      2503.45
          CR  UNION      405.65
                           0.00
                           0.00
```

Continued

```
                            0.00
                            0.00
                            0.00
NEW CASH BALANCE:? 52.05
CASH EXPEND: 10.17
*******************************************************
TYPE P TO PRINT
********
TYPE P TO PRINT
*******************************************************
TYPE P TO PRINT
********
TYPE P TO PRINT
NAME OF FILE TO STORE TOTALS:? FEB
Ok
```

When the computer displays the list of files at the start of the program, notice that the files JAN.FRP and JAN.TRN are now included. We don't have any need to look at the January transaction file again, so we type NEW when it asks us if we would like to start a new transaction file. When the computer asks

TYPE NEW IF YOU ARE STARTING A NEW YEAR

ELSE TYPE 3-LETTER ABBREVIATION FOR PREVIOUS MONTH

we will now type JAN. The computer will then load in the information from the file JAN.FRP. The computer displays the account balances. Note that these balances are the same as they were at the end of the last report. Then we enter the transaction data, using the same procedure as before. This time we do not need to make any corrections to the transactions, so we proceed to enter the new cash balance and have the reports printed. Here are the reports:

```
Feb 28    CURRENT EXPENDITURE REPORT
          CATEGORY     AMOUNT   FRACTION
    1.      HOUSING     456.00     0.895
    2.    GROCERIES      43.42     0.085
    3.         CASH      10.17     0.020
             TOTAL      509.59
Feb 28    CURRENT INCOME REPORT
          CATEGORY     AMOUNT   FRACTION
    1.     PAYCHECK    1200.00     0.995
    2.     INTEREST       6.00     0.005
             TOTAL     1206.00
Feb 28    YEAR TO DATE EXPENDITURE REPORT
          CATEGORY     AMOUNT   FRACTION
    1.      HOUSING     912.00     0.744
    2.    GROCERIES     122.66     0.100
    3.      CHARITY     110.00     0.090
    4.        PHONE      26.00     0.021
    5.  COMP. SUPP       18.45     0.015
    6.         CASH      17.50     0.014
    7.          GAS      12.54     0.010
    8.   ENTERTAIN.       4.50     0.004
```

```
    9.    PARKING        2.00      0.002
   10. NEWSPAPERS        0.25      0.000
          TOTAL       1225.90
Feb 28    YEAR TO DATE INCOME REPORT
          CATEGORY     AMOUNT    FRACTION
    1.    PAYCHECK    2400.00      0.998
    2.    INTEREST       6.00      0.002
          TOTAL       2406.00


BALANCES:
          CASH          52.05
      CHECKING        1057.42
       SAVINGS        1515.85
           IRA        2503.45
      CR UNION         405.65
                        0.00
                        0.00
                        0.00
                        0.00
                        0.00
         TOTAL        5534.42


OLD BALANCE          4838.01
+TOTAL INCOME        1206.00
-TOTAL EXPEND         509.59
=NEW BALANCE         5534.42
```

NOTE   The first time you run the financial program, there will not be any files with extension FRP or TRN on your disk. If the computer came across the command

FILES " ∗ .FRP"

in line 15002 and there were no files with extension FRP on this disk, then a "File not Found" error would result and the program would stop. One solution would be to remove line 15002 the first time you ran the program and then put it back later, since this problem will not arise after the program has been run once and a file with extension FRP has been created. Another possibility is to take advantage of the Microsoft BASIC ON ERROR command. The statement

ON ERROR GOTO 18000

in line 30 tells the computer that if an error occurs in the program, it should go to line 18000. After an error has occurred, the value of a special variable named ERR will be the code number for the error that occurred. The code for a file not found error is 53, so lines 18010–18020 tell the computer to proceed anyway if there was a file not found error. If there was another type of error, then the ON

ERROR command is canceled by the

ON ERROR GOTO 0

statement. The use of the ON ERROR command can be a valuable way to protect your program from stopping in the event of certain types of errors. A similar command (ONERR GOTO) works on Apple computers. Check your manual for more details.

EXERCISES

1. Write a program to balance your checkbook each month.

2. Write a program to keep track of the charges you owe on a credit card. When the credit card bill arrives, your computer can tell you whether the bill is correct.

3. Here are some features you might like to add to the personal financial record program contained in the chapter:

> (a) have the program make pie charts showing what fraction of your expenditures went to each category (look ahead to Chapter 14, which discusses graphics);
>
> (b) have the program compare expenditures for this year with expenditures for prior years;
>
> (c) have the program allow you to establish a budget that forecasts your expenditures in each category, and then compare the actual expenditures with the budgeted expenditures.

4. Write a program that reads in the initial principal value of a mortgage, the monthly payment amount, and the interest rate, and then prints a table showing how much of each payment is required to pay interest and how much is left to reduce the principal.

5. Write a program that calculates financial tables. There are six different tables that are particularly useful: a compound-interest table, which tells how much x dollars will be worth if it is left in the bank to accumulate compound interest for n periods; a table that gives the cumulative amount in a bank account if you add x dollars to your account each period for n periods, leaving all interest earned in the account; a table showing the present value of x dollars received n periods in the future; a table showing the present value of an annuity of x dollars received every period for n periods; a mortgage-amortization table, which shows the payment amount necessary to completely pay off a loan by a series of constant payments; and a table showing the price of a bond with a specified par value and coupon rate. You may consult a book on finance to find the formulas you will need, or you may find the formulas by looking at the program in the answer section at the back of this book.

Your program should display a menu that allows the user to choose which table will be calculated. In each case, your program will need to read in a range of values for the interest rate and the number of periods and then construct the table for those values. The program will also need to read in the number of compounding periods per year. For example, in a table of mortgage payments, there are normally 12 compounding periods per year; in a table of bond prices, there are normally two compounding periods per year.

CHAPTER 12

DATA PROCESSING APPLICATIONS

If you ask what most big computers do most of the time, the answer is that they spend their time on various data processing applications. Data processing operations are the kinds of tasks for which computers are ideally suited: they require many repetitious operations on large masses of data.

The word *datum* refers to a single piece of information, that is, a single fact. The word *data* is the plural of "datum" and means a collection of factual information. The act of data processing consists of manipulating that information in useful ways. Data can be classified according to the following hierarchy. The smallest unit of information is a single character, such as a letter. One character usually occupies one computer *byte*, which is eight *binary digits* (*bits*). A group of characters is called a *field*, or data item. An example of a field is a person's name. A group of fields is called a *record*. For example, in the Census Bureau's monthly survey, all the information on a particular individual is stored as a single record. A group of records is called a *file*, and a group of files is called a *data base*.

EXAMPLES OF DATA PROCESSING

People come in contact with data processing applications of computers all the time, and most of the complaints lodged against computers come from their use in this area. Examples of data processing applications of computers include the following:

1. Maintaining an organization's payroll and printing its paychecks (most people like this particular application the best).
2. Keeping track of the balances of the customers at a bank.
3. Keeping track of airline reservations and seat assignments.
4. Maintaining the records (such as grades) for the students in a school district.
5. Sending out bills to customers with credit cards.
6. Calculating statistics for major league baseball teams.

7.   Maintaining a magazine subscription list.
8.   Keeping track of the books checked out and returned at a library.

Most data processing application programs are not written in the BASIC language because there are other languages, such as COBOL, that were designed for these purposes. A complicated task requires a great deal of data storage, so large organizations usually need large computers to meet their data processing needs. However, there are many data processing tasks you can perform in BASIC with a small computer.

NOTECARDS

We now will write a general data processing program that can be used for many different types of problems. Imagine that we have a lot of information to keep track of, but we do not have a computer. We would probably set up a notecard box. Notecards provide a flexible way of maintaining information. You can easily add new cards or remove obsolete cards. You can sort the cards in alphabetical or numerical order. You can tabulate the cards, counting how many cards fall in a particular category. You can sift through the cards and consider only cards that meet a specific condition. You can cross out old information and write in new information.

As convenient as the cardbox system is, a computer can perform the same tasks more effectively. We will write a program that directs the computer to act as a cardbox. The entire program will be very long, but you should no longer be intimidated by long programs. Each piece of the program will perform a well-defined function, and we will use lots of REM statements to label what is going on. This program is different from our previous programs because it is a general-purpose program. We will not think of every possible use for the program before we write it. Instead, new uses for the program will keep arising the more we use the program and become familiar with it.

Here is a list of the various functions that our cardbox program will perform:

1.   Define the layout for the cards
2.   Read information onto the cards
3.   Provide ways to change information
4.   Save the information in a cardbox on a disk; retrieve a cardbox from a disk
5.   Display information from a card on the screen or on the printer (The program will provide several different options for presenting output)
6.   Set up selection criteria to make it possible to perform an operation on a specified group of cards instead of on the entire box of cards
7.   Sort the cards according to the order of one of the items on the card

8. Search through the box to find all cards that contain a specific string of characters
9. Delete a card from the box or add new cards to the box

Here are some possible types of information you could manage with this program:

> address list
> list of members
> list of customers
> list of suppliers
> list of students in class
> list of tasks that need to be done
> geographic data for different cities or countries

The program listing is at the back of this chapter, starting on page 219. When you read the program, remember to treat each segment as if it was a complete program. By now you should be familiar with BASIC, so you can understand how the computer accomplishes jobs such as sorting, searching, saving to disk files, and so on. The most complicated section of the program is the input section, which uses some tricky cursor movement commands. If you are typing the program yourself, you may leave out sections that you don't expect to use. If you would like to have the program without having to type it in, you can use the coupon at the back of the book to order a disk containing this program and the other programs in this book.

The program listing shown below is written in Microsoft BASIC. This particular program runs on an IBM PC computer. For other versions of BASIC, you will need to change features such as the disk file commands, the use of INKEY$ and LPRINT, and the use of apostrophes to mark comments.

The computer stores the information on the cards in a character string array called A$. In line 100, A$ is dimensioned with 200 rows and 10 columns. Each row represents a single card. The number of cards the computer can store at one time depends on the size of the computer memory. If your computer has less memory, you will not be able to fit as many cards in the memory at one time. Here is one space-saving alternative: Instead of writing the entire program as one giant program, you can write each section as a different program. Then the program itself will not occupy as much memory. You can also change the DIM A$ in any particular case. For example, if you need a cardbox with 400 cards where each card contains only five items, you can change line 100 to:

DIM A$(400,5)

When the program is running, you will give orders to the computer, telling it which job to do next. This program is *menu-driven*, meaning that the computer displays a list of choices (called a *menu*) when it is ready for a command. The subroutine that prints the menu is called in line 210. The user types a code number that corresponds to the desired function. The variable CH represents the number of the choice typed in by the user. The ON GOSUB statements in line 230–240 direct the computer to the action parts of the program.

After you type RUN, you will see the menu displayed on the screen:

ENTER YOUR CHOICE:

1. Set up new box	**2. Load and open box**
3. Save box	**4. Enter items onto cards**
5. Display cards	**6. Set up selection criteria**
7. Sort cards	**8. Copy to new box (reorder option)**
9. Adjust disp. format	**10. Turn printer on**
11. Search	**12. Reverse item**
13. Delete card	**14. Count**
15. Adjust card format	**16. Change specific item**
0. Stop program	

We will demonstrate the program by setting up two cardboxes: one containing information on the 50 states and another containing information on the presidents of the United States. Here is a description of the program's capabilities, organized according to the menu choices:

ENTERING INFORMATION

1. Set up new box

Before any information can be entered in a box, it is necessary to define the format of the items that will be contained on each card (lines 1000–1110). You must type in the number of items on each card, provide the labels for each category, and set the maximum number of characters for the items in that category. For example, the cards with state information will contain eight items. Here is the way we define the layout:

ENTER NAME OF BOX:? STATES

ENTER NUMBER OF ITEMS ON CARD:? 8

ENTER LABEL FOR CATEGORY 1 ? Name

ENTER MAXIMUM NUMBER OF CHARACTERS FOR CATEGORY 1 ? 16

ENTER LABEL FOR CATEGORY 2 ? Capital

ENTER MAXIMUM NUMBER OF CHARACTERS FOR CATEGORY 2 ? 16

ENTER LABEL FOR CATEGORY 3 ? Population

ENTER MAXIMUM NUMBER OF CHARACTERS FOR CATEGORY 3 ? 7

ENTER LABEL FOR CATEGORY 4 ? Elec Votes

ENTER MAXIMUM NUMBER OF CHARACTERS FOR CATEGORY 4 ? 2

ENTER LABEL FOR CATEGORY 5 ? Area

ENTER MAXIMUM NUMBER OF CHARACTERS FOR CATEGORY 5 ? 7

ENTER LABEL FOR CATEGORY 6 ? Inland Water

ENTER MAXIMUM NUMBER OF CHARACTERS FOR CATEGORY 6 ? 12

ENTER LABEL FOR CATEGORY 7 ? Highest elev

ENTER MAXIMUM NUMBER OF CHARACTERS FOR CATEGORY 7 ? 12

ENTER LABEL FOR CATEGORY 8 ? Admitted

ENTER MAXIMUM NUMBER OF CHARACTERS FOR CATEGORY 8 ? 8

(The part of each line before the question mark is the message displayed by the computer; our response follows the question mark.)

After the card format has been defined, we need to start entering the information onto the cards (lines 1200–1720). This section makes use of the cursor control commands to move the cursor up and down the screen. The computer will first display the labels for a card. For example:

CARD 1

Name   _

Capital

Population

Elec Votes

Area

Inland Water

Highest elev

Admitted

Then the cursor will move back up to the position opposite the first label (where the _ mark is) and wait for you to type in the state name for card 1 (which is Alabama). After typing the name, press the <RETURN> key. The cursor will jump down to the second line and wait for you to type the next item. After all of the lines have been typed, it will jump to the next card. Note that the input item is read one character at a time using the INKEY$ function (see lines 1310–1360). This makes it possible to assign specific functions to special key combinations. The computer will interpret any character whose ASCII code is less than 32 (the code for a blank) as a special character. This includes the return key and seven control key combinations: control N, control Z, control U, control D, control R,control E, and control O. If one of the special keys is typed, the computer is directed to line 1380, where it figures out what to do.

Here is a list of the special key functions:

Control-Z: End the input section and return to the main menu.

Control-N: Move on to the next card. (Note that the computer automatically moves to the next card if you type the <RE-TURN> key after entering the last item on the card.)

Control-E: Move to a different card. The computer will ask you for the card number to move to.

Control-D, control-U, and control-R: These keys allow you to change lines that have already been typed. Control-U moves the cursor up one line, and control-D moves the cursor down one line. When you press either of these keys, the cursor moves to the left edge of the screen, away from the typing area. Then you can continue to move it up or down, using control-U or control-D, until you reach the line you want. Then you must type control-R to move the cursor to the right back onto the typing area, where you can enter the new value for the item you want.

Control-O: Restore an old value for an item. If you use control-U or control-D to move to a new line and then use control-R to enter a new value, the old value will be erased. You may use control-O if you want to restore the old value.

In the following description, we will assume that we have already entered the information for the state cards and the presidents cards.

2. Load and open box
The computer will ask you for the name of a box that has been previously stored on the disk. The data files for this program have the file extension BOX. Since the computer automatically adds the BOX extension, you do not type this part when you enter the file name. After the file has been loaded and the box opened, the computer can work with it.

3. Save box
The computer will ask you for the name you wish to give the box when it is saved on the disk. Note that the "save" section (lines 6000–6100) is very similar to the "load" section (lines 5000–5120). The main rule for writing information to a disk file is this: Make sure that you write the information to the file in the same order that you use when you read the information back from the file.

4. Enter items onto cards
Use this option when you want to add new cards to an existing box after you have already loaded it. The computer will tell you how many cards are in the box already and then will take you to the

input section, where you can start entering information for the additional cards (lines 1200–1940). By way of contrast, note that option 1 creates an entirely new box.

OUTPUT

5. Display cards
    Use this option to see what is on the cards (lines 2000–2760). You may choose the output format (see option 9), whether the cards will be printed (see option 10), and whether or not all cards will be displayed (see option 6). When you first choose option 5, you will see:

**Type <RETURN> to see all cards. Else type
number of card to start with and number to stop with**

Pressing <RETURN> will tell the computer to display all of the cards. If we wanted to see only cards 15–18, we could type

15 18

and the screen would display the following:

```
----------
- 15 -
Name:          Iowa
Capital:       Des Moines
Population:    2913
Elec Votes:    8
Area:          56290
Inland Water:  349
Highest elev:  1670
Admitted:      1846
----------
- 16 -
Name:          Kansas
Capital:       Topeka
Population:    2363
Elec Votes:    7
Area:          82264
Inland Water:  477
Highest elev:  4039
Admitted:      1861
----------
- 17 -
Name:          Kentucky
Capital:       Frankfort
Population:    3661
Elec Votes:    9
Area:          40395
Inland Water:  745
Highest elev:  4145
Admitted:      1792
```

```
----------
- 18 -
Name:          Louisiana
Capital:       Baton Rouge
Population:    4204
Elec Votes:    10
Area:          48523
Inland Water:  3593
Highest elev:  535
Admitted:      1812
```

(Population is measured in thousands of people; the total area and inland water area are measured in square miles.)

We have two basic choices when we display cards: We can display the items on the cards vertically, as we did above, or we can display the items horizontally. However, note that it might not be possible to display all items on a card horizontally because the screen might not be wide enough. We can tell the computer not to display all items on the cards and instead have it display only selected items. For example, suppose we would like a table showing each state's population, area, inland water area, and highest elevation. When you see the main menu, choose option 9 (Adjust display format, lines 8000–8290). The screen will show the display format menu:

ENTER CHOICE:

1. **Switch display mode to horizontal**

2. **Stop including labels**

3. **Stop including card numbers**

4. **Select which items to display**

5. **Pause during output**

6. **Change page length, currently 66**

7. **Change space between items, currently 1**

We will choose option 1 to switch the print mode to horizontal. Then we will be returned to the main menu, so we must type 9 again to reenter the "Adjust display format" option. Now we will choose display option 4 ("Select which items to display"). The computer displays the list of items on our cards:

1 **Name**

2 **Capital**

3 **Population**

4 **Elec votes**

5 **Area**

Continued

6 Inland Water

7 Highest elev

8 Admitted

Then it asks:

How many items would you like printed?

We will type 5. Then it says:

Enter items one by one

Since we would like the name, population, area, inland water area, and highest elevation displayed, we will enter these item numbers:

? 1

? 3

? 5

? 6

? 7

Now we are finished using the display format option, so we will see the main menu. Choose option 5 to display cards. This is the result:

	Name	Populat	Area	Inland Water	Highest elev
1.	Alabama	3890	51609	901	2407
2.	Alaska	400	589757	20157	20320
3.	Arizona	2718	113909	492	12633
4.	Arkansas	2286	53104	1159	2753
5.	California	23669	158693	2332	14494
6.	Colorado	2889	104247	481	14433
7.	Connecticut	3108	5009	147	2380
8.	Delaware	595	2057	75	442
9.	Florida	9740	58560	4470	345
10.	Georgia	5464	58876	803	4784
11.	Hawaii	965	6450	25	13796
12.	Idaho	944	83557	880	12662
13.	Illinois	11418	56400	652	1235
14.	Indiana	5490	36291	194	1257
15.	Iowa	2913	56290	349	1670
16.	Kansas	2363	82264	477	4039
17.	Kentucky	3661	40395	745	4145
18.	Louisiana	4204	48523	3593	535
19.	Maine	1125	33215	2295	5268
20.	Maryland	4216	10577	686	3360
21.	Massachussetts	5737	8257	431	3491
22.	Michigan	9258	58216	1399	1980
23.	Minnesota	4077	84068	4779	2301

24.	Mississippi	2521	47716	420	806
25.	Missouri	4917	69686	691	1772
26.	Montana	787	147138	1551	12799
27.	Nebraska	1570	77227	744	5426
28.	Nevada	799	110540	651	13143
29.	New Hampshire	921	9304	277	6288
30.	New Jersey	7364	7836	315	1803
31.	New Mexico	1300	121666	254	13161
32.	New York	17557	49576	1745	5344
33.	North Carolina	5874	52586	3788	6684
34.	North Dakota	653	70665	1392	3506
35.	Ohio	10797	41222	247	1550
36.	Oklahoma	3025	69919	1137	4973
37.	Oregon	2633	96981	797	11239
38.	Pennsylvania	11867	45333	367	3213
39.	Rhode Island	947	1214	165	812
40.	South Carolina	3119	31055	830	3560
41.	South Dakota	690	77047	1092	7242
42.	Tennessee	4591	42244	916	6643
43.	Texas	14228	267338	5204	8749
44.	Utah	1461	84916	2820	13528
45.	Vermont	511	9609	342	4393
46.	Virginia	5346	40817	1037	5729
47.	Washington	4130	68192	1622	14410
48.	West Virginia	1950	24181	111	4863
49.	Wisconsin	4705	56154	1690	1951
50.	Wyoming	471	97914	711	13804

When the computer is done displaying cards, two asterisks **
will appear at the bottom of the screen. The asterisks mean that the
computer is pausing to give you a chance to see what is on the
screen. Type any key when you want to proceed. (In this case, the
main menu will be the next item to appear on the screen.)

Here are notes about the other choices in the adjust display
format section:

2.   Stop including labels

If this option is chosen, the item labels will not appear when
cards are output in vertical format. This option has no effect on
horizontal card output.

3.   Stop including card numbers

No card numbers will be displayed in either vertical or horizontal format.

5.   Pause during output

6.   Change page length, currently 66

If option 5 is chosen, then output will stop every time it has printed the number of lines given by the current page length (66 in this example). You must type any key to continue output. This option allows you to slow down the output that appears on the screen or to adjust the paper if you are using the printer. By choosing option 6 you may adjust the page length.

7.   Change space between items, currently 1

This option determines the number of spaces that will appear between items when cards are displayed in horizontal format.

If you wish to cancel any of these options, enter the display format section again and type the same code number that started the option. The display format menu automatically adjusts to tell you what you can change. (Note how the program accomplishes this in lines 8020–8070). For example, the first time you enter the display format menu the first option is:

1.   Switch display mode to horizontal

If you choose option 1, thereby switching the display mode to horizontal, and then enter the display format menu again, you will see:

1.   Switch display mode to vertical

If you choose option 1 now, you will switch the display mode back to vertical.

Here is an example of a printout from the presidential card box. Each card contains four items: the president's name, party, state of birth, and years in office.

	Name	Par	Br. St.	Years
1.	George Washington	Fed	Va	1789-1797
2.	John Adams	Fed	Mass	1797-1801
3.	Thomas Jefferson	DR	Va	1801-1809
4.	James Madison	DR	Va	1809-1817
5.	James Monroe	DR	Va	1817-1825
6.	John Quincy Adams	DR	Mass	1825-1829
7.	Andrew Jackson	Dem	SC	1829-1837
8.	Martin van Buren	Dem	NY	1837-1841
9.	William Henry Harrison	Whg	Va	1841-1841
10.	John Tyler	Whg	Va	1841-1845
11.	James K. Polk	Dem	NC	1845-1849
12.	Zachary Taylor	Whg	Va	1849-1850
13.	Millard Fillmore	Whg	NY	1850-1853
14.	Franklin Pierce	Dem	NH	1853-1857
15.	James Buchanan	Dem	Penn	1857-1861
16.	Abraham Lincoln	Rep	Ken	1861-1865
17.	Andrew Johnson	Rep	NC	1865-1869
18.	Ulysses S. Grant	Rep	Oh	1869-1877
19.	Rutherford B. Hayes	Rep	Oh	1877-1881
20.	James A. Garfield	Rep	Oh	1881-1881
21.	Chester A. Arthur	Rep	Vt	1881-1885
22.	Grover Cleveland	Dem	NJ	1885-1889
23.	Benjamin Harrison	Rep	Oh	1889-1893
24.	Grover Cleveland	Dem	NJ	1893-1897

25.	William McKinley	Rep	Oh	1897-1901
26.	Theodore Roosevelt	Rep	NY	1901-1909
27.	William Howard Taft	Rep	Oh	1909-1913
28.	Woodrow Wilson	Dem	Va	1913-1921
29.	Warren Harding	Rep	Oh	1921-1923
30.	Calvin Coolidge	Rep	Vt	1923-1929
31.	Herbert Hoover	Rep	Iowa	1929-1933
32.	Franklin D. Roosevelt	Dem	NY	1933-1945
33.	Harry S Truman	Dem	Mo	1945-1953
34.	Dwight Eisenhower	Rep	Tex	1953-1961
35.	John F. Kennedy	Dem	Mass	1961-1963
36.	Lyndon B. Johnson	Dem	Tex	1963-1969
37.	Richard M. Nixon	Rep	Cal	1969-1974
38.	Gerald Ford	Rep	Neb	1974-1977
39.	Jimmy Carter	Dem	Ga	1977-1981
40.	Ronald Reagan	Rep	Ill	1981-1989
41.	George Bush	Rep	Mass	1989-

6. Set up selection criteria

Suppose we need to look only at states with populations greater than 10 million. Option 6 (lines 3000–3755) allows us to establish a set of selection criteria. In all subsequent display, sort, count, and search commands, only those cards that meet the selection criteria will be allowed to take part in the command. When we choose this option, the computer first displays the current selection criteria. It will say "All cards selected" if there is no selection criteria currently in effect. Next the computer will display the list of items on the cards. Then it will display the message:

Type A if you would like to see all cards

Else type N

If we type A in response to this question, the selection criteria will select all cards in the box. Otherwise we will be asked for more specific criteria. The computer next displays:

NUMBER OF ITEMS TO SELECT ON:

We only wish to make a selection by one item: population. (If, for example, we wanted to look only at states with populations greater than 10 million and areas greater than 5000, then we would tell the computer to select on two items.) Next the computer asks:

ENTER CODE NUMBER OF ITEM:

Since population is item number 3 on our card, type 3. Next we're asked:

ENTER LOWEST ALLOWABLE VALUE FOR Population:

Enter 10000. (Remember that we are measuring population in units of 1000 people on our cards.) Next we're asked:

ENTER HIGHEST ALLOWABLE VALUE FOR Population:

Enter 1000000 (This will be sure to cover the largest possible value for the population.)

After we have chosen our selection criterion, we will see the menu again. We can choose option 5 to display the cards, and then we will see:

	Name	Populat	Area	Inland Water	Highest elev
5.	California	23669	158693	2332	14494
13.	Illinois	11418	56400	652	1235
32.	New York	17557	49576	1745	5344
35.	Ohio	10797	41222	247	1550
38.	Pennsylvania	11867	45333	367	3213
43.	Texas	14228	267338	5204	8749

	Name	Populat	Area	Inland Water	Highest elev
9.	Florida	9740	58560	4470	345
10.	Georgia	5464	58876	803	4784
14.	Indiana	5490	36291	194	1257
21.	Massachussetts	5737	8257	431	3491
22.	Michigan	9258	58216	1399	1980
30.	New Jersey	7364	7836	315	1803
33.	North Carolina	5874	52586	3788	6684
46.	Virginia	5346	40817	1037	5729

The top list shows states with populations greater than 10 million. The bottom list shows what happens if we change the selection criterion to include states with populations beteen 5 million and 10 million.

If we want to select cards with a specific value of an item, we enter that value for both the highest and lowest allowable value. For example, if we wanted a list of Republican presidents, we could enter "Rep" as the highest and lowest allowable value for the president's party. Here is a list showing all Republican presidents and another list showing all Democratic presidents:

	Name	Par	Br. St.	Years
16.	Abraham Lincoln	Rep	Ken	1861-1865
17.	Andrew Johnson	Rep	NC	1865-1869
18.	Ulysses S. Grant	Rep	Oh	1869-1877
19.	Rutherford B. Hayes	Rep	Oh	1877-1881
20.	James A. Garfield	Rep	Oh	1881-1881
21.	Chester A. Arthur	Rep	Vt	1881-1885
23.	Benjamin Harrison	Rep	Oh	1889-1893
25.	William McKinley	Rep	Oh	1897-1901
26.	Theodore Roosevelt	Rep	NY	1901-1909

27.	William Howard Taft	Rep		Oh	1909-1913
29.	Warren Harding	Rep		Oh	1921-1923
30.	Calvin Coolidge	Rep		Vt	1923-1929
31.	Herbert Hoover	Rep		Iowa	1929-1933
34.	Dwight Eisenhower	Rep		Tex	1953-1961
37.	Richard M. Nixon	Rep		Cal	1969-1974
38.	Gerald Ford	Rep		Neb	1974-1977
40.	Ronald Reagan	Rep		Ill	1981-1989
41.	George Bush	Rep		Mass	1989-

	Name	Par	Br.	St.	Years
7.	Andrew Jackson	Dem		SC	1829-1837
8.	Martin van Buren	Dem		NY	1837-1841
11.	James K. Polk	Dem		NC	1845-1849
14.	Franklin Pierce	Dem		NH	1853-1857
15.	James Buchanan	Dem		Penn	1857-1861
22.	Grover Cleveland	Dem		NJ	1885-1889
24.	Grover Cleveland	Dem		NJ	1893-1897
28.	Woodrow Wilson	Dem		Va	1913-1921
32.	Franklin D. Roosevelt	Dem		NY	1933-1945
33.	Harry S Truman	Dem		Mo	1945-1953
35.	John F. Kennedy	Dem		Mass	1961-1963
36.	Lyndon B. Johnson	Dem		Tex	1963-1969
39.	Jimmy Carter	Dem		Ga	1977-1981

SORTING AND SEARCHING

7. Sort cards

Suppose you would like a listing of all states displayed in order of highest elevation. First, choose option 6 to change the selection criterion back to "All cards selected". Now choose option 7 (lines 4000-4250). The screen will display the item labels and then ask:

Item number to sort on:

Type 7, since population is item 7. Then you see:

Enter A for ascending order, D for descending order?

Type D, Then:

Enter N for numerical sort, C for character sort?

Type N, since the elevation is a number.

Then the computer sorts the states in order of elevation.

You will see the output displayed as follows:

	Name	Highest elev
1.	Alaska	20320
2.	California	14494
3.	Colorado	14433
4.	Washington	14410
5.	Wyoming	13804
6.	Hawaii	13796
7.	Utah	13528
8.	New Mexico	13161
9.	Nevada	13143
10.	Montana	12799
11.	Idaho	12662
12.	Arizona	12633
13.	Oregon	11239
14.	Texas	8749
15.	South Dakota	7242
16.	North Carolina	6684
17.	Tennessee	6643
18.	New Hampshire	6288
19.	Virginia	5729
20.	Nebraska	5426
21.	New York	5344
22.	Maine	5268
23.	Oklahoma	4973
24.	West Virginia	4863
25.	Georgia	4784
26.	Vermont	4393
27.	Kentucky	4145
28.	Kansas	4039
29.	South Carolina	3560
30.	North Dakota	3506
31.	Massachussetts	3491
32.	Maryland	3360
33.	Pennsylvania	3213
34.	Arkansas	2753
35.	Alabama	2407
36.	Connecticut	2380
37.	Minnesota	2301
38.	Michigan	1980
39.	Wisconsin	1951
40.	New Jersey	1803
41.	Missouri	1772
42.	Iowa	1670
43.	Ohio	1550
44.	Indiana	1257
45.	Illinois	1235
46.	Rhode Island	812
47.	Mississippi	806
48.	Louisiana	535
49.	Delaware	442
50.	Florida	345

We also have the option of sorting the cards in ascending order. For example, we could print a list of states in the order of admission to the Union:

	Name	Admi
1.	Delaware	1787
2.	New Jersey	1787
3.	Pennsylvania	1787
4.	Connecticut	1788
5.	Georgia	1788
6.	Maryland	1788
7.	Massachussetts	1788
8.	New Hampshire	1788
9.	New York	1788
10.	South Carolina	1788
11.	Virginia	1788
12.	North Carolina	1789
13.	Rhode Island	1790
14.	Vermont	1791
15.	Kentucky	1792
16.	Tennessee	1796
17.	Ohio	1803
18.	Louisiana	1812
19.	Indiana	1816
20.	Mississippi	1817
21.	Illinois	1818
22.	Alabama	1819
23.	Maine	1820
24.	Missouri	1821
25.	Arkansas	1836
26.	Michigan	1837
27.	Florida	1845
28.	Texas	1845
29.	Iowa	1846
30.	Wisconsin	1848
31.	California	1850
32.	Minnesota	1858
33.	Oregon	1859
34.	Kansas	1861
35.	West Virginia	1863
36.	Nevada	1864
37.	Nebraska	1867
38.	Colorado	1876
39.	Montana	1889
40.	North Dakota	1889
41.	South Dakota	1889
42.	Washington	1889
43.	Idaho	1890
44.	Wyoming	1890
45.	Utah	1896
46.	Oklahoma	1907
47.	Arizona	1912
48.	New Mexico	1912
49.	Alaska	1959
50.	Hawaii	1959

Continued

8.   Copy to new box (reorder option)

Use this option (lines 7000–7070) if you would like to copy all of the cards in a box into another box. The cards in the new box may be put in the same order as the cards in the existing box, or they may be sorted according to one of the items on the card. The computer asks you:

New box name:

Then it asks:

Enter item number to sort by

Else type 0

Type 0 if you want the cards in the same order as in the original box. If you want a box with state cards sorted in order of population, then type 3 (since 3 is the item number for population in our example.)

Notice how this section uses the same subroutines for sorting and storing on the disk as are used by options 3 and 7.

10.   Turn printer on

If you choose this option (lines 8900–8940), all subsequent output will go to the printer until you choose this option again to turn the printer off.

11.   Search

Suppose we want to look at the card for California, but we don't happen to know the card number. The search option (lines 10000–10130) will search through all of the cards until it finds the one that contains the characters we specify. When you enter this option, the computer first asks:

Enter item number:

Type 1, since we are searching for a state name. Then the computer asks:

Enter characters to search for:

Type "California".

Then the computer starts shuffling through the cards until it finds and displays the card for California:

- 5 -

Name:	California
Capital:	Sacramento
Population:	23669

Elec Votes:	**47**
Area:	**158693**
Inland Water:	**2332**
Highest elev:	**14494**

Type E to edit this card, Type R to repeat search, Else type N

Now we have three choices. If one of the data items for California needs to be changed, we could type E. Then the computer would put us in the edit mode for this card. The cursor will start at the left-hand edge of the screen. Use control-D or control-U to move the cursor up or down, and use control-R to move the cursor to the right onto the typing area. (See the description of the edit mode under option 1.) Type Control-Z when you have completed this card.

If we choose the option "R to repeat search", the computer will look through the cards to see if it can find another card named California. Obviously it will not, so it will display the message "California not found" and then return us to the main menu. This option will be helpful in some cases. For example, we could use the search procedure to look at (or edit) all cards for Democratic presidents.

If we choose option N, we will be returned to the main menu.

The search command will look to see if any part of the string you specify occurs in the specified item on the card. It is not necessary to type the whole word. For example, you could have the computer search for all states with "New" in their names, or you could search for all states with "Dakota" in their names.

12. Reverse items

Suppose you have a cardbox for people where one item is the person's name, written with first name first. If you want to alphabetize according to the last name, you will need to switch the order of the first and last name, which you can do with the "Reverse items" procedure (lines 11000–11090). The computer will first ask you for the item number you wish to reverse. Then it will ask you for the separator character, which is likely to be a blank or a comma, etc.

13. Delete card

The computer asks you for the card number to delete, then asks you to confirm the deletion, then deletes the card (lines 12000–12110).

COUNTING

14. Count

Suppose you would like to know how many presidents were born in Virginia, how many were born in Ohio, and so on. You can use the count procedure (lines 13000–13180), which counts how many cards have each possible value for a particular item. Choose option 14. The computer asks you:

Code number of item to count:

Type 3 (the number for state of birth in the president box). Then you will see:

```
      Va        8
    Mass        4
      SC        1
      NY        4
      NC        2
      NH        1
    Penn        1
     Ken        1
      Oh        7
      Vt        2
      NJ        2
    Iowa        1
      Mo        1
     Tex        2
     Cal        1
     Neb        1
      Ga        1
     Ill        1
TOTAL
```

As you can see, eight presidents were born in Virginia and seven were born in Ohio. (Note that Grover Cleveland is counted twice in this table because he served as president two nonconsecutive terms.)

15. Adjust card format

This option allows you to change the length of one of the items on the card or even to add a new item to each card. If you choose to add a new item, you are asked for the label for the item and the length. Then the computer will display the cards one by one, asking you to type in the value of the new item.

16. Change specific item

Suppose you wish to enter new values for population for every card. Then choose this option and enter the number of the item you wish to change. The computer will display the cards one by one, automatically placing the cursor in the correct position to add the new value of the item. Note: In this option, you cannot move the cursor up or down to change any item on the cards other than the one you selected.

0. Stop the program

This option is self-explanatory. It does contain a valuable feature that prevents the program from stopping if you accidentally choose the stop option. After choosing this option, the computer asks you:

TYPE Y TO CONFIRM YOU ARE DONE WITH PROGRAM

If you are really done, then type Y and the program will end. If you did not mean to stop the program, press any other key and you will be returned to the main menu. It is as good idea to have any program ask for confirmation whenever a user types a command that will lose data (such as stopping the program or deleting cards). Here is the program listing:

```
1 REM   CARD BOX PROGRAM
2 REM     THIS PROGRAM CAUSES THE COMPUTER TO ACT AS A
3 REM     NOTECARD BOX.  THE MENU (STARTING AT LINE 16000)
4 REM     LISTS THE DIFFERENT OPTIONS AVAILABLE.
5 REM     SEE THE TEXT OF THE CHAPTER FOR A DESCRIPTION
6 REM     OF EACH PART OF THE PROGRAM.
7 REM     THIS PROGRAM IS WRITTEN IN MICROSOFT BASIC
99 REM ****** DIMENSION THE ARRAYS USED ******
100 DIM A$(200,10),NUMCH(10),LAB$(10)
101 REM  THE PROGRAM CURRENTLY ALLOWS 200 CARDS WITH 10 ITEMS PER CARD
102 DIM L$(200),L(200),POSTN(200)
105 DIM SEL(200),SEL$(2,10)
108 DIM SEL2(10):FOR I=1 TO 10:SEL2(I)=1:NEXT I
110 DIM CT$(80),CT(80)
114 REM ****************************************
115 REM  IN THIS SECTION YOU NEED TO DEFINE THE CURSOR MOVEMENT
116 REM  CHARACTERS, USING THE COMMAND CODES FOR YOUR COMPUTER.
117 REM  UP$ IS THE CODE TO MOVE THE CURSOR UP; DOWN$ MOVES IT DOWN;
118 REM  RT$ MOVES IT TO THE RIGHT AND BK$ MOVES CURSOR BACK (LEFT).
119 REM  THESE ARE THE CODES FOR THE IBM PC:
120   UP$=CHR$(30)
121   DOWN$=CHR$(31)
122   RT$=CHR$(28)
123   BK$=CHR$(29)
124 REM   USE THESE CODES IF YOUR COMPUTER FOLLOWS THE ANSI
125 REM   SCREEN CONTROL COMMANDS:
126 REM      UP$=CHR$(27)+"[1A"
127 REM      DOWN$=CHR$(27)+"[1B"
128 REM      RT$=CHR$(27)+"[1C"
129 REM      BK$=CHR$(8)
130 RET$=CHR$(13)   'RETURN KEY
131 CTZ$=CHR$(26)   'CONTROL-Z
132 CTU$=CHR$(21):CTD$=CHR$(4):CTR$=CHR$(18) 'CONTROL U,D, AND R
133 CTN$=CHR$(14)   'CONTROL-N
134 CTE$=CHR$(5)    'CONTROL-E
135 CTO$=CHR$(15)   'CONTROL-O
150 ALL=1
155 PRT=0:LBLS=1:HRZ=0:CNUM=1:CRUISE=1
160 PGLEN=66   'PAGE LENGTH
```

Continued

```
165 SPBI=1      'SPACE BETWEEN ITEMS IN HORIZONTAL DISPLAYS
197 '
198 '
199 REM ****************************************
200 REM   PRINT MENU AND READ IN USER'S CHOICE
210  GOSUB 16000    'PRINT MENU
220 INPUT CH
222 IF CH=0 THEN GOTO 900 'END
230 ON CH GOSUB 1000,5000,6000,1200,2000,3500,4000,7000
235 IF CH<=8 THEN GOTO 200 ELSE CH2=CH-8
240 ON CH2 GOSUB 8000,8900,10000,11000,12000,13000,14000,15000
260 GOTO 200
899 '
900 REM -- END OF PROGRAM
910 PRINT "TYPE Y TO CONFIRM YOU ARE DONE WITH PROGRAM"
915 GOSUB 9000
920  IF (K$="Y") OR (K$="y") THEN END ELSE GOTO 200
997 '
998 '
999 REM ****************************************
1000 REM *   START NEW BOX                     *
1001 REM ****************************************
1010 INPUT "ENTER NAME OF BOX:";NM$
1020 INPUT "ENTER NUMBER OF ITEMS ON CARD:";NUM
1028  MAXLAB=0
1030 FOR I=1 TO NUM
1040    PRINT "ENTER LABEL FOR CATEGORY ";I;
1050    INPUT LAB$(I)
1055      IF LEN(LAB$(I))>MAXLAB THEN MAXLAB=LEN(LAB$(I))
1060    PRINT "ENTER MAXIMUM NUMBER OF CHARACTERS FOR CATEGORY ";I;
1070    INPUT NUMCH(I)
1080 NEXT I
1090 NUMCARDS=0
1100 GOSUB 1200
1110 RETURN
1197 '
1198 '
1199 REM ****************************************
1200 REM *   ENTER NEW ITEMS ONTO CARDS        *
1201 REM ****************************************
1209 PRINT:PRINT
1210 PRINT "NAME OF BOX:";NM$;"    NUMBER OF ITEMS PER CARD:";NUM
1211 PRINT "NUMBER OF CARDS:";NUMCARDS
1215  FOR I=1 TO NUM:SEL2(I)=1:NEXT I
1217  CARD=NUMCARDS
1218    CRUISE=1
1220 REM === START NEW CARD =====================
1230     CARD=CARD+1
1240     PRINT:PRINT "----------"
1245     PRINT "CARD ";CARD
1250     FOR I=1 TO NUM:PRINT " ";LAB$(I):NEXT  I
1260     FOR I=1 TO NUM:PRINT UP$;:NEXT I
1270     FOR J=1 TO (MAXLAB+3):PRINT RT$;:NEXT J
1290     I=1   'I IS THE ITEM NUMBER
1300 REM ===== START NEW ITEM   ===================
1305        IF A$(CARD,I)<>"" THEN GOSUB 1850 'PRINT BLANKS
```

```
1310          X$=""
1320          GOSUB 9000    'INKEY SUBROUTINE
1325          REM  K$ REPRESENTS THE KEY THAT WAS PRESSED
1330          IF (K$<" ") THEN GOTO 1380  'A SPECIAL KEY HAS BEEN TYPED
1340          X$=X$+K$
1345          IF LEN(X$)>NUMCH(I) THEN PRINT CHR$(7);
1346          REM   RING BELL IF ITEM TYPED IN IS TOO LONG
1350          PRINT K$;
1360          GOTO 1320       'READ NEXT CHARACTER
1380 REM =========SPECIAL KEY  =====================
1381 IF (CARD<NUMCARDS) AND (I=NUM) AND K$=RET$ THEN GOTO 1320
1382 IF (CH=11) AND K$=RET$ THEN GOTO 1320
1383 REM The Return key is ignored if this section is called
1384 REM from the search section (choice 11) or if we are not
1385 REM at the end of the box of cards.
1386          IF K$=CHR$(8) THEN GOSUB 9020:GOTO 1320 'BACKSPACE KEY
1387          IF K$=CTO$ THEN PRINT A$(CARD,I):I=I+1:GOTO 1700
1388          REM CTL-O MEANS RESTORE OLD VALUE
1390          IF LEN(X$)>NUMCH(I) THEN X$=LEFT$(X$,NUMCH(I))
1400          A$(CARD,I)=X$
1405          IF K$=CTN$ THEN GOTO 1800   'CTL-N MEANS START NEXT CARD
1407          IF K$=CTU$ THEN GOTO 1700   'CTL-U MEANS MOVE UP
1408          IF K$=CTD$ THEN GOTO 1760   'CTL-D MEANS MOVE DOWN
1409          IF K$=CTE$ THEN GOTO 1900   'CTL-E MEANS MOVE TO DIFFERENT CARD
1410          IF K$=RET$ THEN I=I+1:IF I<=NUM THEN GOTO 1600 ELSE GOTO 1220
1411          REM                              1600 - START NEW ITEM
1412          REM                              1220 - START NEW CARD
1420          IF K$=CTZ$ THEN GOTO 1630    'CTL-Z MEANS END THE INPUT SECTION
1490          GOTO 1320  'INVALID KEY HAS BEEN PUSHED IF YOU REACH THIS LINE
1600 REM ======== START NEW ITEM ===================
1610          PRINT:FOR J=1 TO (MAXLAB+3):PRINT RT$;:NEXT J
1620          GOTO 1300
1630 REM ======== END THE INPUT SECTION ============
1640        FOR J=1 TO NUM+1:PRINT:NEXT J
1645        NUMCARDS=CARD
1647        IF NUMCARDS<NUMC2 THEN NUMCARDS=NUMC2
1650 RETURN
1698 '
1699 '
1700 REM ======== MOVE CURSOR UP OR DOWN ===========
1705   PRINT:PRINT UP$;
1710   IF I>1 THEN I=I-1:PRINT UP$;
1720   GOSUB 9000   ' INKEY SUBROUTINE
1725     IF K$=CTZ$ THEN GOTO 1630
1727     IF K$=CTN$ THEN GOTO 1800
1730     IF K$=CTU$ THEN GOTO 1710
1735     IF K$=CTD$ THEN GOTO 1760
1737     IF K$=CTE$ THEN GOTO 1900
1740     IF K$<>CTR$ THEN GOTO 1720
1745     FOR J=1 TO (MAXLAB+3):PRINT RT$;:NEXT J
1750     GOTO 1300    'READY TO TYPE IN NEW ITEM
1760       REM - CONTROL D WAS PUSHED
1765        IF I<NUM THEN I=I+1:PRINT
1770        GOTO 1720
1800 REM ==== CTL-N: START NEW CARD ================
1810   FOR J=I TO (NUM+2):PRINT:NEXT J
```

```
1815    CARD=CARD+1
1820    GOTO 1910
1850 REM ====== PRINT BLANKS ====================
1855      PRINT SPC(NUMCH(I));
1860       FOR J=1 TO NUMCH(I):PRINT BK$;:NEXT J
1865      RETURN
1900 REM ==== CTL-E: MOVE TO NEW CARD ============
1902   FOR J=1 TO NUM:PRINT:NEXT J
1905   INPUT "Card number to move to:";CARD
1910   IF NUMCARDS<CARD THEN NUMCARDS=CARD
1912   NUMC2=NUMCARDS
1915   PRT2=PRT:PRT=0
1920   GOSUB 2500  'PRINT CARD
1922   PRT=PRT2
1925   FOR J=1 TO NUM:PRINT UP$;:NEXT J
1930   I=1
1940   GOTO 1720
1997 '
1998 '
1999 REM ****************************************
2000 REM * DISPLAY ITEMS ON CARDS              *
2001 REM ****************************************
2005   PRINT
2006   LNUM=0
2010   PRINT "Type <RETURN> to see all cards.  Else type"
2011   PRINT "number of card to start with and number to stop with"
2015   INPUT CH$
2020    IF CH$="" THEN STARTT=1:STOPP=NUMCARDS:GOTO 2030
2025    CH2=INSTR(CH$," ")
2026    IF CH2=0 THEN STARTT=VAL(CH$):STOPP=STARTT:GOTO 2030
2027    STARTT=VAL(LEFT$(CH$,CH2-1))
2028    STOPP=VAL(RIGHT$(CH$,LEN(CH$)-CH2))
2029    IF STOPP>NUMCARDS THEN STOPP=NUMCARDS
2030      FOR CARD=STARTT TO STOPP
2035        GOSUB 3000  'SELECT ROUTINE
2037        IF SELECT<>1 THEN GOTO 2080
2050        GOSUB 2400 'PRINT CARD
2080      NEXT CARD
2090   PRINT
2095   PRINT "**":GOSUB 9000
2099   RETURN
2398 '
2399 '
2400 REM ======= PRINT CARDS ====================
2410   IF HRZ=0 THEN GOSUB 2500 ELSE GOSUB 2600
2420 RETURN
2498 '
2499 '
2500 REM ======= PRINT CARD VERTICALLY ============
2505        IF CNUM<>1 THEN PRINT:GOTO 2510
2506        PRINT "----------":PRINT "-";CARD;"-"
2507        IF PRT=1 THEN LPRINT "----------":LPRINT "-";CARD;"-"
2508        LNUM=LNUM+2
2510        FOR I=1 TO NUM
2511   IF (CH=4) OR (CH=11) OR (CH=16)  THEN GOTO 2525 'IF THE SUBROUTINE
2512        REM IS CALLED BY OPTION 4, 11, OR 16 THEN THE LABELS
```

```
2514          REM ARE ALWAYS PRINTED AND EACH ITEM IS ALWAYS PRINTED
2515          IF SEL2(I)<>1 THEN GOTO 2590
2520          IF LBLS<>1 THEN GOTO 2540
2525             PRINT " ";LAB$(I);":";:PRINT TAB(MAXLAB+4);
2530             IF PRT=1 THEN LPRINT LAB$(I);":";:LPRINT TAB(MAXLAB+3);
2540             PRINT A$(CARD,I)
2545             IF PRT=1 THEN LPRINT A$(CARD,I)
2590          NEXT I
2591          IF CRUISE=1 THEN RETURN
2592          LNUM=LNUM+NUM:IF LNUM>PGLEN THEN PRINT "**":LNUM=0:GOSUB 9000
2595       RETURN
2599
2600 REM ======= PRINT CARD HORIZONTALLY ==========
2605   IF LNUM=0 THEN GOSUB 2700   'PRINT HEADINGS AT TOP
2607   LNUM=LNUM+1:IF LNUM>PGLEN THEN LNUM=0
2610   IF CNUM<>1 THEN GOTO 2620
2612   PRINT USING "####";CARD;:PRINT ".   ";
2614   IF PRT=1 THEN LPRINT USING "####";CARD;:LPRINT ".   ";
2620   FOR I=1 TO NUM
2625     IF SEL2(I)<>1 THEN GOTO 2660
2630       S2=NUMCH(I)-LEN(A$(CARD,I))+SPBI
2640       PRINT SPC(S2);:IF PRT=1 THEN LPRINT SPC(S2);
2650       PRINT A$(CARD,I);:IF PRT=1 THEN LPRINT A$(CARD,I);
2660   NEXT I
2670   PRINT :IF PRT=1 THEN LPRINT
2680 RETURN
2697 '
2698 '
2699 '
2700 REM ======= PRINT LABELS ACROSS TOP ==========
2702   IF CRUISE<>1 THEN PRINT "**":GOSUB 9000
2704   PRINT:IF PRT=1 THEN LPRINT
2705   IF CNUM=1 THEN PRINT "        ";:IF PRT=1 THEN LPRINT "       ";
2706   IF CH=7 THEN PRINT "       ";:IF PRT=1 THEN LPRINT "       ";
2710   FOR I=1 TO NUM
2715     IF SEL2(I)<>1 THEN GOTO 2750
2717       L2$=LAB$(I):IF LEN(L2$)>NUMCH(I) THEN L2$=LEFT$(L2$,NUMCH(I))
2720       S2=NUMCH(I)-LEN(L2$)+SPBI
2725       PRINT SPC(S2);:IF PRT=1 THEN LPRINT SPC(S2);
2730       PRINT L2$;:IF PRT=1 THEN LPRINT L2$;
2750     NEXT I
2755   PRINT   : IF PRT=1 THEN LPRINT
2760 RETURN
2997 '
2998 '
2999 REM ***********************************
3000 REM * SELECTION ROUTINE               *
3001 REM ***********************************
3002 REM IF THE VARIABLE SELECT IS SET TO 1, THEN THE ITEM
3003 REM WILL BE SELECTED
3010   IF ALL=1 THEN SELECT=1:RETURN
3020   SELECT=1
3030    J=0
3040    REM START CHECKING ITEMS
3042      J=J+1
3050      IF SEL(J)=-1 THEN RETURN
```

Continued

```
3060        I=SEL(J)
3070        A1$=A$(CARD,I)
3072        IF SELNUM(J)=0 THEN GOTO 3080   'NON-NUMERIC STRING
3074        REM -- SELECTION FOR NUMERIC STRINGS
3076        A1=VAL(A1$):SELN1=VAL(SEL$(1,J)):SELN2=VAL(SEL$(2,J))
3077        IF (A1<SELN1) OR (A1>SELN2) THEN SELECT=0:RETURN
3078        GOTO 3040    'CHECK NEXT ITEM
3079        REM -- SELECTION FOR NON-NUMERIC STRINGS
3080        IF (A1$<SEL$(1,J)) OR (A1$>SEL$(2,J)) THEN SELECT=0:RETURN
3090        GOTO 3040    'CHECK NEXT ITEM
3497  '
3498  '
3499  '
3500  REM ====== SET UP SELECTION CRITERIA =========
3502   GOSUB 3600  'PRINT CURRENT SELECTION CRITERIA
3505   GOSUB 16200 'PRINT LABELS
3506   PRINT "Type A if you would like to see all cards"
3507   INPUT "Else type N  ",Q$
3508   IF Q$="A" THEN ALL=1:RETURN
3509   ALL=0
3510   INPUT "NUMBER OF ITEMS TO SELECT ON:";N
3520   FOR J=1 TO N
3525        SELNUM(J)=0
3530        INPUT" ENTER CODE NUMBER OF ITEM:";CODE
3535        SEL(J)=CODE
3540        PRINT "ENTER LOWEST ALLOWABLE VALUE FOR ";LAB$(CODE);
3550        INPUT SEL$(1,J)
3555        GOSUB 3700  'CHECK TO SEE IF THIS IS A NUMERIC VALUE
3560        PRINT "ENTER HIGHEST ALLOWABLE VALUE FOR ";LAB$(CODE);
3570        INPUT SEL$(2,J)
3580   NEXT J
3585   SEL(N+1)=-1
3590   RETURN
3598  '
3599  '
3600  REM ====== DISPLAY SELECTION CRITERIA ========
3605   PRINT "Current selection criteria:"
3610   IF ALL=1 THEN PRINT "All cards selected":RETURN
3620     I=0
3630    REM - START LOOP
3640     I=I+1
3650     IF SEL(I)=-1 THEN RETURN
3660     PRINT LAB$(SEL(I)),SEL$(1,I);"-";SEL$(2,I)
3670     GOTO 3630
3697  '
3698  '
3699  '
3700    REM CHECK TO SEE IF THIS IS A NUMERIC STRING
3705        SELCH$=SEL$(1,J)
3710        FOR I3=1 TO LEN(SELCH$)
3720            I4$=MID$(SELCH$,I3,1)
3725            IF I4$="." THEN GOTO 3740
3730            IF (I4$<"0") OR (I4$>"9") THEN GOTO 3755
3731            REM IF WE FIND ONE NON-NUMERIC CHARACTER THEN RETURN
3740        NEXT I3
3750        SELNUM(J)=1  'THIS IS A NUMERIC STRING
```

```
3755      RETURN
3997 '
3998 '
3999 REM **************************************
4000 REM *   SORT CARDS                        *
4001 REM **************************************
4005  GOSUB 16200 'PRINT LABELS
4006  INPUT "Item number to sort on:";INUM
4010     REM   SORT ON ITEM NUMBER INUM
4012  INPUT "Enter A for ascending order, D for descending order";X2$
4013  INPUT "Enter N for numerical sort, C for character sort";X3$
4015     J1=0
4020  FOR CARD=1 TO NUMCARDS
4030     GOSUB 3000  'SELECT
4040     IF SELECT<>1 THEN GOTO 4090   'NEXT CARD
4050     J1=J1+1
4060     L$(J1)=A$(CARD,INUM)
4070     POSTN(J1)=CARD
4090  NEXT CARD
4100 REM ======= BUBBLE SORT ROUTINE ===============
4110     N=J1  'NUMBER OF ITEMS TO BE SORTED
4115     IF X3$="N" THEN GOTO 4140   'NUMERICAL SORT
4119    REM -- SORT CHARACTER VALUES
4120    FOR I=1 TO N
4122      FOR J=1 TO N-I
4124        IF L$(J)<=L$(J+1) THEN GOTO 4130
4126        SWAP L$(J),L$(J+1)
4128        SWAP POSTN(J),POSTN(J+1)
4130     NEXT J
4132  NEXT I
4134     GOTO 4185
4140  REM - SORT NUMERICAL VALUES
4142    FOR I=1 TO N:L(I)=VAL(L$(I)):NEXT I
4144    FOR I=1 TO N
4146      FOR J=1 TO N-I
4148        IF L(J)<=L(J+1) THEN GOTO 4154
4150        SWAP L(J),L(J+1)
4152        SWAP POSTN(J),POSTN(J+1)
4154     NEXT J
4156   NEXT I
4185  IF X2$="D" THEN FOR I=1 TO INT(N/2):SWAP POSTN(I),POSTN(N+1-I):NEXT I
4190  IF CH=8 THEN RETURN
4200 REM ======= DISPLAY SORTED ITEMS ===============
4205   IF HRZ=1 THEN GOSUB 2700   'PRINT LABELS ACROSS TOP
4206    LNUM=1
4210    FOR I2=1 TO N
4215      PRINT USING "###";I2;:PRINT ". ";
4216     IF PRT=1 THEN LPRINT USING "###";I2;:LPRINT ". ";
4220      CARD=POSTN(I2)
4230      GOSUB 2400   'PRINT CARD
4240   NEXT I2
4245   PRINT "**":GOSUB 9000
4250   RETURN
4997 '
4998 '
```

Continued

```
4999 REM ****************************************
5000 REM *   LOAD BOX FROM DISK FILE             *
5001 REM ****************************************
5002 PRINT "ENTER NAME OF BOX TO LOAD. TYPE ? TO SEE DIRECTORY"
5003 PRINT "TYPE <RETURN> TO CANCEL"
5004 INPUT NM$: IF NM$="?" THEN FILES "*.BOX":PRINT:GOTO 5002
5006 IF NM$="" THEN RETURN
5010 F$=NM$+".BOX"
5020 OPEN "I",#1,F$
5030 INPUT#1,NUM
5035 INPUT#1,MAXLAB
5040 FOR I=1 TO NUM:INPUT#1,LAB$(I),NUMCH(I):NEXT I
5045 INPUT#1,NUMCARDS
5050 FOR CARD=1 TO NUMCARDS
5060    INPUT#1,CARD1
5070    FOR I=1 TO NUM:INPUT#1,A$(CARD,I):NEXT I
5080 NEXT CARD
5090 CLOSE#1
5100 PRINT "NAME OF BOX:";NM$;"     NUMBER OF ITEMS ON CARD:";NUM
5110 PRINT "NUMBER OF CARDS:";NUMCARDS
5120 RETURN
5998 '
5999 REM ****************************************
6000 REM *   SAVE BOX ON DISK FILE              *
6001 REM ****************************************
6005 PRINT "Type <RETURN> if ";NM$;" is the name you want to give the box."
6006 PRINT "Else type name of box."
6007 INPUT F2$: IF F2$<>"" THEN NM$=F2$
6010 F$=NM$+".BOX"
6020 OPEN "O",#1,F$
6030 PRINT#1,NUM
6035 PRINT#1,MAXLAB
6040 FOR I=1 TO NUM:PRINT#1,LAB$(I):PRINT#1,NUMCH(I):NEXT I
6045 PRINT#1,NUMCARDS
6047  IF CH=3 THEN N=NUMCARDS
6050 FOR CARD=1 TO N
6060   PRINT#1,CARD
6065   IF CH=3 THEN C2=CARD ELSE C2=POSTN(CARD)
6070   FOR I=1 TO NUM
6072    IT$=A$(C2,I)
6074    IF INSTR(IT$,",") <>0 THEN IT$=CHR$(34)+IT$+CHR$(34)
6076     PRINT#1,IT$
6078   NEXT I
6080 NEXT CARD
6090 PRINT#1,-1
6095 CLOSE#1
6100 RETURN
6998 '
6999 REM ****************************************
7000 REM * COPY TO NEW BOX - REORDER IF DESIRED*
7001 REM ****************************************
7005  NM1$=NM$:INPUT "New box name:";NM$
7010  GOSUB 16200
7015  PRINT "Enter item number to sort by"
7020  PRINT "Else type 0"
7025  INPUT INUM
```

```
7030   IF INUM=0 THEN CH=3:GOTO 7060
7040   GOSUB 4010   'SORTING SUBROUTINE
7060   GOSUB 6010   'SAVE ON DISK
7065   NM$=NM1$
7070   RETURN
7999 REM *************************************
8000 REM *   ADJUST DISPLAY FORMAT            *
8001 REM *************************************
8009 PRINT:PRINT
8010 PRINT "ENTER CHOICE:"
8020 PRINT "1 - Switch display mode to ";
8025    IF HRZ=1 THEN PRINT "vertical" ELSE PRINT "horizontal"
8030 IF LBLS=1 THEN GOTO 8031 ELSE GOTO 8032
8031 PRINT "2 - Stop including labels":GOTO 8040
8032 PRINT "2 - Include labels"
8040 IF CNUM=1 THEN GOTO 8041 ELSE GOTO 8042
8041 PRINT "3 - Stop including card numbers":GOTO 8050
8042 PRINT "3 - Include card numbers"
8050 PRINT "4 - Select which items to display"
8060 IF CRUISE=1 THEN GOTO 8061 ELSE GOTO 8062
8061 PRINT "5 - Pause during output":GOTO 8065
8062 PRINT "5 - Stop pausing during output"
8065 PRINT "6 - Change page length, currently ";PGLEN
8070 PRINT "7 - Change space between items, currently ";SPBI
8100 INPUT CH
8110 IF CH=1 THEN HRZ=1-HRZ:RETURN
8120 IF CH=2 THEN LBLS=1-LBLS:RETURN
8130 IF CH=3 THEN CNUM=1-CNUM:RETURN
8140 IF CH=5 THEN CRUISE=1-CRUISE:RETURN
8150 IF CH=6 THEN INPUT "New page length:",PGLEN:RETURN
8155 IF CH=7 THEN INPUT "New space between items:";SPBI:RETURN
8200  REM -- SELECT WHICH ITEMS ON CARD TO DISPLAY
8210  FOR I=1 TO NUM:PRINT USING "####";I;
8215     PRINT ".  ";LAB$(I):NEXT I
8220  INPUT "How many items would you like printed?";NUM2
8230  PRINT "Enter item numbers one by one"
8240  FOR I=1 TO NUM2:INPUT INUM:SEL2(INUM)=2:NEXT I
8250  FOR I=1 TO NUM
8255     IF SEL2(I)=2 THEN SEL2(I)=1 ELSE SEL2(I)=0
8260 NEXT I
8290 RETURN
8897 '
8898 '
8899 REM *************************************
8900 REM *    TURN PRINTER ON OR OFF          *
8901 REM *************************************
8910  PRT=1 - PRT
8920 PRINT "The printer is now ";
8930 IF PRT=1 THEN PRINT "on" ELSE PRINT "off"
8940 RETURN
8997 '
8998 '
8999 REM *************************************
9000 REM * INKEY SUBROUTINE                   *
9001 REM *************************************
9005 PRINT " ";:PRINT BK$;
```

Continued

```
9010 K$=INKEY$:IF K$="" THEN GOTO 9010
9012 PRINT " ";:PRINT BK$;
9015 RETURN
9018 '
9019 REM ****************************************
9020 REM *   BACKSPACE KEY                      *
9021 REM ****************************************
9030 PRINT BK$;" ";BK$;
9040 IF LEN(X$)>0 THEN X$=LEFT$(X$,LEN(X$)-1)
9050 RETURN
9998 '
9999 REM ****************************************
10000 REM *    SEARCH                           *
10001 REM ****************************************
10005 PRT3=PRT:PRT=0:CRUISE=1
10010 GOSUB 16200 'LIST LABELS
10015 INPUT "Enter item number:";INUM
10020 INPUT "Enter characters to search for:";X1$
10027  STARTT=1
10030 FOR CARD=STARTT TO NUMCARDS
10032  GOSUB 3000:IF SELECT<>1 THEN GOTO 10040
10035   IF INSTR(A$(CARD,INUM),X1$)>0 THEN GOTO 10050
10040  NEXT CARD
10045 PRINT X1$;" not found":GOTO 10077 ' RETURN
10050  PRINT "Card number:";CARD
10055  GOSUB 2500  'PRINT CARD
10057 EDOK=1   'OK TO EDIT THIS CARD
10060 PRINT "Type E to edit this card, ";
10065 PRINT "Type R to repeat search. Else type N"
10070  GOSUB 9000
10072  IF EDOK=1 THEN IF (K$="E") OR (K$="e") THEN GOTO 10100
10075   IF (K$="R") OR (K$="r") THEN STARTT=CARD+1:GOTO 10030
10077 PRT=PRT3
10080 RETURN
10099 '
10100 REM ==== MOVE FROM SEARCH TO EDIT ===========
10105 PRINT "Type Ctl-Z when you are done editing"
10110 FOR J=1 TO NUM+2:PRINT UP$;:NEXT J
10115 I=1
10120 NUMC2=NUMCARDS
10125 GOSUB 1720 'EDIT ROUTINE
10127 EDOK=0   'IT'S NOT OK TO EDIT THE SAME CARD AGAIN
10130 GOTO 10065
10997 '
10998 '
10999 REM ****************************************
11000 REM *    REVERSE ITEM                      *
11001 REM ****************************************
11005 GOSUB 16200  'LIST LABELS
11010 INPUT "Item number:";INUM
11015 INPUT "Separator character (blank, comma, etc.:";X1$
11018  IF LEN(X1$)=0 THEN X1$=" "
11020 FOR CARD=1 TO NUMCARDS
11025    GOSUB 3000 'SELECT ROUTINE
11030    X2$=A$(CARD,INUM)
11035    LX=LEN(X2$)
```

```
11040    X2=INSTR(X2$,X1$)
11045    IF X2=0 THEN GOTO 11080
11050    X3$=LEFT$(X2$,X2-1)
11060    X4$=RIGHT$(X2$,LX-X2)
11070    A$(CARD,INUM)=X4$+X1$+X3$
11080    NEXT CARD
11090   RETURN
11997 '
11998 '
11999 REM ***********************************
12000 REM *   DELETE CARD                   *
12001 REM ***********************************
12010   INPUT "Card number to delete:";CARD
12020   GOSUB 2400   'PRINT CARD
12030   INPUT "Type Y to confirm deletion";X1$
12040   IF (X1$="Y") OR (X1$="y") THEN GOTO 12050 ELSE RETURN
12050   FOR C1=CARD TO NUMCARDS
12060     FOR I=1 TO NUM
12070       A$(C1,I)=A$(C1+1,I)
12080     NEXT I
12090   NEXT C1
12100   NUMCARDS=NUMCARDS-1
12110   RETURN
12997 '
12998 '
12999 REM ***********************************
13000 REM *   COUNT                         *
13001 REM ***********************************
13010   GOSUB 16200   'PRINT LABELS
13020   INPUT "Code number of item to count:";INUM
13030   FOR I=1 TO 80:CT$(I)="":CT(I)=0:NEXT I
13040   FOR CARD=1 TO NUMCARDS
13050     GOSUB 3000   'SELECT
13060     IF SELECT<>1 THEN GOTO 13100
13070     FOR I1=1 TO 80
13080       IF CT$(I1)=A$(CARD,INUM) THEN CT(I1)=CT(I1)+1:GOTO 13100
13090       IF CT$(I1)="" THEN CT$(I1)=A$(CARD,INUM):CT(I1)=1:GOTO 13100
13095     NEXT I1
13100   NEXT CARD
13120 REM ======= DISPLAY OUTPUT ===================
13125     GOSUB 3600   'PRINT SELECTION CRITERIA
13127     TOTCARDS=0
13130     FOR I1=1 TO 80
13135       IF CT$(I1)="" THEN GOTO 13175
13140       PRINT SPC(NUMCH(INUM)-LEN(CT$(I1)));
13150       PRINT CT$(I1);
13160       PRINT USING "######";CT(I1)
13165       TOTCARDS=TOTCARDS+CT(I1)
13170     NEXT I1
13175     PRINT "TOTAL",TOTCARDS
13177     PRINT "**" : GOSUB 9000
13180   RETURN
13997 '
13998 '
13999 REM ***********************************
14000 REM *    ADJUST CARD FORMAT           *
```

Continued

```
14001 REM ************************************
14010  PRINT "Current format:"
14015  FOR I=1 TO NUM:PRINT I;"  ";LAB$(I),NUMCH(I):NEXT I
14020 PRINT "Enter your choice"
14025 PRINT "1 - Change length of item"
14030 PRINT "2 - Add new item to card"
14100 INPUT CH2
14110  IF CH2=1 THEN GOTO 14200
14115  IF CH2=2 THEN GOTO 14300
14200 REM - CHANGE LENGTH OF ITEM
14205   INPUT "Enter item number:";INUM
14210   INPUT "New length:";NUMCH(INUM)
14215  RETURN
14300 REM ====== ADD NEW ITEM TO EACH CARD ========
14305   INPUT "New item label:";X$
14310   INPUT "New item length:";X1
14315   NUM=NUM+1
14320   LAB$(NUM)=X$
14325   IF LEN(X$)>MAXLAB THEN MAXLAB=LEN(X$)
14330   NUMCH(NUM)=X1
14332   CH=16 'WE WILL NOW USE OPTION 16
14335   INUM=NUM:GOSUB 15010:RETURN
14997 '
14998 '
14999 REM ************************************
15000 REM *  CHANGE SPECIFIC ITEM ON EACH CARD *
15001 REM ************************************
15003   GOSUB 16200  'PRINT LABELS
15005   INPUT "Enter item number:";INUM
15007   CH=4 '4 IS THE CHOICE NUMBER FOR THE ENTER SECTION
15010   FOR CARD=1 TO NUMCARDS
15015   GOSUB 3000 :IF SELECT<>1 THEN GOTO 15080
15019   PRT2=PRT:PRT=0
15020   GOSUB 2500   'PRINT CARD
15021   PRT=PRT2
15030   FOR J=1 TO (NUM-INUM+1):PRINT UP$;:NEXT J
15040   FOR J=1 TO (MAXLAB+3):PRINT RT$;:NEXT J
15045   I=INUM:GOSUB 1850  'PRINT BLANKS
15050   INPUT "",X$
15060   IF X$="" THEN RETURN
15065   A$(CARD,INUM)=X$
15070   FOR J=INUM TO NUM:PRINT:NEXT J
15080  NEXT CARD
15090  RETURN
15997 '
15998 '
15999 REM ************************************
16000 REM *      DISPLAY MENU                   *
16001 REM ************************************
16005 PRINT "ENTER YOUR CHOICE:"
16010 PRINT " 1 - Set up new box        2 - Load and open box"
16015 PRINT " 3 - Save box              4 - Enter items onto cards"
16020 PRINT " 5 - Display cards         6 - Set up selection criteria"
16025 PRINT " 7 - Sort cards            8 - Copy to new box (reorder option)"
16030 PRINT " 9 - Adjust disp. format  10 - Turn printer ";
16040    IF PRT=1 THEN PRINT "off" ELSE PRINT "on"
```

```
16045 PRINT "11 - Search          12 - Reverse item"
16050 PRINT "13 - Delete card     14 - Count"
16052 PRINT "15 - Adjust card format  16 - Add single item to cards"
16055 PRINT " 0 - Stop the program"
16070 RETURN
16200 REM ======  LIST LABELS  =====================
16210  FOR I=1 TO NUM:PRINT I,LAB$(I):NEXT I
16215 RETURN
```

As you use this program, you will undoubtedly think of new features to add to make the program meet your needs better. The exercises include some suggestions.

If you plan on working in the field of data processing, you will need to learn much more about data management methods. One important concept is *data base management*. It would be very awkward if each department in a large organization required its own data bank arranged in its own special way. For example, it would be much easier if the payroll office could read data from the same place from which the personnel office reads data. A collection of data that is common to more than one program is called a *data base,* and data base management is a challenging job.

Designing a good data base is difficult because you need to be sensitive to the potential information requirements of many different tasks. Some of the information will always be changing, and it has to be possible to make changes in the data base. One obvious advantage of data base management for a large organization is that it greatly reduces redundancy, as compared to the situation where each department maintains its own records. In a well-designed system, the user can access the data by referring to it by name without having to worry about the physical location of the data.

If you anticipate doing a great deal of work with large data bases, you can obtain a software package specifically designed for data base management.

So far most of our programs have performed serious functions. In the next two chapters we will look at two entertaining applications of computers: playing games and drawing pictures.

EXERCISES

1.   Here are some tasks you can perform with the cardbox program included in this chapter:

(a) Design a box containing information about the countries of the world. Include information such as population, area, gross national product, capital city, form of government, continent, and so on.

(b) Design a box containing information on the largest companies in a national list, such as the Fortune 500. Include information on sales, assets, profits, employees, and type of industry.

(c) Set up a system for keeping track of the tasks that need to be done in an office. Each card will correspond to one specific task. The information you include on each card should include such items as a description of the task, to whom the task is assigned, the date the task was assigned, the date the task is due, and whether or not the task has been completed. Label the last two items on the card "comments" and leave room to add any comments you wish to include.

(d) Keep track of your personal address book information. For each person include information such as address, telephone number, birthday, and so on.

2. Write a program that keeps track of the books that have been checked out of a library. The program will need to maintain a list of library patrons and a list of books. The program should be menu-driven. Some of the options on the menu should include: check out books; return books; add new books; add new patrons; print a list of patrons with overdue books; record fines that are collected from patrons; and keep track of reserve requests for people wishing to obtain books that are checked out at the moment.

3. Write a personal appointment reminder program. The program should be able to keep track of appointments that you make for each day, and it also should be able to remind you of regular daily, weekly, or monthly events. You can make the program even more useful by including other features. For example, you could have the program keep track of all holidays and remind you of birthdays and anniversaries. (If you have a busy schedule and you spend a lot of time close to your computer, you probably will find this type of program very useful. However, most people are likely to find that it is easier to keep track of their schedules in a small appointment book. Entering the appointments into the computer is likely to take more time than it saves.)

4. Write a program to keep track of your store discount coupons. Whenever you get a new coupon, give it a number and store it in a box by its number. Type into the computer the number of the coupon, what it is good for, and the expiration date. Before you go to the store, type in the names of the items that you intend to buy, and the computer will tell you if you have coupons for any of those items and, if you do, what their numbers are.

5. Write a program that allows you to type in all your recipes on the computer and then displays the recipe you need when you type in its name.

6. A coliseum has tickets at five different prices. Write a program that reads in the five prices, then reads in the number of tickets sold at each price, and finally calculates the total revenue from the ticket sales each day.

7. Suppose you are directing a table tennis tournament for 20 players. Write a program that designs a 19-day schedule. Each player plays one game each day, and at the end of the tournament each player will have played every other player exactly once.

8. Write a program to keep track of the standings for the tournament in exercise 7. The program should read in the winners and losers of all the games each day. Every day, it should print a listing of all the players in the order of their win-loss records.

9. Write a program to keep track of reservations and seat assignments for an airline.

10. Write a program to keep track of the inventory in a book store.

11. Write a program to keep track of the attendance records of the members of a club.

12. Write a program to read in the test scores from a class of students who take 10 tests during the year and to calculate their average scores and their ranks relative to the rest of the class.

13. Write a payroll program to handle a company where different employees have different hourly rates.

14. Write a program to keep track of your current Christmas or Hanukkah card mailing list.

15. Write a program to keep track of statistics for your local basketball, football, or baseball team. Read the statistics

into the computer after each game, and then print out the cumulative season statistics.

16. Write a program that will enable you to type in the names of restaurants in your town and then displays the appropriate establishments when you input any of the following criteria: the name of the neighborhood in which the restaurant is located, the price range for a meal, the type of food, and your overall rating of the quality of the food and service.

CHAPTER 13

GAMES

Computers can play many different types of games. Many computer games allow you to move pictures around the screen by using a special input device, such as a joystick. We will discuss computer graphics in the next chapter, but we will not write any game programs involving moving graphics. Those programs require advanced programming techniques, which are very machine-specific.

In another type of computer game (known as an adventure game), the computer places the player in an imaginary situation with some objective, such as finding a treasure buried in a cave. The player can type in sentences such as "Look around" or "Walk forward" and the computer will tell what will happen. These programs will be very complicated because the program will need to keep track of many different possible actions by the player.

Computers have been taught to play strategy games. Some games, such as tic-tac-toe, are simple enough that it is possible to develop an unbeatable strategy. For very complicated games, such as chess, there is no perfect strategy. Computer chess programs cannot always beat human chess players. Computer scientists have put a lot of effort into writing chess strategy programs, but they do not do this just for fun. Studying the strategy for a game such as chess helps scientists understand how to make a computer "think" (and they can also learn the limitations that prevent a computer from ever thinking like a person). The field that studies computer thought is known as *artificial intelligence*.

SCOREBOARD TIMER

Even when the computer is not actually playing the game, it can provide assistance to the players (by keeping track of the time, for example). We will write three programs in this chapter: a scoreboard timer program, a quick trivia game program, and a football game program. There are many games that require timers, so it will be fun to have the computer screen act as a scoreboard timer. You initially set the timer by typing in the amount of time the timer will run. You can stop the clock at any time, then restart the clock when you are ready to resume play. Here is the program, written for a Commodore 64:

```
1 REM   SCOREBOARD TIMER PROGRAM
2 REM   THIS PROGRAM DISPLAYS A SCOREBOARD
3 REM   TIMER ON THE SCREEN.
4 REM   THE USER ENTERS THE AMOUNT OF TIME THE
5 REM   TIMER WILL RUN.  THE TIMER CAN BE STOPPED
6 REM   AT ANY TIME BY PRESSING ANY KEY.
7 REM   IT CAN BE RESTARTED BY PRESSING ANY KEY
10 REM   THIS PROGRAM RUNS ON A COMMODORE 64 COMPUTER
12 REM   IT USES THE BUILT-IN FUNCTION TI, WHICH
13 REM   CALCULATES THE TIME THAT HAS ELAPSED SINCE
14 REM   THE COMPUTER WAS TURNED ON,
15 REM   MEASURED IN 60THS OF A SECOND
20 REM    KEY VARIABLES:
21 REM    TS   TIME AT START
22 REM    TE   TIME AT END
23 REM    TN   TIME NOW
24 REM    TL   TIME LEFT
50 INPUT "MINUTES,SECONDS:";M,S
60 TL = 60*M+S
72 OS=S+1
75 GOSUB 600 : REM DISPLAY TIME
77 GET K$ : IF K$ = "" THEN GOTO 77
78 GOSUB 500 : REM CALCULATE TN
80 TS = TN
90 TE = TL + TN
99 REM **********************
100 REM CLOCK RUNNING LOOP
110 GOSUB 500 : REM  CALCULATE TN
120 TL = TE - TN
130 IF TL<1 THEN GOTO 990 : REM TIME UP
140 GOSUB 600 : REM DISPLAY TIME
150 GOSUB 900 : REM SEE IF KEY IS PRESSED
160 IF K$ = "" THEN GOTO 100
170 GOTO 200 : REM STOP CLOCK
199 REM   **************************
200 REM  CLOCK STOPPED LOOP
205 GOSUB 500 : REM CALCULATE TN
210 IF TE<TL+TN THEN TE=TL+TN
220 GOSUB 600 : REM DISPLAY TIME
230 GOSUB 900 : REM SEE IF KEY IS PRESSED
240 IF K$ = "" THEN GOTO 200
250 GOTO 100 : REM RESTART CLOCK
499 REM   **************************
500 REM   CALCULATE TN
510 TN=TI/60
511 REM TI IS THE BUILT-IN TIMER
520 RETURN
599 REM **************************
600 REM  DISPLAY TIME
610 M=INT(TL/60) : REM MINUTES
615 M1$ = STR$(M)
620 S = INT(TL-60*M):REM SECONDS
625 IF S<10 THEN S1$="0"+RIGHT$(STR$(S),1)
630 IF S>=10 THEN S1$=RIGHT$(STR$(S),2)
640 IF S=OS THEN GOTO 690
641 REM DON'T DISPLAY THE TIME AGAIN IF
```

```
642 REM THE SECONDS HAVE NOT CHANGED
650 PRINT CHR$(147) : REM CLEAR SCREEN
660 PRINT M1$;":";S1$
670 OS=S
690 RETURN
899 REM ******************************
900 REM   CHECK TO SEE IF KEY IS PRESSED
910 FOR I = 1 TO 50
920 GET K$
925 IF K$<>"" THEN RETURN
930 NEXT I
940 RETURN
989 REM ******************************
990 REM   TIME UP
995 PRINT CHR$(147): REM CLEAR SCREEN
998 PRINT " 0:00"
999 PRINT "TIME UP" : END
```

The Commodore contains a timer, represented by the built-in function TI. The timer measures the time that has elapsed since the computer was turned on, measured in sixtieths of a second. Note that the program operates around two loops: a clock-running loop, where the time left is constantly reduced, and a clock-stopped loop, where the time left is kept constant and the ending time is constantly increased. You may stop or restart the clock by pressing any key.

QUICK TRIVIA GAME

Now we will write a quick trivia game program in which the computer acts as the referee for two human players. The computer displays a question on the screen. The first player to signal the computer is allowed to give an answer to the question. To do well at this game you have to be quick as well as knowledgeable.

Here is the program, written in Microsoft BASIC:

```
1 REM QUICK TRIVIA GAME
2 REM    This program conducts a trivia game between two players.
3 REM    At the start of the game both players type in their names
4 REM    and they type the key they will use to signal the computer.
5 REM    The two keys should be at opposite ends of the keyboard.
6 REM    For example, one player may be "Z" and the other player may
7 REM    be "?".  The question will appear on the screen. The
8 REM    first player to press the key gets the chance to answer it.
9 REM    After answering the question that player needs to state the
10 REM   degree of confidence:  P (positive), S (fairly sure), G (guess).
11 REM   The degree of confidence chosen determines how many points
12 REM   will be gained or lost:
13 REM       Degree of Confidence    Answer Correct   Answer Incorrect
14 REM               P                   +20              -50
15 REM               S                   +10              -10
16 REM               G                   +5               -2
```

Continued

```
17 REM        You will enter your own trivia questions into the
18 REM        computer by using the "Enter question" section.
19 REM        Note - when you use this program you must have the
20 REM        Caps-lock key set for capital letters.
25 RANDOMIZE  'This command is necessary in Microsoft BASIC
27 DIM Q$(100,2),A$(100),ASKED(100)
30 PRINT "Type G to play game"
40 PRINT "Type E to enter questions"
45 PRINT "Type S to stop"
50 INPUT R1$
60 IF R1$="G" THEN GOTO 100
70 IF R1$="E" THEN GOSUB 3000
75 IF R1$="S" THEN END
80 GOTO 30
98 '
99 '
100 REM START NEW GAME
110 GOSUB 1000 'READ  IN PLAYER NAMES
120 GOSUB 2000 'READ IN QUESTIONS/ANSWERS
130 GOSUB 500 'PLAY GAME
140 PRINT "Type L if you would like to load some more questions"
150 INPUT R1$
160 IF R1$="L" THEN GOTO 120
170 END
498 '
499 '
500 REM PLAY GAME
505 GOSUB 800   'PRINT SCORE
507 IF J>=NUM THEN RETURN
510 QNUM=INT(NUM*RND+1)
520 IF ASKED(QNUM)=1 THEN GOTO 510
521 REM   THIS STATEMENT IS INCLUDED TO MAKE SURE NO
522 REM   QUESTION IS ASKED MORE THAN ONCE
530 ASKED(QNUM)=1
540 J=J+1
545 PRINT CHR$(7);   'BELL
549 CLS
550 REM   AT THIS POINT INSERT THE COMMANDS FOR YOUR
552 REM   COMPUTER TO CLEAR THE SCREEN AND PUT THE CURSOR HOME
555 K$=INKEY$
560 PRINT J;". ";
570 PRINT Q$(QNUM,1):PRINT Q$(QNUM,2)
575 FOR T=1 TO 750:K$=INKEY$
576   REM    YOU MAY INCREASE OR DECREASE THE TIME THE PLAYERS
577   REM    HAVE TO PRESS THEIR KEYS  BY CHANGING THE VALUE 750
580 IF (K$=K1$(1)) OR (K$=K1$(2)) THEN GOTO 590
585 NEXT T
586 PRINT CHR$(7); 'THIS BELL MEANS TIME IS UP
587 PRINT A$(QNUM):GOTO 505
590 PRINT CHR$(7);   'BELL
600 IF K$=K1$(1) THEN P=1:GOTO 630
610 IF K$=K1$(2) THEN P=2:GOTO 630
630 PRINT:PRINT:PRINT N$(P):PRINT:PRINT
640 PRINT "What is your answer?"
650 PRINT   "Type P for positive, S for fairly sure, G for guess:";
```

```
655 GOSUB 900
656 IF (K$="P") OR (K$="S") OR (K$="G") THEN GOTO 659
658 GOTO 655
659 PRINT K$;:C$=K$
664 PRINT
665 PRINT "Answer:"
670 PRINT A$(QNUM)
680 PRINT "Enter Y if your answer was correct, else N"
690 GOSUB 900
700 IF K$="Y" THEN GOTO 750
705 IF K$="N" THEN GOTO 715
710 GOTO 680
714 '
715 REM -- ANSWER WAS NOT CORRECT
720 IF C$="P" THEN S(P)=S(P)-50
730 IF C$="S" THEN S(P)=S(P)-10
735 IF C$="G" THEN S(P)=S(P)-2
745 GOTO 505
749 '
750 REM -- ANSWER WAS CORRECT
760 IF C$="P" THEN S(P)=S(P)+20
770 IF C$="S" THEN S(P)=S(P)+10
780 IF C$="G" THEN S(P)=S(P)+5
790 GOTO 505
798 '
799 '
800 REM -- PRINT SCORE
801 PRINT
810 PRINT N$(1),N$(2)
820 PRINT S(1),S(2)
830 PRINT "Type space to continue:":GOSUB 900
840 PRINT "Get Ready"
850 FOR K=1 TO 800:NEXT K
851 REM STATEMENT 850 IS INCLUDED TO INTRODUCE A DELAY
852 REM YOU MAY MAKE THE DELAY LONGER OR SHORTER IF YOU WISH
853 REM BY CHANGING THE NUMBER 800
860 RETURN
898 '
899 '
900 REM INKEY$ SUBROUTINE
905 K$=INKEY$
910 IF K$="" THEN GOTO 905
915 RETURN
998 '
999 '
1000 REM READ IN PLAYER NAMES
1010 FOR P=1 TO 2
1020 PRINT "Name of player ";P;" ";
1030 INPUT N$(P)
1040 PRINT "Type key for player ";P
1050 GOSUB 900
1060 PRINT K$
1070 K1$(P)=K$
1080 SC(P)=0
1090 NEXT P
1092 J=0   'J IS THE NUMBER OF QUESTIONS ASKED SO FAR
```

Continued

```
1095 RETURN
1998 '
1999 '
2000 REM READ IN QUESTIONS/ANSWERS
2010 FILES "*.TRV"
2020 PRINT:INPUT "Name of question file to load?";F$
2025 F1$=F$+".TRV"
2030 OPEN "I",#1,F1$
2040 INPUT#1,NUM
2041 REM  The first line of the question file contains the
2042 REM  number of questions in that file.
2050 FOR I=1 TO NUM
2060 LINE INPUT#1,Q$(I,1)
2062 LINE INPUT#1,Q$(I,2)
2064 LINE INPUT#1,A$(I)
2065 REM   The LINE INPUT command in Microsoft BASIC causes
2066 REM   the entire data line to be read, even if it contains
2067 REM   a comma.
2070 NEXT I
2080 CLOSE#1
2085 FOR I=1 TO 100:ASKED(I)=0:NEXT I
2090 RETURN
2998 '
2999 '
3000 REM ENTER NEW QUESTIONS AND ANSWERS
3010 J=0
3020 J=J+1
3025 PRINT "  (Type S to stop)"
3030 PRINT "Enter question ";J
3040 PRINT "Two lines"
3050 INPUT Q$(J,1)
3055   IF (Q$(J,1)="S") OR (Q$(J,1)="s") THEN GOTO 3200
3060 INPUT Q$(J,2)
3070 PRINT "Enter answer (one line)"
3080 INPUT A$(J)
3090 IF J>=100 THEN GOTO 3200
3100 GOTO 3020
3200 REM SAVE QUESTIONS AND ANSWERS ON DISK
3210 IF J<100 THEN NUM=J-1 ELSE NUM=J
3220 INPUT "Name of file:";F$
3225 F1$=F$+".TRV"
3230 OPEN "O",#1,F1$
3235 PRINT#1,NUM
3240 FOR J=1 TO NUM
3250 PRINT#1,Q$(J,1)
3260 PRINT#1,Q$(J,2)
3270 PRINT#1,A$(J)
3280 NEXT J
3290 CLOSE#1
3300 RETURN
```

The rules for the game are described by the comments at the start of the program. Note how the INKEY$ function is used to see which player signals first (lines 575–585). If neither player signals, the computer will display the answer after a certain amount of time has passed.

In order to play this game, you will need someone to type some trivia questions. The trivia program also provides an option that allows you to type in questions and answers and to store them on a disk file. You may type in questions that relate to any subjects you think will be interesting for your friends or family. If you want your friends to continue playing with you, remember that the questions should not be too hard or too easy. Here are some sample questions you may use:

```
   Who is the youngest person to have served as
President of the U.S.?
Theodore Roosevelt (age 42)
   Which borough of New York City is
not on an island?
The Bronx
   Name two of the first three people to
orbit the moon
Borman Lovell Anders    (Apollo 8)
   What state will Captain James T. Kirk of the
U.S.S. Enterprise be from?
Iowa
   What are the only four states that meet at a place
where four states touch?
Arizona New Mexico Colorado Utah
   What did Charles Babbage design but was
unable to build?
The Analytic Engine -- a kind of computer
   What is especially unique about Grover Cleveland's eight
years as President of the U.S.?
They were not consecutive
   What 20th century President was inaugurated inside
the Capitol because of extreme cold?
Ronald Reagan (1985)
   What are the two galaxies nearest our
Milky Way galaxy?
The Large and Small Magellenic Clouds
   Which cabinet department is located across the street
from the White House?
The Treasury Department
   Name one of the two officers whose signatures
appear on U.S. dollar bills?
The Secretary of the Treasury and the Treasurer of the U.S.
   What Boston church was hung with lanterns:
One if by land, two if by Sea?
Old North Church
   Name the highest and lowest Great Lakes
in elevation?
highest: Superior (600 ft)  lowest: Ontario (245 ft)
   What river separates Minneapolis and
St. Paul?
```

Continued

```
Mississippi
   What lake is Chicago located
next to?
Lake Michigan
   What city is Disneyland
located in?
Anaheim California
   What city is located next to two
mile-long floating bridges?
Seattle Washington
   What body of water does the Golden
Gate Bridge cross?
The Golden Gate
   What lame stuttering man was the fourth
emperor of the Roman Empire?
Claudius
   Who was the first Roman Emperor (ruling from
30 BC to 14 AD)?
Augustus
   He was secret agent 86 of Control in the
1960s
Don Adams playing Maxwell Smart
   He played a role as an astronaut with a magic
Jeannie before playing an oil executive
Larry Hagman
   Who was the evil governor who ordered Princess Leia's planet
be blown up?
Grand Moff Tarkin
   Who was the Ewok from Endor who first
befriended Princess Leia?
Wicket
   What did Sgt. Phil Esterhaus always say to the
policemen at the end of roll call?
Let's be careful out there!   (on Hill St. Blues)
   Nobody knows the real name of this t.v. detective
played by Pierce Brosnan.
Remington Steele
```

These questions cover topics such as geography, history, television, movies, and science.

COMPUTER FOOTBALL

Here's an example of a football strategy game program. We will use the computer to referee a game between two people. We'll set up the game so that the offensive player has a choice of 13 plays and the defensive player has a choice of 7 defensive strategies. Each player will type in a strategy number without letting the other person see it. Then the computer will calculate the results of the play. If, for example, the offensive player chooses play 1 (run over center) and the defensive player chooses defense 1 (crowd the center), the play will not gain many yards. However, if the offensive player chooses play 10 (throw a long pass) and the defensive player is using defense 1, the play will probably go for a long gain. The game is therefore basically a game of psychology: the idea is to guess what strategy your opponent will use while making sure that your own strategy is a surprise.

To keep the game from becoming predictable, we'll add a random element. We can use the RND function to add to or subtract from the result of the play before it is printed. We'll also use RND function to determine whether a fumble is made (the probability of a fumble on a running play is .05); whether a pass is complete (the probability of completion depends on the type of pass and the type of defense); and whether a field goal or extra point is good (the probability that an extra point will be good is .95 and the probability that a field goal will be good depends on the distance of the attempt).

We can use the program just to tell us the results of the plays if we were willing to keep track of the yard line, the down, and the score ourselves. However, we can also let the computer perform these bookkeeping tasks.

Here is the program:

```
1    REM ********FOOTBALL GAME PROGRAM*******
2    REM THIS PROGRAM CONDUCTS A FOOTBALL GAME BETWEEN
3    REM TWO PLAYERS -- THE VISITING TEAM PLAYER AND THE
4    REM HOME TEAM PLAYER.
5    REM FOR EACH PLAY, BOTH THE OFFENSIVE PLAYER AND THE
6    REM DEFENSIVE PLAYER INPUT THEIR PLAY NUMBERS.
7    REM THEN THE COMPUTER CALCULATES THE RESULTS OF THE PLAY.
8    REM OFFENSIVE STRATEGIES ARE:
9    REM           1: RUN OVER CENTER
10   REM           2: RUN OFF TACKLE -- STRONG SIDE
11   REM           3: RUN OFF TACKLE -- WEAK SIDE
12   REM           4: RUN END SWEEP -- STRONG SIDE
13   REM           5: RUN END SWEEP -- WEAK SIDE
14   REM           6: DRAW
15   REM           7: SCREEN PASS
16   REM           8: PASS TO TIGHT END
17   REM           9: SHORT PASS PATTERN
18   REM          10: DEEP PASS PATTERN
22   REM          12: PUNT
23   REM          13: FIELD GOAL ATTEMPT
24   REM
25   REM       DEFENSIVE STRATEGIES ARE:
26   REM             1: CROWD CENTER
27   REM             2: CROWD STRONG SIDE
28   REM             3: CROWD WEAK SIDE
29   REM             4: STANDARD 3-4
30   REM             5: BLITZ
31   REM             6: PASS COVERAGE EMPHASIS
32   REM             7: PREVENT
34   REM
35   RANDOMIZE  '(COMMAND NEEDED FOR MICROSOFT BASIC)
36   REM
37   GOSUB 1100    '  ***** READ IN VALUES
40   HS = 0  : VS = 0   ' HS IS HOME TEAM SCORE, VS IS VISITING TEAM SCORE
```

Continued

```
45    M = -1  : Z = 70    '  M = -1 FOR VISITOR'S BALL, M = 1 FOR HOME BALL
46    REM          Z = DISTANCE OF BALL FROM HOME TEAM GOAL LINE
47    REM          VISITOR STARTS GAME WITH BALL AT ITS OWN 30 YARD LINE
49    REM ........RESET AT FIRST DOWN...............
50    DN = 1  :  YTG = 10    ' DN IS DOWN, YTG IS YARDS TO GO FOR FIRST DOWN
51  PRINT : PRINT  "VISITOR: ";VS;"HOME: ";HS
52    REM
53    REM -----------PRINT  CURRENT POSITION -----------
54 PRINT
55    IF M = -1 THEN PRINT  "VISITING TEAM BALL ";
56    IF M = 1 THEN PRINT   "HOME TEAM BALL      ";
60    PRINT  DN;" DOWN,  ";
61    GOSUB 900   ' DETERMINE WHAT YARD LINE BALL IS AT
62    IF YTG < YTTD THEN PRINT  YTG;" YARDS TO GO  ";
64    IF YTG > YTTD THEN PRINT  " GOAL TO GO  ";
70    PRINT  X$;W;" YARD LINE"
71    REM---------------------------------------------------------
72    REM
75    PRINT  "INPUT OFFENSIVE PLAY:";
76    INPUT OP: PRINT OP
77    IF OP<0 THEN END   ' ENTER A NEGATIVE  NUMBER TO END THE GAME
78    IF OP = 12 THEN GOTO 200   '*****PUNTING SITUATION
79    IF OP = 13 THEN GOTO 300   '*****FIELD GOAL ATTEMPT
80    PRINT  "INPUT DEFENSIVE PLAY:";
81    INPUT DP : PRINT DP
85    PRINT  OPL$(OP);"       ";DPL$(DP)
89    REM
90    GOSUB 400     ' *****PLAY RESULT SUBROUTINE
91    REM
99    REM ----------UPDATE POSITION OF BALL
100   Z = Z + M * Y    ' Y IS YARDS GAINED ON PLAY
110 IF (Z <= 99) AND (Z >= 1) THEN GOTO 130 'GOAL LINE NOT CROSSED
115 IF (Z>99) THEN GOTO 125 'VISITING TEAM GOAL LINE CROSSED
119 REM    HOME TEAM GOAL LINE CROSSED
120 IF M=-1 THEN GOTO 960 ELSE GOTO 940
121 REM          LINE 960: VISITOR TOUCHDOWN        LINE 940: VISITOR SAFETY
125 REM    VISITING TEAM GOAL LINE CROSSED
126 IF M=1 THEN GOTO 950 ELSE GOTO 930
127 REM          LINE 950: HOME TOUCHDOWN        LINE 930: HOME SAFETY
130   YTG = YTG - Y
140 IF YTG < 1 THEN GOTO 50    '  FIRST DOWN HAS BEEN MADE
150   DN = DN + 1      ' DOWN INCREASES BY 1
155   IF DN > 4 THEN GOTO 780
160 GOTO 53 ' READY FOR NEXT PLAY
161   REM ---------------------------------------------------------
162   REM
163   REM
200   REM:********* PUNT *********************
210   Q = INT(35 + 8 * RND)
212 PRINT  Q;" YARD PUNT"
215   Z = Z+ M * Q
220   IF Z > 99 THEN LET Z = 80
230   IF Z < 1 THEN LET Z = 20
240   M = -M
250   GOTO 50
251   REM ---------------------------------------------------------
```

```
252   REM
253   REM
254   REM
300   REM ************ FIELD GOAL ATTEMPT ****************
310   Y2 = YTTD      ' YARDS TO GOAL LINE
317   PRINT  (Y2+17);" YARD ATTEMPT"
320   Y3 = 10 + 35 * RND
325   IF Y3 < Y2 THEN GOTO 370
330   PRINT  "KICK IS GOOD"
340   IF M = 1 THEN LET HS = HS + 3
345   IF M = -1 THEN LET VS = VS + 3
350   IF M=1 THEN GOTO 45
360   Z = 30   : M = 1  : GOTO 50
370   PRINT  "KICK IS NO GOOD"
375   IF M = 1 THEN GOTO 390
380   M = 1  : Z = 20  : GOTO 50
390   M = -1  : Z = 80  : GOTO 50
391   REM ------------------------------------------------
392   REM
394   REM
400   REM ------- PLAY SUBROUTINE ------------------
420   IF OP > 6 THEN GOTO 470       ' ***** PASSING PLAY
421   REM
422   REM
430   REM --------- RUNNING PLAY --------------------
440   C = RND
450   IF C < .05 THEN GOTO 770   ' FUMBLE
460   Y = INT(D(DP,OP)+2*(RND-.5))  ' PLAY RESULT COMES FROM ARRAY D
461   GOTO 750
462   REM
463   REM
470   REM --------- PASSING PLAY -------------------
480   G = OP - 6  : P2 = F(DP,G) ' P2 IS PROB OF INTERCEPTION
490   C = RND
510   IF C < P2 THEN GOTO 771 ' INTERCEPTION
520   P3 = E(DP,G)     ' *** PROBABILITY OF COMPLETION
530   IF ( C < (P2 + P3) ) THEN GOTO 580      ' **** COMPLETION
540   C = RND
550   P4 = .2  :  IF DP = 5 THEN LET P4 = .75
551   REM  P4 IS THE PROBABILITY OF A SACK
560   IF C < P4 THEN GOTO 572
570   PRINT  "INCOMPLETE" : Y = 0 :  GOTO 750
572   PRINT  "SACK"
573   Y = -8
574   GOTO 750
580   REM ****** COMPLETE PASS *****************
581   Y = D(DP,OP)
582   GOTO 750
583   REM -----------------------------------------------------------
584   REM
585   REM
750   IF Y>YTTD THEN Y=YTTD
755   PRINT  "YARDS GAINED: ";Y
756   RETURN
770   PRINT  "FUMBLE"  : Y = 0 : M = -M : YTG = -100 : RETURN
```

Continued

```
771   PRINT  "INTERCEPTION"  : Y = 0  : M = -M  : YTG = -100  : RETURN
778   REM
779   REM ***** CHANGE OF POSSESSION
780   M = -M  : GOTO 50
899   REM
900 REM   SUBROUTINE TO CALCULATE YARD LINE
905    IF M=1 THEN YTTD = 100 - Z ELSE YTTD = Z
906    REM     YTTD = YARDS TO TOUCHDOWN
910   IF Z < 50 THEN GOTO 915 ELSE GOTO 920
915    W = Z : X$ = "HOME" : RETURN
920    W = 100 - Z : X$ = "VISITOR" : RETURN
921   REM  W IS THE YARD LINE NUMBER
925   RETURN
926   REM--------------------------------
930 REM   HOME SAFETY
931    PRINT  "SAFETY"
932    HS=HS+2:M=1:Z=45:GOTO 50
940 REM   VISITOR SAFETY
941    PRINT  "SAFETY"
942    VS=VS+2:M=-1:Z=55:GOTO 50
950   PRINT  "HOME TOUCHDOWN" : HS = HS + 6 : GOSUB 980 : GOTO 45
960   PRINT  "VISITOR TOUCHDOWN"  : VS = VS + 6
970   Z = 30 : GOSUB 980 : M = 1  : GOTO 50
976   REM
977   REM--------------------------------------------
980   REM ***** EXTRA POINT ATTEMPT
981   IF RND < .95 THEN GOTO 990
982   PRINT  "EXTRA POINT ATTEMPT IS NO GOOD" : RETURN
990   PRINT  "EXTRA POINT ATTEMPT IS GOOD"
991   IF M = 1 THEN LET HS = HS + 1
992   IF M = -1 THEN LET VS = VS + 1
993   RETURN
994   REM--------------------------------------------
995   REM
1100 REM******** SUBROUTINE TO READ IN VALUES FOR PLAYS ****
1101 DIM D(8,11),F(8,4),E(8,4)
1110 FOR I = 1 TO 8 : FOR J = 1 TO 11 : READ D(I,J) : NEXT J : NEXT I
1120 DATA -5,0,0,6,5,0,0,6,8,100,.3
1130 DATA 2,-4,6,-6,8,2,6,0,6,20,.6
1140 DATA 2,6,-4,8,-6,2,6,21,6,20,0
1150 DATA 1,2,1,2,1,2,6,6,6,12,.2
1160 DATA 2,3,3,3,3,30,32,0,0,0,.7
1170 DATA 3,6,6,4,4,0,0,5,4,6,.2
1180 DATA 9,11,11,7,7,5,0,0,0,0,0
1190 DATA 1,0,4,0,2,1,0,8,9,20,1
1200 REM
1210 REM
1220 REM READ IN DATA FOR COMPLETION PERCENTAGES
1230 FOR I = 1 TO 8 : FOR J = 1 TO 4 : READ E(I,J) : NEXT J : NEXT I
1240 DATA 0,.4,.4,.7
1250 DATA .5,0,.6,.4
1260 DATA .5,.6,.6,.4
1270 DATA .3,.5,.6,.3
1280 DATA .8,0,0,0
1290 DATA 0,.2,.2,.3
1300 DATA 0,0,0,0
```

```
1310 DATA 0,.8,.8,.5
1320 REM
1330 REM
1350 REM*** DATA FOR INTERCEPTION PERCENTAGES
1360 FOR I = 1 TO 8 : FOR J = 1 TO 4 : READ F(I,J) : NEXT J : NEXT I
1370 DATA .2,.2,.2,0
1380 DATA .1,.8,.1,0
1390 DATA .1,0,.1,0
1400 DATA .1,.1,.1,.1
1410 DATA 0,.3,.3,.3
1420 DATA .5,.3,.3,.3
1430 DATA .7,.7,.7,.7
1440 DATA .1, 0, 0, .1
1450 REM ** DATA FOR PLAYS
1455 DIM OPL$(13), DPL$(7)
1460 FOR I=1 TO 12:READ OPL$(I):NEXT I
1465 DATA "RUN OVER CENTER"
1466 DATA "RUN OFF TACKLE -- STRONG SIDE"
1467 DATA "RUN OFF TACKLE -- WEAK SIDE"
1468 DATA "RUN END SWEEP -- STRONG SIDE"
1469 DATA "RUN END SWEEP -- WEAK SIDE"
1470 DATA "DRAW"
1471 DATA "SCREEN PASS"
1472 DATA "PASS TO TIGHT END"
1473 DATA "SHORT PASS PATTERN"
1474 DATA "DEEP PASS PATTERN"
1475 DATA "PUNT"
1476 DATA "FIELD GOAL ATTEMPT"
1480 FOR I=1 TO 7:READ DPL$(I):NEXT I
1481 DATA "CROWD CENTER"
1482 DATA "CROWD STRONG SIDE"
1483 DATA "CROWD WEAK SIDE"
1484 DATA "STANDARD 3-4"
1485 DATA "BLITZ"
1486 DATA "PASS COVERAGE EMPHASIS"
1487 DATA "PREVENT"
1495 RETURN
```

Here is a sample run of the program:

```
VISITOR:  0 HOME:  0

VISITING TEAM BALL 1  DOWN,   10  YARDS TO GO  VISITOR 30  YARD LINE
INPUT OFFENSIVE PLAY: 2
INPUT DEFENSIVE PLAY: 3
RUN OFF TACKLE -- STRONG SIDE    CROWD WEAK SIDE
YARDS GAINED:  5

VISITING TEAM BALL 2  DOWN,   5  YARDS TO GO  VISITOR 35  YARD LINE
INPUT OFFENSIVE PLAY: 9
INPUT DEFENSIVE PLAY: 5
SHORT PASS PATTERN    BLITZ
SACK
YARDS GAINED: -8
```

Continued

```
VISITING TEAM BALL  3  DOWN,   13  YARDS TO GO  VISITOR 27  YARD LINE
INPUT OFFENSIVE PLAY: 6
INPUT DEFENSIVE PLAY: 5
DRAW     BLITZ
YARDS GAINED:  29


VISITOR:  0 HOME:  0

VISITING TEAM BALL  1  DOWN,   10  YARDS TO GO  HOME 44  YARD LINE
INPUT OFFENSIVE PLAY: 8
INPUT DEFENSIVE PLAY: 3
PASS TO TIGHT END    CROWD WEAK SIDE
YARDS GAINED:  21


VISITOR:  0 HOME:  0

VISITING TEAM BALL  1  DOWN,   10  YARDS TO GO  HOME 23  YARD LINE
INPUT OFFENSIVE PLAY: 5
INPUT DEFENSIVE PLAY: 1
RUN END SWEEP -- WEAK SIDE    CROWD CENTER
YARDS GAINED:  5

VISITING TEAM BALL  2  DOWN,   5  YARDS TO GO  HOME 18  YARD LINE
INPUT OFFENSIVE PLAY: 9
INPUT DEFENSIVE PLAY: 2
SHORT PASS PATTERN    CROWD STRONG SIDE
YARDS GAINED:  6


VISITOR:  0 HOME:  0

VISITING TEAM BALL  1  DOWN,   10  YARDS TO GO  HOME 12  YARD LINE
INPUT OFFENSIVE PLAY: 1
INPUT DEFENSIVE PLAY: 4
RUN OVER CENTER    STANDARD 3-4
YARDS GAINED:  1

VISITING TEAM BALL  2  DOWN,   9  YARDS TO GO  HOME 11  YARD LINE
INPUT OFFENSIVE PLAY: 2
INPUT DEFENSIVE PLAY: 4
RUN OFF TACKLE -- STRONG SIDE    STANDARD 3-4
YARDS GAINED:  2

VISITING TEAM BALL  3  DOWN,   7  YARDS TO GO  HOME 9  YARD LINE
INPUT OFFENSIVE PLAY: 6
INPUT DEFENSIVE PLAY: 6
DRAW     PASS COVERAGE EMPHASIS
YARDS GAINED:  0

VISITING TEAM BALL  4  DOWN,   7  YARDS TO GO  HOME 9  YARD LINE
INPUT OFFENSIVE PLAY: 13
 26  YARD ATTEMPT
KICK IS GOOD

VISITOR:  3 HOME:  0
```

```
HOME TEAM BALL       1  DOWN,    10  YARDS TO GO  HOME 30   YARD LINE
INPUT OFFENSIVE PLAY: 10
INPUT DEFENSIVE PLAY: 5
DEEP PASS PATTERN     BLITZ
SACK
YARDS GAINED: -8


HOME TEAM BALL       2  DOWN,    18  YARDS TO GO  HOME 22   YARD LINE
INPUT OFFENSIVE PLAY: 7
INPUT DEFENSIVE PLAY: 7
SCREEN PASS      PREVENT
INCOMPLETE
YARDS GAINED:  0


HOME TEAM BALL       3  DOWN,    18  YARDS TO GO  HOME 22   YARD LINE
INPUT OFFENSIVE PLAY: 8
INPUT DEFENSIVE PLAY: 7
PASS TO TIGHT END     PREVENT
INTERCEPTION


VISITOR:  3 HOME:  0


VISITING TEAM BALL  1  DOWN,    10  YARDS TO GO  HOME 22   YARD LINE
INPUT OFFENSIVE PLAY: 4
INPUT DEFENSIVE PLAY: 4
RUN END SWEEP -- STRONG SIDE    STANDARD 3-4
YARDS GAINED:  1


VISITING TEAM BALL  2  DOWN,    9  YARDS TO GO  HOME 21   YARD LINE
INPUT OFFENSIVE PLAY: 10
INPUT DEFENSIVE PLAY: 1
DEEP PASS PATTERN     CROWD CENTER
YARDS GAINED:  21
VISITOR TOUCHDOWN
EXTRA POINT ATTEMPT IS GOOD


VISITOR:  10 HOME:  0


HOME TEAM BALL       1  DOWN,    10  YARDS TO GO  HOME 30   YARD LINE
INPUT OFFENSIVE PLAY: 1
INPUT DEFENSIVE PLAY: 4
RUN OVER CENTER     STANDARD 3-4
YARDS GAINED:  0

HOME TEAM BALL       2  DOWN,    10  YARDS TO GO  HOME 30   YARD LINE
INPUT OFFENSIVE PLAY: 2
INPUT DEFENSIVE PLAY: 4
RUN OFF TACKLE -- STRONG SIDE    STANDARD 3-4
YARDS GAINED:  1

HOME TEAM BALL       3  DOWN,    9  YARDS TO GO  HOME 31   YARD LINE
INPUT OFFENSIVE PLAY: 3
INPUT DEFENSIVE PLAY: 6
RUN OFF TACKLE -- WEAK SIDE     PASS COVERAGE EMPHASIS
YARDS GAINED:  6
```

Continued

```
HOME TEAM BALL      4  DOWN,    3  YARDS TO GO  HOME 37   YARD LINE
INPUT OFFENSIVE PLAY: 12
 39   YARD PUNT

VISITOR:  10 HOME:   0

VISITING TEAM BALL  1  DOWN,   10  YARDS TO GO  VISITOR 24   YARD LINE
INPUT OFFENSIVE PLAY: 1
INPUT DEFENSIVE PLAY: 4
RUN OVER CENTER      STANDARD 3-4
YARDS GAINED:   1

VISITING TEAM BALL  2  DOWN,    9  YARDS TO GO  VISITOR 25   YARD LINE
INPUT OFFENSIVE PLAY: 1
INPUT DEFENSIVE PLAY: 6
RUN OVER CENTER      PASS COVERAGE EMPHASIS
YARDS GAINED:   3

VISITING TEAM BALL  3  DOWN,    6  YARDS TO GO  VISITOR 28   YARD LINE
INPUT OFFENSIVE PLAY: 6
INPUT DEFENSIVE PLAY: 7
DRAW      PREVENT
YARDS GAINED:   5

VISITING TEAM BALL  4  DOWN,    1  YARDS TO GO  VISITOR 33   YARD LINE
INPUT OFFENSIVE PLAY: 12
 40   YARD PUNT

VISITOR:  10 HOME:   0

HOME TEAM BALL      1  DOWN,   10  YARDS TO GO  HOME 27   YARD LINE
INPUT OFFENSIVE PLAY: 10
INPUT DEFENSIVE PLAY: 4
DEEP PASS PATTERN    STANDARD 3-4
INCOMPLETE
YARDS GAINED:   0

HOME TEAM BALL      2  DOWN,   10  YARDS TO GO  HOME 27   YARD LINE
INPUT OFFENSIVE PLAY:-1
```

This program does not have any kickoffs. Instead, the receiving team always starts with the ball on its own 30-yard line. The program as it is now written runs in an infinite loop. You will have to decide in advance how long you want to play and then interrupt the program execution at the end of that time period.

There are, of course, many commercially available game programs. However, now that you know how to program, you can be creative and write your own programs to play your own games.

EXERCISES

1. Write a tic-tac-toe strategy program. The computer will play against a human player. The game of tic-tac-toe is simple enough that it is possible to make a chart showing every possible game outcome, so your task will be translating this information into

a form that allows the computer to know how to respond to every possible opponent's move in every possible situation.

2.   Here are some extra modifications you may like to add to the football program:

(a) Include occasional penalties and the choice of whether or not to accept them.

(b) Include kickoffs and the possibility of an onside kick.

(c) Include a coin toss at the beginning of the game to determine who will have possession of the ball.

(d) Keep track of team statistics, such as total yardage and first downs.

(e) Keep track of the time left in each quarter, subtracting a certain amount for each play depending on whether it was a passing play or a running play.

(f) Include the effect of the wind on kicks. The wind will add to the distance of kicks with the wind but shorten the distance of kicks against the wind. If you include this option, you also must include a coin toss and a timer dividing the game into quarters, so you can have the teams switch directions at the end of each quarter. At the start of each half, the team that does not choose who will receive the kickoff will choose the direction in which the teams will go.

(g) The program has room for you to add an option play (offensive play 11) in which the offensive player could select the option for the play after seeing what the defense is; however, this play is risky and has a much higher chance of resulting in a fumble.

3.   Write a computer program that deals out the cards in a blackjack (21) game.

4.   Write a Clue strategy program. As you play the game Clue, you slowly gather more information about the identity of the killer. Have the program read in each piece of evidence and then tell you when it has narrowed down the choices so that it knows who the killer is.

5.   Write a program that referees a Monopoly game. For example, the program will have to keep track of the position of each player's marker on the board, the properties that each player owns, and the amount of money each player has.

6.   Write a program to play Hangman.

7.   (This will be *very* hard.) Try to write your own checkers strategy program. Your program will not be able to consider every single possible checkers game. Instead, it will have to have some

rule that allows it to evaluate alternative game positions and then make the move that leads to the best game position. This type of problem is important in *artificial intelligence*. Don't attempt it unless you are serious about learning quite a bit about this field. (See the next chapter to learn how to use the computer's graphics capabilities to draw the checkerboard on the screen.)

8.   Write your own StarShip program. Have the program keep track of the position of your starship in the galaxy, the position of the other obstacles, and the amount of power your ship has left. You will have to think of an objective for the game to make it interesting. Be as creative as you can!

9.   Write a program that tries to predict the results of major league baseball games by reading in the batting averages and pitching averages for two real teams, and then conducts a simulated game between them.

10.   Write a program that keeps track of the scores during a bowling game.

11.   Write a program that keeps track of the cards that have already been turned up in a blackjack game, and then tells you whether you should ask for another card in a given situation.

12.   Write a program to referee a game of Black Box. The computer needs to know the position of the markers. When the searching player types in the position from which he or she wants to fire a ray, the program will tell what happens to that ray. Is it a hit, is it a reflection, or will the ray come out of the board at another location?

CHAPTER 14

GRAPHICS

DRAWING LINES

To draw pictures with computers, we need to have a way to control the location on the screen (or on the page) where the computer will put output. One simple way to direct picture drawing is with the TAB command. With the TAB command, we can control how much space the computer will leave between the left margin and the symbol we want typed. For example, we can write a program to trace out the rough equivalent of a straight line, using an asterisk, *, to represent each point on the line.

```
1    REM   PROGRAM TO DRAW A STRAIGHT LINE
10   FOR I = 1 TO 20
20   PRINT TAB(I);" * "
30   NEXT I
40   END
```

The output looks like the following:

```
*
 *
  *
   *
    *
     *
      *
       *
        *
         *
          *
           *
            *
             *
              *
               *
                *
                 *
                  *
                   *
```

DRAWING CURVES

Now suppose that we want to make a graph of the motion of a ball thrown in the air. The path of the ball will be shaped like a parabola. If we tried to draw a graph manually, it would take a long time. We would first have to calculate the position of each point on the path and then mark each point on graph paper. That is the tedious kind of work for which the computer is well suited.

We will again use asterisks, *, to represent the points, and we will use the TAB command to control the placement of the asterisks. We will draw a graph of a sideways parabola, because then we will need to put only one asterisk on each line. When we draw this kind of graph, we need to adjust the scaling so that the graph fills up as much of the page as possible. If the TAB values become too large, the graph won't fit on the screen. If the TAB values are too small, the graph will not be very easy to read. The program is as follows:

```
1   REM   PROGRAM TO DRAW A PARABOLA
10  S = 50/100
20  FOR Y = -10 TO 10
30     H = INT(S * Y * Y)
40     PRINT TAB(H);" * "
50  NEXT Y
60  END
```

The output looks like this:

```
                                        *
                                     *
                                 *
                              *
                           *
                        *
                     *
                  *
               *
             *
            *
           *
            *
             *
               *
                  *
                     *
                        *
                           *
                              *
                                 *
```

For some purposes it will help if we draw coordinate axes on the graph. In this case, we are graphing the parabola $x = \frac{1}{2}y^2$, so we would like to have the computer draw in the vertical y axis and the horizontal x axis. The following program does this:

```
10    S = 50/100
20    FOR Y = –10 TO 10
30       IF Y = 0 THEN GOTO 80
35    REM
36    REM
40    X = Y * Y
50    H =INT(X * S)
60    IF H>0 THEN PRINT "Y";TAB(H);"*"
62    IF H = 0 THEN PRINT "*"
70      GOTO 90
75    REM
76    REM
80    FOR Y2=1 TO 50: PRINT "X"; : NEXT Y2
82    PRINT
90    NEXT Y
99    END
```

Here is the output:

```
Y                                                                    *
Y                                                              *
Y                                                        *
Y                                                  *
Y                                            *
Y                                     *
Y                              *
Y                       *
Y           *
*
XXXXXXXXXXXXXXXXXXXXXXXXXXXXXXXXXXXXXXXXXXXXXXXXXXXX
*
Y           *
Y                 *
Y                       *
Y                            *
Y                                  *
Y                                        *
Y                                              *
Y                                                    *
Y                                                          *
```

Suppose we want to make a graph of a billiard ball as it bounces off the side of the table. We will need to make a V-shaped graph, using two TAB commands in each line. The following program does this:

```
1    REM   PROGRAM TO TRACE OUT PATH OF BILLIARD BALL
10   FOR Y = 18 TO 2 STEP –1
20     X1 = INT((20 – Y)/2)
30   X2 = INT(20 – 2 * X1)
40   PRINT TAB(X1);" * ";
50   PRINT TAB(X1 + X2 – 1);" * "
60   NEXT Y
70   END
```

Here is the output:

The graphics programs that we have written so far will work on any computer. A computer operating in this fashion is said to be in text mode. In text mode, the screen is divided into about 25 rows and 40 or 80 columns, and the computer can put one character at each of these locations. (Note that all of the programs we have done up to now have been in text mode.) Some computers have built-in graphics characters, such as squares, circles, diamonds, or triangles. The availability of these characters greatly expands your capabilities for text-mode graphics. You should explore the upper range of your computer's character set to see what characters are represented by ASCII codes above 130.

GRAPHICS MODE

There is one big disadvantage to text-mode graphics: you cannot draw pictures that have fine detail. If you look closely at your screen, you will see that your display is made of a great many little dots. In order to draw sharp pictures, we need to control each dot on the screen. Many computers can be switched into *graphics mode*, which allows you this kind of control. If you have a monochrome screen, you can decide which dots will be lit up; if you have a color screen, you can also control the color of each dot. The graphics mode often includes commands to draw lines and other shapes as well. Unfortunately, the graphics commands are different for different computers. You will need to check your manual to see what graphics commands are available on your computer. In the rest of this chapter, we will describe some sample programs that illustrate the graphics capabilities of the Commodore 64, Apple II, and IBM PC.

In general, there are three things you need to know in order to use the graphics commands for any computer:

1. How many dots are on the screen. You need to know the height and width of the screen (measured in dots). The table shows what is available on four common versions:

Version	Screen Height	Screen Width	Total Dots
Commodore 64			
Bit Mapped Graphics	200	320	64,000
Apple II High			
Resolution Graphics	160	280	44,800
IBM PC Medium			
Resolution Graphics	200	320	64,000
IBM PC High			
Resolution Graphics	200	640	128,000

A larger value for the number of dots means you can include more fine detail in your pictures.

2. How to put the computer in graphics mode and how to return it to text mode. On the Apple II, the command HGR turns on high-resolution graphics and the command TEXT returns the screen to text mode. On the IBM PC, the command SCREEN 1 turns on medium-resolution graphics, SCREEN 2 turns on high-resolution graphics, and SCREEN 0 returns the computer to text mode. On the Commodore 64, you need to use a set of commands that directly addresses the computer's memory using POKE and PEEK commands. You should write these commands as a subroutine so that you can call them whenever you need to write a graphics program. The following programs demonstrate this procedure. (You may be wondering, What are POKE and PEEK commands? The PEEK command allows you to examine the contents of a specific location in the computer's memory, and the POKE command allows you to put a specific value into a specific memory location. If you use a PEEK or POKE command, you must carefully consult your manual to learn the layout of the memory. We have not included any other POKE or PEEK commands in this book because they are very machine-specific.)

3. How to light up a dot at a specified location on the screen. When you want to light up a dot that is *y* units down from the top of the screen and *x* units away from the left edge of the screen, use the command PSET(*x,y*) on the IBM PC or the command HPLOT *x,y* on the Apple II. The Commodore 64 procedure involves several statements that should be written as a subroutine.

DRAWING LOOPS

Here is a program that can draw very interesting roselike loop patterns on the screen. The pattern is governed by the formula

$$R = SIN(N * RD)$$

which is plotted in polar coordinates. *R* represents the distance of the point from the origin, and *RD* represents the angle of orientation of the point, measured in radians. The nature of the pattern depends on the value of *N*, which can be a whole number or a fraction. If you have studied trigonometry and polar coordinates, then you can figure out why this formula works, but you do not need to know anything about the math involved in order to run the program and observe the patterns it forms. Here is the program:

```
1 REM   THIS PROGRAM DRAWS LOOPS
2 REM   YOU TYPE IN THE NUMBER N, WHICH
3 REM   DETERMINES THE NUMBER OF LOOPS
4 REM   YOU TYPE IN THE NUMBER S, WHICH
5 REM   DETERMINES THE SIZE OF THE LOOPS.
6 REM   THIS PROGRAM RUNS ON A COMMODORE 64
8 INPUT "N:";N
9 INPUT "SIZE: (0 TO 1):";S: S = S * 90
10 GOSUB 3000  : REM  INITIALIZE GRAPHICS
20 SH = 200 : SW = 320
21 REM  SH IS SCREEN HEIGHT
22 REM  SW IS SCREEN WIDTH
30 FOR T = 1 TO 360
31 REM  T IS THE ANGLE MEASURED IN DEGREES
40 RD = 3.14159*T/180
41 REM  RD IS THE ANGLE MEASURED IN RADIANS
50 R = S * SIN(N * RD)
59 REM NOW CONVERT TO RECTANGULAR COORDINATES
60 X = (SW/2) + R*COS(RD)
70 Y = (SH/2) - R*SIN(RD)
80 GOSUB 2000 : REM  PLOT X,Y
90 NEXT T
100 END
1999 REM ********************
2000 REM  LIGHT UP THE POINT AT (X,Y)
2010 CH=INT(X/8)
2020 RO=INT(Y/8)
2030 LN=YAND7
2040 BY=BASE+RO*320+8*CH+LN
2050 BI=7-(XAND7)
2060 POKEBY,PEEK(BY)OR(2^BI)
2070 RETURN
2999 REM ********************
```

```
3000 REM   INITIALIZE GRAPHICS
3005 BASE=2*4096:POKE53272,PEEK(53272)OR8
3010 POKE53265,PEEK(53265)OR32
3020 FOR I=BASE TO BASE+7999:POKEI,0:NEXT
3030 FOR I=1024 TO 2023:POKEI,3:NEXT
3040 RETURN
```

Try running the program with several different values of N. Can you discover a relation that determines how the number of loops depends on the value of N? See if you can make the program draw a circle and a heart shape. Note that you can change the size of the patterns by changing the value of S.

Both of these programs could be written in another version of BASIC with the appropriate changes made in the graphics initialization command and the plotting command.

DRAWING GRAPHS

In many cases, pictures provide the best way to present information. As they say, "One picture is worth a thousand words." In particular, numerical information is often more meaningful when it is presented as a graph instead of a table of numbers. Two particularly useful types of graphs are *pie charts* and *bar graphs*.

A pie chart is the best way to illustrate what share of the total is contained in each category. For example, if you want to illustrate the costs for a company, you could draw a pie chart showing the fraction that goes for wages, the fraction for supplies, the fraction for rent, and so on. A pie chart is a circular diagram where each category is represented as a wedge-shaped piece of pie. The angular size of the wedge is determined by the fraction of the total that belongs to that category. Here is an Apple II program that reads in a list of numbers and then draws a pie chart:

```
1   REM   PIE CHART PROGRAM
2   REM   THIS PROGRAM DRAWS A PIE CHART
3   REM   FOR A LIST OF NUMBERS TYPED IN
4   REM   BY THE USER.  THIS PROGRAM RUNS
5   REM   ON AN APPLE IIE COMPUTER.
50 SH = 160 : REM SCREEN HEIGHT
55 SW = 280 : REM SCREEN WIDTH
60 C1 = SW/2 : C2 = SH/2
61 REM C1,C2 ARE COORDINATES OF CENTER
70 R = 70 : REM RADIUS OF PIE CHART
100 INPUT "HOW MANY NUMBERS ";N
105 T = 0
110 FOR I = 1 TO N
120 PRINT I; : INPUT K(I)
130 T = T + K(I)
140 NEXT I
145 PRINT : PRINT : PRINT
146 PRINT "-----------------"
150 FOR I = 1 TO N
155 PRINT K(I);",";
```

Continued

```
160 K(I) = K(I)/T
170 NEXT I
199 REM *********************
200 REM  DRAW SPOKES
202 HGR : REM TURN ON HIGH RESOLUTION GRAPHICS
205 K(0) = 0
206 S = 0
210 FOR I = 0 TO N-1
215 S = S + K(I)
220 A = S * 2 * 3.14159
230 X = C1 + R * COS(A)
240 Y = C2 - R * SIN(A)
250 HPLOT C1,C2, TO X,Y
260 NEXT I
299 REM *********************
300 REM  DRAW CIRCLE
302 X2 = C1 + R : Y2 = C2
305 FOR T = 0 TO 2 * 3.14159 STEP 0.05
310 X = C1 + R * COS(T)
320 Y = C2 - R * SIN(T)
330 HPLOT X2,Y2 TO X,Y
335 X2 = X : Y2 = Y
340 NEXT T
350 END
```

The numbers are read in lines 100–140. Note that no DIM statement is included for the array K. Many computers will automatically dimension an array to include ten elements if no DIM statement is included. If you will be using the program in a situation with more than ten numbers, you will have to include a DIM statement.

The program takes advantage of one Apple II feature that makes it possible to display the numbers themselves on the screen below the pie chart. When the computer is switched to high-resolution graphics mode, the bottom four lines of the screen remain in text mode. Therefore, you can print output to those lines, as is done in lines 145–170.

The Apple II HPLOT command can be used to draw lines (line 250). The command HPLOT C1, C2 TO X,Y will draw a line from the point C1,C2 to the point X,Y. After the spokes of the pie chart are drawn, the computer draws the circle that forms the boundary of the chart (lines 300–340).

Another useful type of diagram is a bar graph. In a bar graph, the relative sizes of a group of numbers are shown by the heights of different bars. Here is an Apple II program that draws a bar graph:

```
1  REM  BAR DIAGRAM PROGRAM
2  REM  THIS PROGRAM DRAWS A BAR DIAGRAM
3  REM  FOR A SET OF NUMBERS TYPED IN BY
4  REM  THE USER.  THIS PROGRAM IS FOR
5  REM  AN APPLE IIE COMPUTER
50 SH = 160 : REM SCREEN HEIGHT
55 SW = 280 : REM SCREEN WIDTH
```

```
60 W = 24   : REM WIDTH OF EACH BAR
70 G = 12   : REM GAP BETWEEN BARS
80 M = 2    : REM SIZE OF THE MARGINS
100 INPUT "HOW MANY NUMBERS ";N
110 FOR I = 1 TO N
120 PRINT I; : INPUT K(I)
140 NEXT I
145 INPUT "SCALE:";S
147 PRINT : PRINT : PRINT
148 PRINT "---------------"
150 FOR I = 1 TO N
155 PRINT K(I);",";
160 K(I) = SH * K(I)/S
170 NEXT I
180 HGR : REM TURN ON HIGH RESOLUTION GRAPHICS
199 REM **********************
200 REM  DRAW AXES
210 HPLOT M,0 TO M,SH-M
220 HPLOT TO SW-M,SH-M
230 REM DRAW BARS
235 X = M - 1
240 FOR I = 1 TO N
250 FOR K1 = 1 TO W
260 HPLOT (X+K1),(SH-M) TO (X+K1),(SH-M-K(I))
270 NEXT K1
280 X = X + W + G
290 NEXT I
300 END
```

As in the last program, the numbers are read and then displayed at the bottom of the screen (lines 100–170). You also need to specify the vertical scale of the diagram. The number you type in for the scale should be a bit larger than the largest number in the list.

The computer draws the two axes in lines 200–220. The command HPLOT M,0 TO M,SH-M draws a line along the left-hand edge of the screen—the point (2,0) to the point (2,158). Note that the command HPLOT TO SW-M,SH-M does not specify where the line is to begin. In that case, the computer will use the point that was last referred to as the beginning of the line. Here, the point last referenced was (M,SH-M) from line 210. Therefore, line 220 will draw a line along the bottom of the graphics area, from the point (2,158) to the point (278,158). The bars are drawn in lines 230–290.

Graphs provide a valuable tool for understanding the behavior of mathematical equations, so we will write a general program that can draw the graph of any function you choose. (Even if you are not mathematically inclined, you can still use this program and experiment with the interesting curves that can be drawn.) As is usual in math, the horizontal axis will be called the x axis and the vertical axis will be called the y axis. Our program will draw graphs of equations of the form $y = f(x)$. (In other words, y will be a function of *x*.) In order to make the program fully general, we need to be able to shift the location of the origin and change the vertical and horizontal scales. Here is the program:

```
1    REM   GENERAL CURVE DRAWING PROGRAM
2    REM   THIS APPLE IIE PROGRAM WILL DRAW A GRAPH OF A CURVE THAT
3    REM   REPRESENTS Y AS A FUNCTION OF X. THE USER CAN CHOOSE
4    REM   THE SCALE OF THE DRAWING AND THE COORDINATES OF THE
5    REM   CENTER OF THE SCREEN.
14   SH = 160  : REM SCREEN HEIGHT
15   S2 = SH/2 : REM HALF OF SCREEN HEIGHT
20   SW = 280  : REM SCREEN WIDTH
30   PRINT "DO YOU WANT AXES SHOWN?"
40   INPUT "Y OR N ";QA$
50   REM   SET INITIAL SPECIFICATIONS
60   XC = 0 : YC = 0
61   REM   THE CENTER IS AT (0,0)
70   W = 20 : H = 16
71   REM W IS WIDTH, H IS HEIGHT
99   REM ************************
100  REM INPUT SPECIFICATIONS
105  HOME
110  VTAB 21
115  LIST 1000
120  PRINT "W:";W;"  H:";H;
130  PRINT " CENTER:";XC;",";YC;
140  PRINT "   ?";
150  GET X$
160  IF X$="G" THEN GOSUB 500 : GOTO 110
170  IF X$="W" THEN GOTO 210
175  IF X$="H" THEN GOTO 220
180  IF X$="X" THEN GOTO 230
185  IF X$="Y" THEN GOTO 240
187  IF X$="S" THEN END
190  GOTO 150
199  REM *************************
200  REM   CHANGE SPECIFICATIONS
210  INPUT "NEW WIDTH:";W
215  GOTO 100
220  INPUT "NEW HEIGHT:";H
225  GOTO 100
230  INPUT "NEW X CENTER:";XC
235  GOTO 100
240  INPUT "NEW Y CENTER:";YC
245  GOTO 100
499  REM *************************
500  REM   DRAW DIAGRAM
505  HGR : REM TURN ON HIGH RES. GRAPHICS
508  IF QA$ = "Y" THEN GOSUB 700 : REM PLOT AXES
510  XS = XC - W/2 : REM STARTING X VALUE
520  DX = W/SW : REM X INCREMENT
530  X2 = 0
540  FOR X = XS TO (XS+W) STEP DX
550  X2 = X2 + 1
560  GOSUB 1000 : REM CALCULATE Y
```

```
570 Y2 = INT(S2 - SH*(Y-YC)/H)
571 REM   NOW CHECK TO MAKE SURE WE'RE
572 REM   NOT OVER THE EDGE
573 IF X2<1 THEN GOTO 590
574 IF X2>=SW THEN GOTO 590
576 IF Y2<1 THEN GOTO 590
578 IF Y2>=SH THEN GOTO 590
580 HPLOT X2,Y2
590 NEXT X
600 RETURN
699 REM ******************************
700 REM   PLOT AXES
710 XA = SW * (W/2 - XC)/W
715 XA = INT(XA + 0.5)
720 YA = SH - (SH * (H/2 - YC)/H)
725 YA = INT(YA + 0.5)
730 IF (XA<1) OR (XA>=SW) THEN GOTO 750
740 HPLOT XA,0 TO XA,SH-1
750 IF (YA<1) OR (YA >= SH) THEN GOTO 770
760 HPLOT 0,YA TO SW-1,YA
770 RETURN
990 REM ******************************
991 REM   LINE 1000 DETERMINES THE CURVE
992 REM    THAT WILL BE DRAWN.  TO CHANGE
993 REM    THE CURVE, YOU MUST CHANGE LINE
994 REM    1000.  IN THIS EXAMPLE, THE
995 REM    CURVE DRAWN IS Y = SIN(X)
1000  Y = SIN(X)
1010  RETURN
```

Line 1000 defines the function that will be graphed. When you want to graph a different function, you will need to change that line. There are several variables that determine the position and scale of the graph: W: width, H: height, XC: x coordinate of center of screen, YC: y coordinate of center of screen. Initially, W = 20, H = 16, XC = 0, and YC = 0. This means that the origin is at the center of the screen. The screen is 20 units wide (meaning x values from −10 to 10 are shown) and 16 units high (meaning y values from −8 to 8 are shown). If you want to blow up the vertical scale of the graph, make the value of H smaller. For example, if H is 4, then y values from −2 to 2 will be shown (assuming YC is still 0). This will stretch the curve vertically. Of course, if you make H too small, parts of the curve will be cut off and will not appear on the screen. If you want to move the x axis down, make YC bigger; if you want to move the y axis to the left, make XC bigger. If the point you choose for (XC,YC) is too far from the origin, the axes will not appear on the screen.

Before the computer draws the curve, it will display the specifications for the curve at the bottom of the screen. Note that line 115 contains the instructions LIST 1000. This will cause line 1000 to be displayed, showing the equation of the curve. Then the values of W, H, XC, and YC are displayed. You have six options, depending on which key you press:

Key	Action
G	go ahead and draw curve with the current specifications
W	computer will ask you for new value of W
H	computer will ask you for new value of H
X	computer will ask you for new value of XC
Y	computer will ask you for new value of YC
S	stop the program

The subroutine that draws the curve starts at line 500. There is one important difference between plotting points on the screen and normal mathematical plotting: on the screen, the values of Y become bigger when you move down.

There are many interesting functions that you may experiment with. The function $y = \sin x$ is particularly interesting because you will see a wave pattern on the screen. You may adjust the height of the waves by changing the value of H, and you may adjust the number of waves on the screen by adjusting the value of W. It is also interesting to look at third-degree polynomial functions, such as $y = x^3 + 3x^2 - 9x + 3$, which changes direction twice. Polynomial equations of higher degree can change direction even more times.

IBM PC GRAPHICS

Here are some examples of graphics programs in IBM PC BASIC. This program draws a spiral pattern on the screen:

```
 1   REM   This program draws a spiral pattern on the screen.
 2   REM   This is IBM PC BASIC.
10   XMAX = 639
15   XBAR = XMAX/2
20   YMAX = 199
25   YBAR = YMAX/2
40   INPUT "Time delay betwee dots:";DELAY
50   INPUT "Spiral factor:";SF
51   REM   SF should be a number close to 1, such as 1.01
100  CLS        'Clear screen
105  SCREEN 2   ' Set screen to high resolution graphics
110  R = 4
117  TMAX = 3600
120  FOR T = 1 TO TMAX STEP 5
125     R = SF*R
130     RAD = 3.14159*T/180
140     X = R*COS(RAD)
150     Y = R*SIN(RAD)
160     X1 = XBAR + X
```

```
170     Y1 = YBAR + Y
180     PSET(X1,Y1)
190      FOR J = 1 TO DELAY : NEXT J
200   NEXT T
210   END
```

SCREEN 2 (line 5) is the command to turn on high-resolution graphics; CLS (line 100) is the command to clear the screen; and PSET(X1,Y1) (line 180) is the command to plot the point given by the coordinates (X1,Y1).

If you have a color monitor, you can write color graphics programs. Many computers allow you to change the background color and the foreground color. Check your manual to see how color commands work on your computer. Here is one program that demonstrates the use of color on an IBM PC:

```
1   REM  COLOR DEMONSTRATION PROGRAM
2   REM      FOR THE IBM PC
3   REM  THIS PROGRAM DRAWS 16 STRIPES
4   REM      ACROSS THE SCREEN, ILLUSTRATING
5   REM      EACH OF THE COLORS AVAILABLE
6   REM      IN TEXT MODE.
10  SCREEN 0  ' SET TO TEXT MODE
20  FOR J=1 TO 25
30     FOR C=0 TO 15
40       COLOR C
41  REM  THE COMMAND "COLOR C" IN TEXT MODE
42  REM      SETS THE FOREGROUND COLOR TO
43  REM      COLOR NUMBER C.
50  PRINT CHR$(219);CHR$(219);
51  REM  219 IS THE CHARACTER CODE
52  REM      FOR A SOLID SQUARE.
60     NEXT C
70  PRINT
80  NEXT J
90  END
```

Here is another program that uses color:

```
1 REM   CHECKERBOARD PROGRAM
2 REM   THIS PROGRAM DRAWS A COLORED
3 REM   CHECKERBOARD ON THE SCREEN
4 REM   THIS IS IBM PC BASIC
60 INPUT "PALETTE: (0 OR 1)";P
62 IF P=1 THEN PRINT "1 - CYAN    2 - MAGENTA    3 - WHITE"
64 IF P=0 THEN PRINT "1 - GREEN   2 - RED        3 - BROWN"
70 INPUT "SQUARE COLOR:";CL
72 INPUT "BORDER COLOR:";BCL
75 CLS    'CLEAR SCREEN
80 SCREEN 1   'SET SCREEN TO GRAPHICS
90 COLOR 0,P 'SET BACKGROUND COLOR AND PALETTE
100 SW = 320 'SCREEN WIDTH
110 SH = 200 'SCREEN HEIGHT
120 S = SH/8 'SQUARE SIZE
130 FOR R=1 TO 8
135    SR = (R-1)*S+1
140    IF (R/2)=INT(R/2) THEN ST=S+1 ELSE ST=1
150    FOR C=1 TO 4
160       SC=ST+(C-1)*S   'COLUMN OF UPPER LEFT CORNER
170       LINE (SC,SR) - (SC+S,SR+S),CL,BF
171       REM SC IS THE STARTING COLUMN
172       REM SR IS THE STARTING ROW
173       REM CL IS THE COLOR CODE
174       REM BF MEANS "FILL BOX"
175       ST=ST+S
180    NEXT C
190 NEXT R
194 REM DRAW BORDER AROUND SCREEN
195 LINE (1,1)-(8*S+1,8*S-1),BCL,B
196 REM   B MEANS "DRAW BOX"
200 Q$=INKEY$ : IF Q$="" THEN GOTO 200
205 CLS
210 END
```

In medium-resolution graphics mode (SCREEN 1), the IBM PC provides two different color palettes, each with three colors. In this program you choose which palette you wish to use, then choose which color you would like for the checkerboard squares and which color for the border.

The versatile LINE command is used to draw the squares. You can draw a line on the screen by specifying two points. For example, LINE (X1,Y1) – (X2,Y2) will draw a line from the point (X1,Y1) to (X2,Y2). (This form of the LINE command is the same as the Apple II HPLOT command with two points specified.) You can choose the color of the line by specifying the color number after the points. You can draw a rectangle on the screen by specifying two points at opposite corners of the rectangle and including the option

B (for box) at the end of the command. Line 195 draws a box with color determined by BCL to form the border of the checkerboard. You can draw a solid rectangle by including the option BF (for filled-in box). Line 170 draws the checkerboard squares. CL is the color number.

IBM PC BASIC also includes a command to draw circles and a command to paint a specified area with a certain color. Here is an example program:

```
1 REM   DARTBOARD PROGRAM
2 REM   THIS PROGRAM DRAWS A DARTBOARD ON THE SCREEN
3 REM   THIS IS IBM PC BASIC
60 INPUT "SIZE OF STRIPES:";SS
70 INPUT "PALETTE: (0 OR 1)";P
72 IF P=1 THEN PRINT "0 - BLACK   1 - CYAN   2 - MAGENTA   3 - WHITE"
74 IF P=0 THEN PRINT "0 - BLACK   1 - GREEN  2 - RED       3 - BROWN"
80 FOR CH=1 TO 2
82    PRINT "INPUT COLOR ";CH
84    INPUT CL(CH)
86 NEXT CH
90 CLS   'CLEAR SCREEN
92 SCREEN 1   'SET SCREEN TO GRAPHICS
94 COLOR 0,P
95 CH = 1
100 SW = 320   'SCREEN WIDTH
110 SH = 200   'SCREEN HEIGHT
120 XC = SW/2 : YC = SH/2
130 R = SH/2 + SS
131 NS = SH/(2*SS)    'NUMBER OF STRIPES
132 FOR I = 1 TO NS
134    R = R-SS
136    CH = 3 - CH : C = CL(CH)
140    CIRCLE(XC,YC),R,C
145    PAINT(XC,YC),C
150 NEXT I
200 Q$=INKEY$: IF Q$="" THEN GOTO 200
205 CLS
210 END
```

The command CIRCLE (XC,YC),R,C (line 140) draws a circle with center at the point (XC,YC), radius equal to R, using the color number given by C. The command PAINT (XC,YC),C will paint the region that contains the point (XC,YC) with color given by C.

By now you have an appreciation for the types of graphics programs that can be written in BASIC. Many computers contain additional graphics commands; if you are interested, you should investigate further the capabilities of your computer.

EXERCISES   *Write programs to draw the following shapes:*

1. parallelogram
2. triangle
3. regular polygon (let the user enter the number of sides for the polygon)
4. crescent moon
5. spiral galaxy
6. cube (create a perspective drawing that makes the cube look three-dimensional)
7. eye
8. the border around the edge of the screen
9. football
10. football field
11. donut
12. comet with a long tail
13. snowflake

14. If you have a color screen, write a pie-chart program that draws the wedges in different colors.

15. Write a program that allows two people to play a game of checkers on the computer. The computer will first draw the checkerboard with the pieces set up in the initial position. Then, as players enter their moves into the computer, the screen will show the pieces moving around the board.

16. Write a program that uses the RND function to display geometric shapes at random locations on the screen.

17. Write a program that draws a circle and then draws line segments connecting pairs of points on the circle. Investigate what patterns you can form by changing the distance between the pairs of points that are connected.

18. Write a program that draws a scatter diagram of a set of points. Then use the program to plot the relationship between height and weight for a group of people, or the relationship between inflation and unemployment in the economy, or the relation between temperature and precipitation for different cities.

19. Write a program that reads in a set of time series data (such as the population in a city every year for 20 years) and then makes a graph of the data, showing time on the horizontal axis and the data you're measuring on the vertical axis.

20. Write a program that draws Saturn's rings. Allow the user to choose the angle at which the rings are viewed. For example, if you are directly above Saturn, the rings appear as circles; if you look at Saturn from the side, the rings appear as a straight line segment. In general, the rings will have the shape of an ellipse.

Exercises 21–24 contain suggestions for programs that make use of moving graphics. Check you manual to see what moving graphics capabilities are available on your computer. For example, the Commodore 64 allows you to define shapes (called sprites) *that can be moved around the screen.*

21. Write a program that follows the path of a ball as it moves around the screen. When the ball hits one of the walls, have it bounce back.

22. Add some more obstacles off which the ball in exercise 21 can bounce.

23. Write a program that allows two balls to move around the screen and bounce off each other.

24. Write a program to draw a cube, and then make it possible to rotate the cube as if you were viewing it from different angles. (This will be difficult.)

25. Write a program that displays large numbers or letters on the screen.

CHAPTER 15

SCIENTIFIC APPLICATIONS

Computers play an important role in scientific research. Scientists use computers to construct models that allow them to investigate the implications and predictions of their theories. Then they can conduct experiments and perform observations to test whether the theoretical predictions are correct in the real world. And, of course, students encounter many interesting scientific problems that can be solved with computers.

COMPUTER MODELS

For example, computer models have been essential tools for understanding the way that the sun works. Astronomers make some assumptions about what the center of the sun might be like. For example, they guess what the temperature and pressure at the center of the sun might be, and they guess what the composition might be, that is, how much hydrogen, helium, and so on, the sun contains. Then astronomers need to answer the following question: "If the center of the sun really were like this, what would it look like to observers on Earth?" The computer performs the necessary calculations to tell the astronomers how bright the theoretical sun would be and what its spectrum would look like. These theoretical predictions can be compared with the actual results for the real sun. If the theoretical predictions agree with what the real sun looks like, then the theory is a promising model and deserves to be investigated further. However, if the theoretical predictions are not correct, then the model is no good. For example, if the model predicts that the sun will look purple, we know that it's back to the drawing board to develop another model.

Computers can also play an important part in medicine. A doctor diagnoses a patient's illness by observing the patient's symptoms. Most doctors have memorized the symptoms for most common diseases. However, when a patient has an obscure disease with unusual symptoms, the doctor will need to consult a reference manual. A computer program has been developed that acts like a medical reference manual. The doctor types in the patient's symptoms, and the computer responds by telling the doctor what further symptoms to test for. Finally, the computer tells the doctor what possible diseases could be causing these symptoms.

Computers are essential research tools for social sciences such as economics and psychology. Theoretical models in economics are usually written for computers.

Here is an example of an important economics problem: Suppose we change the money supply by *x* percent, we change the amount of government spending by *y* percent, and we change the tax rates by *z* percent. What will happen to the inflation rate? to the unemployment rate? to the interest rate? Ideally, we would like to know the answers to these questions for many different values of *x,* *y,* and *z* so that we could pick the best policy. However, we can't very easily experiment on the real world by varying the level of actual government spending and actual taxes just to see what happens. It would help greatly if a theoretical model capable of being solved by a computer could be developed that could answer this kind of question. However, that is very difficult to do because nobody understands economics well enough.

All scientists must do statistical calculations. When they perform an experiment many times or when they collect many observations, they need to estimate the uncertainty in the results. Computers are essential to perform the long calculations involved.

To write a scientific application program, you need to know a lot about the subject you are investigating. (Sometimes, however, a scientist will describe his or her model to a computer programmer, and the programmer will be left to write the program.) Often you need to know a lot of math. For example, computers are needed to solve many problems involving special types of equations known as *differential equations.* Problems involving motion usually require differential equations. Most differential equations don't have simple solutions that a mathematician can derive, so the only way to solve them is with the computer.

Another interesting type of model is a simulation model, or Monte Carlo model. Sometimes a scientist will not be able to predict for certain whether an event will happen, but it is possible to predict the probability that the event will happen. When the program is being run, the random number function will be used to determine whether the event occurs. This method is called the Monte Carlo method because it is like a game of chance. An example is the football game program in Chapter 13. We know what the probability of a fumble occurring is, so the program uses a random number to determine whether a fumble actually occurs on a particular play.

Computers can be even more valuable for scientific purposes when they don't have to wait for users to type in data. In many scientific applications, the computers themselves automatically read the data from the measuring devices. And instead of merely printing results, the computers can be designed to control the movements of machines. For example, the Voyager probes were controlled by computers.

There are many scientific programs that can be written in BASIC, although BASIC is not, on the whole, the best language for scientific problems. The FORTRAN programming language was originally designed mainly for scientific and engineering problems. PL/I is another good language for these purposes. It is more versastile than FORTRAN. APL is often the best language for advanced mathematical research. Unlike BASIC, however, these languages are usually not available on small computers. Pascal is a language that is commonly used to solve scientific problems on microcomputers.

HOW FAR IS IT FROM HERE TO THERE?

Here is an example of a scientific problem with important practical applications. If you are planning to fly an airplane between two cities, you would like to know the shortest possible distance between them. Because Earth is a sphere, the shortest distance between two cities is not always obvious. For example, the shortest route between cities in the United States and cities in Europe sometimes involves flying over the North Pole.

First, our program will read in the latitudes and longitudes of the two cities. Then it will use a defined function to convert these figures from degrees into radians. Next it will calculate the *rectangular coordinates* for the two cities, with the origin at the center of Earth, the z axis pointing to the North Pole, and the x axis pointing to 0 degree longitude (which is the longitude of the observatory at Greenwich, England). Once we know the rectangular coordinates of the two points, we can calculate the straight-line distance (d) between the two cities. The straight-line distance doesn't help us too much, since we can't travel in a straight line through the middle of Earth. However, we can use the straight-line distance to calculate the surface distance (s) from the formula:

$$s = 2r \arcsin\left(\frac{d}{2r}\right)$$

Here is the program. Note that, if one city is west of Greenwich and the other is east of Greenwich, we need to convert the east longitude into a west longitude using the formula

west longitude = 360 − east longitude

```
1   REM   PROGRAM TO CALCULATE THE DISTANCE BETWEEN
2   REM      TWO CITIES
10  R = 3960   'R IS THE RADIUS OF THE EARTH
15  DEF FNAS(X)=ATN(X/SQR(1−X*X))'ARCSINE
20  DEF FNR (X) = X * 3.14159/180
21  REM   FNR CONVERTS A NUMBER FROM DEGREES TO RADIANS
30  INPUT "FIRST CITY:" ;C1$
40  INPUT "LONGITUDE OF FIRST CITY:" ;N1:N1 = FNR(N1)
```

```
50   INPUT "LATITUDE OF FIRST CITY:" ;T1:T1 = FNR(T1)
60   INPUT "SECOND CITY:" ;C2$
70   INPUT "LONGITUDE OF SECOND CITY:" ;N2:N2 = FNR(N2)
80   INPUT "LATITUDE OF SECOND CITY:" ;T2:T2 = FNR(T2)
99   REM    .....................................
100   REM    NOW, CONVERT COORDINATES OF THE TWO CITIES
101   REM       INTO RECTANGULAR COORDINATES
110   X1 = R * COS(T1) * COS(N1)
120   Y1 = R * COS(T1) * SIN(N1)
130   Z1 = R * SIN(T1)
140      REM .....................................
150   X2 = R * COS(T2) * COS(N2)
160   Y2 = R * COS(T2) * SIN(N2)
170   Z2 = R * SIN(T2)
180      REM .....................................
190   REM   D IS THE STRAIGHT LINE DISTANCE BETWEEN
200   REM      THE CITIES, ASSUMING THAT WE CAN TRAVEL
210   REM      RIGHT THROUGH THE EARTH
220   X = ABS(X1 – X2)
221   Y = ABS(Y1 – Y2)
222   Z = ABS(Z1 – Z2)
230   D = SQR(X ↑ 2 + Y ↑ 2 + Z ↑ 2)
240   S = 2 * R * FNAS(D/(2 * R))
250   PRINT "THE DISTANCE BETWEEN" ;C1$;" AND";C2$;"IS"
260   PRINT INT(S);"MILES."
270   END
```

Here is a sample run of the program:

```
RUN
FIRST CITY:NEW YORK
LONGITUDE OF FIRST CITY:73.98
LATITUDE OF FIRST CITY:40.75
SECOND CITY:LOS ANGELES
LONGITUDE OF SECOND CITY:118.23
LATITUDE OF SECOND CITY:34.05
```

Continued

THE DISTANCE BETWEEN NEW YORK AND LOS ANGELES IS 2447 MILES.

  RUN

FIRST CITY:LOS ANGELES

LONGITUDE OF FIRST CITY:118.23

LATITUDE OF FIRST CITY:34.05

SECOND CITY:TOKYO

LONGITUDE OF SECOND CITY:220.25

LATITUDE OF SECOND CITY:35.75

THE DISTANCE BETWEEN LOS ANGELES AND TOKYO IS 5475 MILES.

  RUN

FIRST CITY:NEW YORK

LONGITUDE OF FIRST CITY:73.98

LATITUDE OF FIRST CITY:40.75

SECOND CITY:LONDON

LONGITUDE OF SECOND CITY:0

LATITUDE OF SECOND CITY:51.50

THE DISTANCE BETWEEN NEW YORK AND LONDON IS 3465 MILES.

CALCULATING STAR POSITIONS

Our next program will tell us where in the sky stars and planets will appear. To us, the sky appears to be a giant sphere with Earth at the center. This imaginary sphere is called the *celestial sphere*. The position of a star or planet on this sphere is measured by two numbers called *right ascension* and *declination*. Right ascension is similar to the longitude of an object as seen from Earth, and declination is similar to the latitude. If a star is in the plane of Earth's equator, it has a declination of 0°. The declination of other objects is the angular distance between the object and the plane of the equator. Positive declinations mean that the object is north of the equator, and negative declinations mean that the object is south of the equator. For example, the North Star (Polaris) has a declination of almost +90°. The right ascension of an object is the angle between the object and a special point in the constellation Pisces (this special point is actually the point where the sun is on the first day of spring).

Instead of being measured in degrees, right ascension is usually measured in hours, where 1 hour = 15° and 24 hours = 360°. (Don't confuse this type of hour with the hours we use to measure

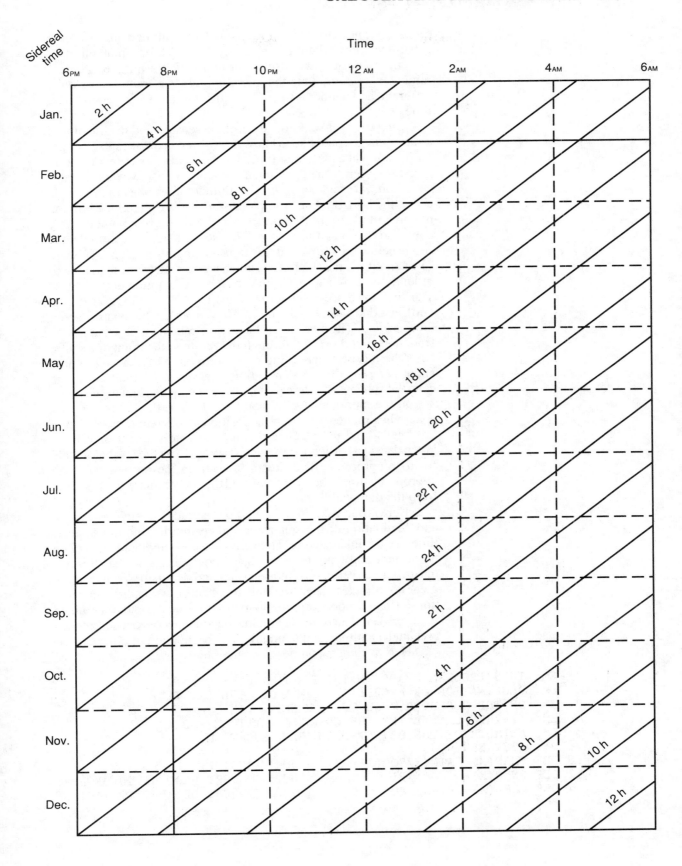

time.) If we need to measure very small intervals of declination, we can use *minutes*, where 1 minute = $\frac{1}{60}°$. To measure small intervals of right ascension, we also use a unit called a minute, where 1 minute = $\frac{1}{60}$ hour. Note that these two types of minutes are quite different, and neither is the same as the minutes we use to measure time.

Suppose that we know the right ascension and declination of a star, and we would like to know its position in the sky as seen from our location at a particular time. To identify the location of a point in the sky seen from a particular location, we use two coordinates called *altitude* and *azimuth*. The altitude of an object is its angle above the horizon. For example, a star that is right on the horizon has an altitude of 0°. A star that is at the zenith (the point directly overhead) has an altitude of 90°. If a star has negative altitude, the star is below the horizon at this time and therefore cannot be seen. The azimuth of the star tells us in what direction we need to look in order to see it. A star that is due north has an azimuth of 0° or 360°. The direction due east has an azimuth of 90°, due south is at azimuth 180°, and due west is at azimuth 270°. We also need to know about the *meridian*. The meridian is the great circle in the sky that passes from the point due north through the zenith to the point due south.

There is one more thing we need to know. We need to know about *sidereal time*. Sidereal time measures the rotation of the celestial sphere. At sidereal time 0, the stars with right ascension 0 are on the meridian. At sidereal time 1 hour, the entire celestial sphere has rotated 15° from its position at sidereal time 0. Figure 15–1 tells how to calculate the approximate sidereal time for a given date at a particular time. Read across from the left-hand scale for the appropriate date. Read down from the top scale for the appropriate time. Then you may read the approximate sidereal time from the diagonal lines.

Here is our task. We will enter our latitude, the right ascension and declination of the star we are interested in, and the sidereal times we are interested in. Then we want the computer to calculate the altitude and azimuth of the object. For it to be able to do this, we must first convert the right ascension and declination into rectangular coordinates. Then we have to perform two coordinate rotations. (See a book on trigonometry to learn about coordinate rotations.) And then we convert the rectangular coordinates into the two angles altitude and azimuth.

Here is the program:

```
1 REM  THIS PROGRAM READS IN THE RIGHT ASCENSION AND
2 REM  DECLINATION OF A CELESTIAL OBJECT, THE LATITUDE
3 REM  OF THE OBSERVER, AND THE SIDEREAL TIME.
4 REM   IT THEN CALCULATES THE CURRENT ALTITUDE AND
5 REM  AZIMUTH OF THE OBJECT FROM YOUR LOCATION.
45 PI = 3.14159
50 DEF FNAS(X)= ATN(X/SQR(1-X*X))    :REM ARCSINE
52 DEF FNDG(X)= 180*X/PI             :REM CONVERT RADIANS TO DEGREES
54 DEF FNRD(X)= PI*X/180             :REM CONVERT DEGREES TO RADIANS
99 REM
```

```
100 REM MAIN PROGRAM BLOCK
110 INPUT "Enter latitude (in degrees):";LAT
120 COLAT = LAT-90   :REM NEGATIVE OF COMPLEMENT OF LATITUDE
130 COLAT = FNRD(COLAT)   :REM CONVERT TO RADIANS
140 REM   SET SIDEREAL TIME
150      INPUT "Enter starting sidereal time (in hours):";S1
160      INPUT "Enter stopping sidereal time (in hours):";S2
170         IF S2<S1 THEN S2 = S2+24
180         S1 = S1*PI/12 : S2 = S2*PI/12   :REM CONVERT TO RADIANS
190      INPUT "Enter sidereal time interval:";STI
200         STI = STI*PI/12
210      REM ENTER RIGHT ASCENSION AND DECLINATION
215         INPUT "Name of object:";N$
216         PRINT N$
220         INPUT "Enter RA (in hours):";RA
230         INPUT "Enter DEC (in degrees):";DEC
240            RA = RA*PI/12   :REM CONVERT TO RADIANS
250            DEC = FNRD(DEC) :REM CONVERT TO RADIANS
260            TIME = S1
270               GOSUB 2000   :REM CALCULATE SUBROUTINE
280               TIME = TIME+STI
290            IF TIME<= S2 THEN GOTO 270
300      INPUT "Type R to see new object. Else type S";Q$
310      IF Q$<>"S" THEN GOTO 210
320   INPUT "Type R to reset sidereal time. Else type S";Q2$
330   IF Q2$<>"S" THEN GOTO 140
340 END
999   REM
1000 REM ARCTANGENT SUBROUTINE
1001 REM   THIS SUBROUTINE CALCULATES THE ARCTANGENT
1002 REM   OF Y9/X9 WITH THE RESULT PLACED IN THE CORRECT QUADRANT
1003 REM   THE VARIABLE Q9 IS THE RESULT OF THE FUNCTION
1010 Q9 = ATN(Y9/X9)
1020 IF X9<0 THEN Q9 = Q9+PI
1030 IF Q9<0 THEN Q9 = Q9+2*PI
1040 RETURN
1999 REM
2000 REM CALCULATION SUBROUTINE
2010   X1 = COS(DEC)*COS(RA)
2020   Y1 = COS(DEC)*SIN(RA)
2030   Z1 = SIN(DEC)
2031 REM    X1,Y1,Z1:  COORDINATES WITH X AXIS POINTING
2032 REM     AT 0 DEGREES RIGHT ASCENSION AND Z AXIS POINTING
2033 REM     AT NORTH POLE
2040   X2 = X1*COS(TIME) + Y1*SIN(TIME)
2050   Y2 = Y1*COS(TIME) - X1*SIN(TIME)
2060   Z2 = Z1
2061 REM    X2,Y2,Z2:  COORDINATES WITH X AXIS POINTING
2062 REM     AT MERIDIAN AND Z AXIS POINTING AT NORTH POLE
2070   X3 = X2*COS(COLAT) + Z2*SIN(COLAT)
2080   Y3 = Y2
2090   Z3 = Z2*COS(COLAT) - X2*SIN(COLAT)
2091 REM    X3,Y3,Z3:  COORDINATES WITH X AXIS POINTING
2092 REM     DUE SOUTH AND Z AXIS POINTING TO ZENITH
2100   ALT = FNAS(Z3)    :REM ARCSINE FUNCTION
2101 REM     ALT IS THE ALTITUDE
```

Continued

```
2110      X9 = X3:Y9 = Y3:GOSUB 1000    :REM ARCTAN SUBROUTINE
2120      AZI = PI - Q9                 :REM AZI IS THE AZIMUTH
2130      IF AZI < 0 THEN AZI = 2*PI  + AZI
2140 REM  CONVERT TO DEGREES:
2150      ALT = FNDG(ALT)
2160      AZI = FNDG(AZI)
2170 REM  CONVERT TO HOURS
2180      HOURS = TIME*12/PI
2190      IF HOURS > 24 THEN HOURS = HOURS - 24
2200 REM OUTPUT
2210     PRINT "Sidereal time:   ";
2215     PRINT USING "###.#";HOURS;
2220     PRINT "   Altitude:  ";
2225     PRINT USING "####.##";ALT;
2230     PRINT "   Azimuth:  ";
2235     PRINT USING "####.##";AZI
2240 RETURN
```

Let's try some sample runs of this program. Suppose we are at latitude 40° North, which is the latitude of New York, Chicago, and northern California. Let's say we are observing in mid-June. The sidereal time at midnight is 18, in the early evening is 12, and in the early morning is 24. So, we will look at the sky for three-hour intervals from sidereal time (S.T.) 12 to S.T. 24. We will look at three constellations: Sagittarius (which is in the direction of the center of the Milky Way galaxy) at right ascension 18.5 and declination −30; the Big Dipper (in Ursa Major) at right ascension 12 and declination 55; and Orion at right ascension 5.5 and declination 0. Here is the output:

```
Sagittarius
Sidereal time:   12.0    Altitude:   -24.08    Azimuth:   109.87
Sidereal time:   15.0    Altitude:     4.73    Azimuth:   136.42
Sidereal time:   18.0    Altitude:    19.65    Azimuth:   173.11
Sidereal time:   21.0    Altitude:    11.83    Azimuth:   212.59
Sidereal time:   24.0    Altitude:   -13.58    Azimuth:   242.04


Big Dipper
Sidereal time:   12.0    Altitude:    75.00    Azimuth:     0.00
Sidereal time:   15.0    Altitude:    56.85    Azimuth:   312.13
Sidereal time:   18.0    Altitude:    31.77    Azimuth:   317.57
Sidereal time:   21.0    Altitude:    12.47    Azimuth:   335.46
Sidereal time:   24.0    Altitude:     5.00    Azimuth:   360.00
```

```
Orion
Sidereal time:    12.0    Altitude:     -5.74    Azimuth:    274.84
Sidereal time:    15.0    Altitude:    -37.43    Azimuth:    309.95
Sidereal time:    18.0    Altitude:    -49.42    Azimuth:     11.57
Sidereal time:    21.0    Altitude:    -27.80    Azimuth:     63.75
Sidereal time:    24.0    Altitude:      5.74    Azimuth:     94.84
```

Sagittarius is below the horizon at S.T. 12, has just risen at S.T. 15, and is just about to set at S.T. 22. The highest altitude it reaches during the night occurs near S.T. 18, when it is almost due south.

The Big Dipper is special because it is visible all night from this latitude. Its lowest point during the night occurs at S.T. 24, when it has an altitude of 5° and an azimuth of 360 degrees (due north).

Orion cannot be seen at all in June. It rises just before S.T. 24, when it is almost due east, but the sun will have already risen by this time.

An especially interesting result occurs if we look at the point at declination 90°. This point is called the north celestial pole. It is very close to the position of the North Star, Polaris. The point is at altitude 40° and azimuth 0 all night. In fact, this point appears to remain in the same position all of the time. All the stars seem to move in circles around this point.

CALCULATING PLANETARY MOTION

Here is a more complicated example of a scientific application. We'll write a program that predicts the motion of a planet as seen from Earth. As in any scientific program, this one requires a great deal of specialized knowledge. However, we can use the same general strategy that we've used for the other programs we've written. The planetary motion program is very complicated, but it will help to divide the problem into smaller parts. Some physics ideas will be introduced as we go along.

We need to know that the planets move along orbits shaped like ellipses, with the sun at one focus. Our first task will be to figure out where along its ellipse a planet will be at a particular time. Since we need to know where the planet will be as seen from Earth, we'll calculate its right ascension and declination. Figure 15–2 shows our strategy at the most general level.

Now we'll begin work on a subroutine to trace the motion of a planet in its own orbit. To figure out the shape of the ellipse, (see Figure 15–3), we need to know the *semimajor axis* (*a*) and the *eccentricity* (*e*). From these values we can determine the *semiminor axis* (*b*):

$$b = a \sqrt{1 - e^2}$$

We'll draw in a standard *x–y* coordinate system, putting the *x* axis along the major axis of the ellipse. The origin of the coordinate system will be at the sun. That means that the center of the ellipse

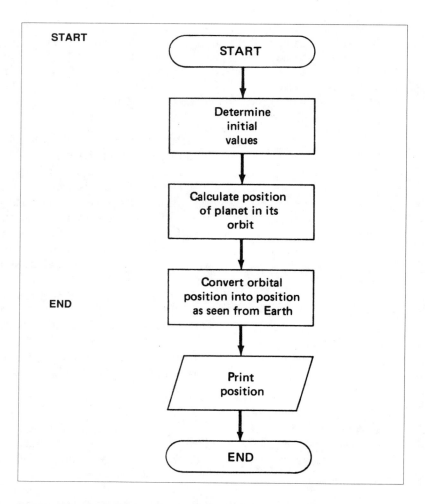

START

END

Figure 15-2

is the point $(-ea,0)$, so the equation of the ellipse becomes

$$\frac{(x + ea)^2}{a^2} + \frac{y^2}{b^2} = 1$$

We need to decide what units of measure to use. It will be awkward to measure the distances in miles or kilometers because then the numbers would be very big. Let's measure distance in million-kilometer units. It will be most convenient to measure time in units of days. Also, we'll need to know the position of the planet on the first day that we run the program. For example, if we start running the program on November 15, 1989, we'll need to know the position of the planet we're interested in on that date.

We'll use v_x to stand for the speed at which the planet is moving in the x direction, expressed in millions of kilometers per day. Then, in half an hour, the change in the x position will be

$$x = x + v_x \left(\frac{1}{48}\right)$$

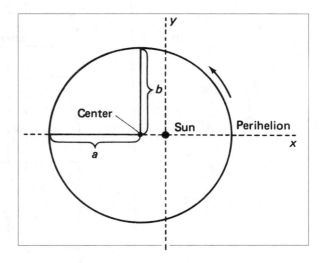

Figure 15-3

But v_x also changes during that half hour, according to the equation

$$v_x = v_x + a_x \left(\frac{1}{48}\right)$$

In this case, a_x is the *acceleration* in the x direction, which is given by

$$-\frac{Gx}{r^3}$$

where r is the distance from the planet to the sun, and $G = 991.047$, which is the gravitational constant multiplied by the mass of the sun.

Figure 15–4 shows the flowchart for the planetary motion subroutine.

We still need to perform the second general task. We must convert the planet's orbital motion into its position as seen from Earth. We need to break this job into four parts. First, we must calculate the sun-centered coordinates of the planet, relative to the plane of Earth's orbit, with the x axis pointed in a standard direction. We'll call these coordinates X1, Y1, and Z1. To perform this calculation, we need to know three numbers that determine the orientation of the planet's orbit: I, the angle of inclination, which tells how much the planet's orbit is tilted with respect to the orbit of Earth; L, the longitude of the ascending node, which tells the longitude of the point where the planet crosses the plane of Earth's orbit when the planet is going up; and M, the longitude of perihelion, which tells the longitude of the point where the planet is closest to the sun. (See Figures 15–5 and 15–6.) These calculations are carried out in the subroutine starting at line 500.

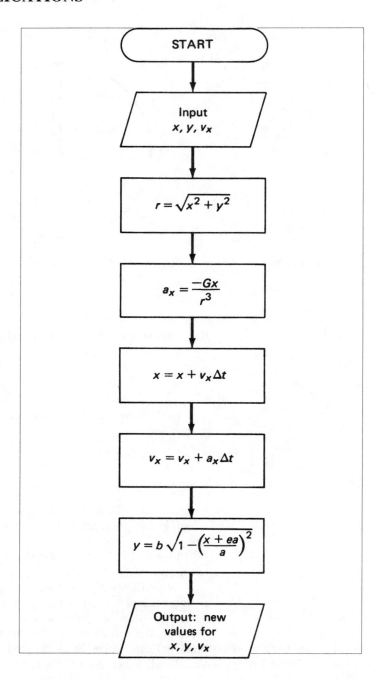

Figure 15-4

Second, we have to repeat exactly the same planetary motion program to find the position of Earth. We'll call the coordinates of Earth X5, Y5, and Z5. Third, once we know the sun-centered coordinates of Earth and the other planet, we need to calculate the Earth-centered coordinates of the planet. We'll call these coordinates X3, Y3, and Z3. Fourth, we need to convert the Earth-centered rectangular coordinates into right ascension and declination. (We should add one more task—we'll need to convert the day

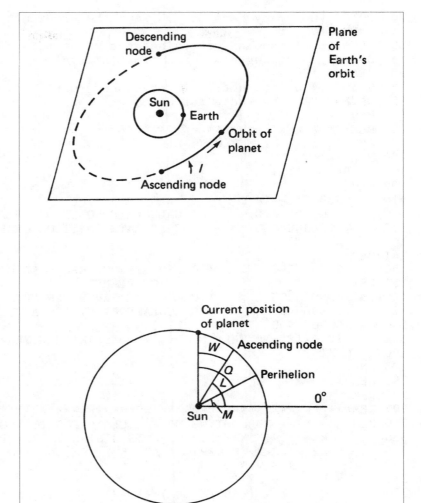

Figure 15-5

Figure 15-6

number we've been using in the calculations into a regular month and day of the month. Fortunately, we've already written a subroutine to do this. See Chapter 6.

Now that our strategy is all set, we need to go ahead and write the program:

```
1 REM   ********  PROGRAM TO CALCULATE PLANETARY POSITIONS
2 REM     This program calculates the motion of a selected
3 REM     planet and determines its position (right ascension
4 REM     and declination) as seen from earth.
5 REM     All distances are measured in units of
6 REM     million-kilometers.  All times are measured in
7 REM     units of days.  The program updates the position
8 REM     of the planet and the earth every half hour, and
9 REM     it displays the results once each day.  The
10 REM    program starts on November 15, 1989.
11 REM    This is Microsoft BASIC
50  GOSUB 1200    ' ***** INITIALIZE VALUES ***********
```

Continued

```
70    PRINT "How many days do you want the program to run";
75    INPUT T9
80    NP = 48      'number of periods per day
85    D=1/NP       'length of each time interval
90    YEAR = 1988
92    GOSUB 1700 'subroutine to start new year
95    DATE=318     'yeardate for November 14
97    REM
98    REM ****************************
99    REM    START MAIN BLOCK
100 FOR T=1 TO T9
105     DATE=DATE+1
109 REM
110     FOR T1 = 1 TO NP
120        GOSUB 300        ' CALCULATE POSITION OF PLANET
130        GOSUB 400        ' CALCULATE POSITION OF EARTH
140     NEXT T1
141 REM
150     GOSUB 500          ' CALCULATE SUN-CENTERED COORDINATES
151 REM                          OF PLANET
160     GOSUB 600          ' CALCULATE EARTH-CENTERED COORDINATES
170     GOSUB 700          ' CALCULATE RIGHT ASC AND DECLINATION
180     GOSUB 800          ' OUTPUT
185     IF DATE>=ND THEN GOSUB 1700 'START NEW YEAR
190    NEXT T
200 END
295 REM
296 REM
297 REM*****************************************************
300 REM----------SUBROUTINE TO CALCULATE POSITION OF PLANET--------
310      R = SQR(X*X+Y*Y)    ' R IS DISTANCE FROM PLANET TO SUN
320      A2 = -G*X/(R*R*R)   ' A2 IS X COMPONENT OF ACCELERATION
330      X = X + V * D
340      V = V + A2 * D
350      Q2 = 1 - ((ABS(X+E*A)/A))^2      ' Q2 IS A TEMPORARY VARIABLE
351         IF Q2<0 THEN LET Q2 = 0
352         Y = B*SQR(Q2)
353         IF V>0 THEN LET Y = -Y
360 RETURN
361 REM-----------------------------------------------
362 REM
363 REM
364 REM
399 REM*****************************************************
400 REM -------------SUBROUTINE TO CALCULATE POSITION OF EARTH
410      R0 = SQR(X0*X0+Y0*Y0)
420      A3 = -G * X0/(R0*R0*R0)
430      X0 = X0 + V0 * D
440      V0 = V0 + A3 * D
450      Q3 = 1 - (ABS((X0+E0*A0)/A0))^2
451         IF Q3<0 THEN LET Q3 = 0
452         Y0 = B0 * SQR(Q3)
453         IF V0 > 0 THEN LET Y0 = -Y0
460 RETURN
461 REM----------------------------------------
462 REM
```

```
463 REM
464 REM
499 REM*********************************************************
500 REM-------SUBROUTINE TO CALCULATE --------------------
501 REM          SUN-CENTERED COORDINATES OF PLANET
505    X9=X : Y9=Y : GOSUB 1000 : Q = Q9
506 REM          SUBROUTINE 1000 IS THE ARCTANGENT SUBROUTINE
507 REM          Q IS THE ANGLE FROM THE PLANET TO PERIHELION
510    W = Q - L + M    ' W IS ANGLE FROM PLANET TO ASCENDING NODE
519 REM
520    X2 = R * COS(W)
525    Z2 = R * SIN(W) * SIN (I)
530    Y2 = (SQR(R*R*SIN(W)*SIN(W) - Z2*Z2)) * SGN(SIN(W))
531 REM     X2,Y2,Z2 ARE COORDINATES IN PLANE OF EARTH'S ORBIT WITH
532 REM      X AXIS POINTING TO ASCENDING NODE
533 REM
549 REM
550  X1 = X2*COS(L) - Y2*SIN(L)
555  Y1 = X2*SIN(L) + Y2*COS(L)
560  Z1 = Z2
561 REM          X1,Y1,Z1 ARE THE COORDINATES OF THE PLANET
562 REM          WITH THE X AXIS POINTING TO 0 DEGREES
563 REM          HELIOCENTRIC LONGITUDE
564 REM
570 RETURN
571 REM--------------------------------------------------------
572 REM
573 REM
574 REM*****************************************************
600 REM--------SUBROUTINE TO CALCULATE EARTH CENTERED----------
601 REM                     COORDINATES
605    X5 = X0*COS(M0) - Y0 * SIN(M0)
610    Y5 = Y0 * COS(M0) + X0 * SIN(M0)
615    Z5 = 0
616 REM    X5,Y5,Z5 ARE COORDINATES OF EARTH WITH X AXIS
617 REM     POINTING TO 0 DEGREES HELIOCENTRIC LONGITUDE
618 REM . . . . .
630    X3 = X1 - X5
635    Y3 = Y1 - Y5
640    Z3 = Z1 - Z5
641 REM  X3,Y3,Z3 ARE RECTANGULAR COORDINATES AS SEEN FROM EARTH
650 RETURN
651 REM-------------------------------------------------
653 REM
654 REM*****************************************************
700 REM-------SUBROUTINE TO CALCULATE RA AND DEC---------
705          X4 = X3
710          Y4 = Y3 * COS(H) - Z3 * SIN(H)
715          Z4 = Y3 * SIN(H) + Z3 * COS(H)
720 REM    CALCULATE RIGHT ASCENSION
721          Y9 = Y4 : X9 = X4 : GOSUB 1000 : RA = Q9
730 REM    CALCULATE DECLINATION
731          Y9 = Z4 : X9 = SQR(X4*X4 + Y4*Y4)
732            GOSUB 1000 :     DEC = Q9
740 REM    CONVERT RA TO HOURS
741            RA = RA * 12/PI
```

Continued

```
750 REM    CONVERT DEC TO DEGREES
751            DEC = DEC * 180/PI
755         IF DEC>180 THEN LET DEC = DEC - 360
760 RETURN
761 REM--------------------------------------------
762 REM
763 REM
764 REM*********************************************
800 REM----------OUTPUT------------------------
810    GOSUB 1100      ' CALCULATE MONTH AND DAY
820    LPRINT "          ";M1$; : LPRINT USING "###";MD;
824    REM    CONVERT RA TO HOURS/MINUTES
825    RH=INT(RA):RM=(RA-RH)*60
829    REM    CONVERT DEC TO DEGREES/MINUTES
830    D2=ABS(DEC):DD=INT(D2):DM=(D2-DD)*60:DD=DD*SGN(DEC)
835    LPRINT USING "######";RH;
836    LPRINT USING "####.#";RM;
837    LPRINT USING "########";DD;
838    LPRINT USING "####.#";DM
851 REM-----------------------------------
853 REM
854 IF O2 = 0 THEN GOTO 870
855 REM     -- DETAILED OUTPUT --
856 PRINT "X=";X;" Y=";Y
857 PRINT "X0=";X0;" Y0=";Y0
858 PRINT "X2=";X2;" Y2=";Y2;" Z2=";Z2
860 PRINT "X1=";X1;" Y1=";Y1;" Z1=";Z1
862 PRINT "X5=";X5;" Y5=";Y5;" Z5=";Z5
864 PRINT "X3=";X3;" Y3=";Y3;" Z3=";Z3
866 PRINT "X4=";X4;" Y4=";Y4;" Z4=";Z4
870 RETURN
998 REM
999 REM *********************************
1000 REM --------ARCTANGENT SUBROUTINE------------
1001 REM: THIS SUBROUTINE CALCULATES THE ARCTANGENT OF
1002 REM Y9/X9, WITH THE RESULT PLACED IN THE CORRECT QUADRANT
1010 Q9 = ATN(Y9/X9)
1020 IF X9 < 0 THEN LET Q9 = Q9 + PI
1030 IF Q9 < 0 THEN LET Q9 = Q9 + 2*PI
1040 RETURN '------------------------------------
1042 REM
1099 REM*********************************************
1100 REM--------DATE CONVERSION SUBROUTINE---------------
1110 FOR M8 = 1 TO 12
1120 IF DATE <= (M1(M8+1)) THEN GOTO 1140
1130 NEXT M8
1140    MD = DATE - M1(M8)
1150 M1$ = M2$(M8)
1160 RETURN
1198 REM
1199 REM*********************************************
1200 REM-------------INITIALIZE----------------------
1205 REM              DATA FOR EARTH
1208 REM POSITIONS ARE FOR NOVEMBER 15, 1989
1210 X0=94.646
1220 V0= 1.9798
1225 M0 = 1.78979    '   LONGITUDE OF PERIHELION
```

```
1230 A0 = 149.5      '   SEMIMAJOR AXIS
1240 E0 = 0.01673    '   ECCENTRICITY
1260 B0 = A0*SQR(1 - E0*E0)
1270    Q2 = 1 - (ABS((X0 + E0*A0)/A0))^2
1275    IF Q2 < 0 THEN LET Q2 = 0
1280 Y0 = B0*SQR(Q2)
1285    IF V0 > 0 THEN LET Y0 = -Y0
1288 H = 0.40928    'TILT OF EARTH'S AXIS (IN RADIANS)
1289 G = 991.047    'GRAV CONSTANT TIMES MASS OF SUN
1290 PI = 4*ATN(1)  'PI = 3.14159 ...
1295 DIM D9(4,7)     'D9 HOLDS ORBITAL DATA FOR THE PLANETS
1300 FOR J1 = 1 TO 4 : FOR J2 = 1 TO 7 : READ D9(J1,J2)
1302           NEXT J2   : NEXT J1
1305 REM DATA ARRAY
1306 REM DATA FOR EACH PLANET ARE IN THIS ORDER:
1307 REM: X COORD, VELOCITY, SEMI-MAJOR AXIS, ECCENTRICITY
1308 REM: LONG ASCENDING NODE, LONG PERIHELION, INCLINATION
1309 REM . . . . . .VENUS. . . . . . . .
1310 DATA  -48.899, 2.707, 108.1, 0.00679
1312 DATA  1.3356, 2.2858, 0.059236
1315 REM
1319 REM    MARS
1320 DATA  -145.945, 1.662, 227.8, 0.09337
1322 DATA  0.86268, 5.86067, 0.03229
1325 REM
1329 REM        JUPITER
1330 DATA 175.874, -1.010, 778, 0.04844
1332 DATA 1.7508, 0.2648, 0.022776
1335 REM
1339 REM        SATURN
1340 DATA -1465.12, 0.1866, 1426, 0.05568
1342 DATA 1.98105, 1.6612, 0.043459
1345 REM
1350 PRINT "TYPE YES IF YOU WANT DETAILED OUTPUT"
1355 O2 = 0
1360 INPUT O3$ : IF O3$ = "YES" THEN O2 = 1
1400 PRINT "INPUT NAME OF PLANET:"
1405 INPUT P5$
1408    P6 = 0
1410 IF P5$ = "VENUS" THEN LET P6 = 1
1412 IF P5$ = "MARS" THEN LET P6 = 2
1414 IF P5$ = "JUPITER" THEN LET P6 = 3
1416 IF P5$ = "SATURN" THEN LET P6 = 4
1418 IF P6 = 0 THEN GOTO 1400
1450 X = D9(P6,1)    ' INITIAL X COORDINATE OF PLANET
1460 V = D9(P6,2)    ' INITIAL X COMPONENT OF VELOCITY
1470 A = D9(P6,3)    ' SEMIMAJOR AXIS OF PLANET
1480 E = D9(P6,4)    ' ECCENTRICITY OF PLANET'S ORBIT
1490 L = D9(P6,5)    ' LONGITUDE OF ASCENDING NODE
1500 M = D9(P6,6)    ' LONGITUDE OF PERIHELION
1510 I = D9(P6,7)    ' INCLINATION OF PLANET'S ORBIT
1520 B = A* SQR(1 - E * E)
1530    Q2 = 1 - (ABS((X + E*A)/A))^ 2
1540    IF Q2 < 0 THEN LET Q2 = 0
1550 Y = B * SQR(Q2)
1560    IF V > 0 THEN LET Y = -Y
```

Continued

```
1562 IF O2 = 0 THEN GOTO 1570
1564   PRINT   "A=";A;" B= ";B;" E=";E
1566   PRINT   "L=";L;" M= ";M;" X=';X
1568   PRINT   "Y=";Y;" V=";V  : PRINT " " : PRINT " "
1569 REM
1570 REM
1600 REM --- INITIALIZE DATE SUBROUTINE VARIABLES
1610 DIM M2$(12)
1620 FOR M8 = 1 TO 12
1630 READ M2$(M8)
1640 NEXT M8
1650 DATA "Jan","Feb","Mar","Apr","May","Jun"
1652 DATA "Jly","Aug","Sep","Oct","Nov","Dec"
1660 DIM M1(13),M7(13)
1670 FOR M8 = 1 TO 13
1680 READ M7(M8)
1685 NEXT M8
1690 DATA 0,31,59,90,120,151,181,212,243,273,304,334,365
1695 RETURN '--------------------
1696 REM
1697 REM
1699 REM ********************************
1700 REM     SUBROUTINE TO START NEW YEAR
1705    YEAR=YEAR+1
1710    GOSUB 1800   'PRINT HEADINGS
1720    DATE=0
1730    FOR M8=1 TO 13:M1(M8)=M7(M8):NEXT M8
1740    ND=365
1745    IF (YEAR/4)<>INT(YEAR/4 )THEN RETURN
1749    REM - LEAP YEAR
1750    ND=366
1755    FOR M8=3 TO 13:M1(M8)=M1(M8)+1:NEXT M8
1760 RETURN
1799 REM ********************************
1800 REM   SUBROUTINE TO PRINT HEADINGS
1810    PRINT TAB(15);P5$;"  ";YEAR
1820    PRINT "        Date        RA         Dec"
1825    PRINT "                  Hrs   Min    Deg   Min"
1830 RETURN
```

Here are some samples of the output from this program:

```
        VENUS    1989
  Date          RA          Dec
             Hrs   Min     Deg   Min
Nov 15      18   45.3     -26   35.5
Nov 16      18   49.5     -26   30.1
Nov 17      18   53.6     -26   24.1
Nov 18      18   57.7     -26   17.7
Nov 19      19    1.7     -26   10.7
Nov 20      19    5.7     -26    3.1
```

Date	RA Hrs	Min	Dec Deg	Min
Nov 21	19	9.6	-25	55.1
Nov 22	19	13.5	-25	46.7
Nov 23	19	17.3	-25	37.7
Nov 24	19	21.1	-25	28.3
Nov 25	19	24.7	-25	18.5
Nov 26	19	28.4	-25	8.2
Nov 27	19	31.9	-24	57.5
Nov 28	19	35.4	-24	46.4
Nov 29	19	38.8	-24	35.0
Nov 30	19	42.1	-24	23.2
Dec 1	19	45.3	-24	11.0
Dec 2	19	48.5	-23	58.6
Dec 3	19	51.5	-23	45.8
Dec 4	19	54.5	-23	32.7
Dec 5	19	57.4	-23	19.4
Dec 6	20	0.2	-23	5.8
Dec 7	20	2.9	-22	52.0
Dec 8	20	5.5	-22	37.9
Dec 9	20	8.0	-22	23.7
Dec 10	20	10.4	-22	9.3
Dec 11	20	12.6	-21	54.8
Dec 12	20	14.8	-21	40.1
Dec 13	20	16.8	-21	25.3
Dec 14	20	18.8	-21	10.4
Dec 15	20	20.5	-20	55.5
Dec 16	20	22.2	-20	40.5
Dec 17	20	23.8	-20	25.5
Dec 18	20	25.2	-20	10.4
Dec 19	20	26.5	-19	55.4
Dec 20	20	27.6	-19	40.4
Dec 21	20	28.6	-19	25.4
Dec 22	20	29.5	-19	10.4
Dec 23	20	30.2	-18	55.5
Dec 24	20	30.9	-18	40.7

MARS   1989

Date	RA Hrs	Min	Dec Deg	Min
Nov 15	14	23.4	-13	49.0
Nov 16	14	26.0	-14	2.6
Nov 17	14	28.7	-14	16.1
Nov 18	14	31.3	-14	29.5
Nov 19	14	34.0	-14	42.7
Nov 20	14	36.7	-14	55.9
Nov 21	14	39.3	-15	9.0
Nov 22	14	42.0	-15	21.9
Nov 23	14	44.7	-15	34.8
Nov 24	14	47.4	-15	47.5
Nov 25	14	50.1	-16	0.1
Nov 26	14	52.8	-16	12.6
Nov 27	14	55.5	-16	25.0
Nov 28	14	58.3	-16	37.3
Nov 29	15	1.0	-16	49.4
Nov 30	15	3.8	-17	1.4
Dec 1	15	6.5	-17	13.3
Dec 2	15	9.3	-17	25.1

Continued

```
Dec   3    15   12.1      -17   36.7
Dec   4    15   14.8      -17   48.2
Dec   5    15   17.6      -17   59.6
Dec   6    15   20.4      -18   10.8
Dec   7    15   23.2      -18   21.9
Dec   8    15   26.0      -18   32.8
Dec   9    15   28.9      -18   43.6
Dec  10    15   31.7      -18   54.2
Dec  11    15   34.5      -19    4.7
Dec  12    15   37.4      -19   15.0
Dec  13    15   40.3      -19   25.2
Dec  14    15   43.1      -19   35.2
Dec  15    15   46.0      -19   45.1
Dec  16    15   48.9      -19   54.8
Dec  17    15   51.8      -20    4.4
Dec  18    15   54.7      -20   13.7
Dec  19    15   57.6      -20   23.0
Dec  20    16    0.5      -20   32.0
Dec  21    16    3.5      -20   40.9
Dec  22    16    6.4      -20   49.6
Dec  23    16    9.4      -20   58.1
Dec  24    16   12.3      -21    6.5
```

JUPITER   1989

Date	RA		Dec	
	Hrs	Min	Deg	Min
Nov 15	6	43.7	22	50.9
Nov 16	6	43.4	22	51.3
Nov 17	6	43.1	22	51.8
Nov 18	6	42.8	22	52.2
Nov 19	6	42.5	22	52.6
Nov 20	6	42.1	22	53.1
Nov 21	6	41.7	22	53.5
Nov 22	6	41.4	22	54.0
Nov 23	6	41.0	22	54.5
Nov 24	6	40.6	22	55.0
Nov 25	6	40.1	22	55.5
Nov 26	6	39.7	22	56.0
Nov 27	6	39.3	22	56.5
Nov 28	6	38.8	22	57.0
Nov 29	6	38.4	22	57.6
Nov 30	6	37.9	22	58.1
Dec 1	6	37.4	22	58.7
Dec 2	6	36.9	22	59.2
Dec 3	6	36.4	22	59.8
Dec 4	6	35.9	23	0.3
Dec 5	6	35.4	23	0.9
Dec 6	6	34.8	23	1.4
Dec 7	6	34.3	23	2.0
Dec 8	6	33.7	23	2.6
Dec 9	6	33.2	23	3.1
Dec 10	6	32.6	23	3.7
Dec 11	6	32.0	23	4.3
Dec 12	6	31.4	23	4.8
Dec 13	6	30.8	23	5.4
Dec 14	6	30.2	23	5.9
Dec 15	6	29.6	23	6.5

Date	RA Hrs	Min	Dec Deg	Min
Dec 16	6	29.0	23	7.0
Dec 17	6	28.4	23	7.6
Dec 18	6	27.8	23	8.1
Dec 19	6	27.2	23	8.7
Dec 20	6	26.6	23	9.2
Dec 21	6	25.9	23	9.7
Dec 22	6	25.3	23	10.2
Dec 23	6	24.7	23	10.7
Dec 24	6	24.0	23	11.2

SATURN   1989

Date	RA		Dec	
	Hrs	Min	Deg	Min
Nov 15	18	59.8	-22	31.0
Nov 16	19	0.2	-22	30.5
Nov 17	19	0.6	-22	30.1
Nov 18	19	1.0	-22	29.6
Nov 19	19	1.4	-22	29.1
Nov 20	19	1.8	-22	28.6
Nov 21	19	2.2	-22	28.1
Nov 22	19	2.6	-22	27.6
Nov 23	19	3.0	-22	27.0
Nov 24	19	3.4	-22	26.5
Nov 25	19	3.8	-22	25.9
Nov 26	19	4.3	-22	25.4
Nov 27	19	4.7	-22	24.8
Nov 28	19	5.1	-22	24.2
Nov 29	19	5.6	-22	23.6
Nov 30	19	6.0	-22	23.0
Dec 1	19	6.4	-22	22.4
Dec 2	19	6.9	-22	21.7
Dec 3	19	7.3	-22	21.1
Dec 4	19	7.8	-22	20.4
Dec 5	19	8.2	-22	19.8
Dec 6	19	8.7	-22	19.1
Dec 7	19	9.2	-22	18.4
Dec 8	19	9.6	-22	17.7
Dec 9	19	10.1	-22	17.0
Dec 10	19	10.6	-22	16.3
Dec 11	19	11.0	-22	15.6
Dec 12	19	11.5	-22	14.9
Dec 13	19	12.0	-22	14.1
Dec 14	19	12.5	-22	13.4
Dec 15	19	13.0	-22	12.6
Dec 16	19	13.4	-22	11.9
Dec 17	19	13.9	-22	11.1
Dec 18	19	14.4	-22	10.3
Dec 19	19	14.9	-22	9.5
Dec 20	19	15.4	-22	8.7
Dec 21	19	15.9	-22	7.9
Dec 22	19	16.4	-22	7.1
Dec 23	19	16.9	-22	6.2
Dec 24	19	17.4	-22	5.4

These results are not perfectly accurate, since there are other factors that complicate planetary motion that we have not considered.

THIS IS ONLY THE BEGINNING

By now you have seen some examples of the many tasks that can be done by computers, and you have seen how to give instructions to a computer to get it to do what you want it to do. Your skill with programming will grow even more with further practice. If you have a home computer, you will most likely think of many more jobs that you would like your computer to do for you. Or you might be interested in one of the many jobs that involve working with computers, in which case your knowledge of BASIC will help you understand computers.

Once you have a computer to spare you from having to do boring work, you are free to concentrate on much more creative and interesting tasks. This is only the beginning of what you might be able to accomplish.

EXERCISES

1. Suppose P is a one-dimensional array in which $P(I)$ is the number of people in the country of age I. Suppose that, for every 1,000 people from ages 20 to 35, there are 66 people born each year. Suppose that, from ages 0 to 50, 90% of the people will survive to the next age; and that for people over age 51, 60% will survive to the next age. Write a program that calculates what the age distribution of the population will look like each year for the next 20 years.

2. Follow the same procedure as for Exercise 1, using the current age distribution of the United States population, as well as actual values for the birth rate and death rate by age. Forecast what the age distribution of the population will look like every year for the next 30 years. For each year, calculate the ratio of working-age people (ages 20 to 64) to retirement age people (ages 65 and above).

3. Follow the same procedure as for exercise 2, but compare the effects of the following contrasting assumptions:

Assumption 1: The birth rate at all ages falls to 80% of its current value, and the death rate at all ages falls to 80% of its current value.

Assumption 2: The birth rate at each age rises to 120% of its current value, and the death rate at each age also rises to 120% of its current value.

4. Write a program that demonstrates Kepler's law of planetary motion, which states that the ratio of the cube of a planet's mean distance from the sun divided by the square of its orbital period is the same for all nine planets in the solar system.

5. Write a program that reads in the values for the coefficients a, b, c, d, e, and r, and then performs the division problem

$$\frac{ax^4 + bx^3 + cx^2 + dx + e}{x - r}$$

by using synthetic division. (Refer to a book on algebra to see how synthetic division works.)

6. Write a program that reads in the size of an object and its distance and then computes its apparent angular size. Here are some sample objects:

Object	Size	Distance
Mt. Rainier, seen from Seattle	2.7 miles	60 miles
Width of Central Park, seen from the Empire State Building	3,000 feet	8,000 feet
Moon	3500 kilometers	384,000 kilometers
Sun	864,000 miles	93 million miles
Saturn	75,000 miles	800 million miles
Star Antares	5.5×10^8 miles	2.3×10^{15} miles
Andromeda galaxy	130,000 light years	2.2 million light years

7. Suppose an economy is governed by these three equations:

$$Y_t = C_t + I_t$$
$$C_t = 50 + 0.5\ Y_t$$
$$I_t = 0.5 * (Y_{t-1} - Y_{t-2})$$

where Y_t is gross national product (GNP) in year t, Y_{t-1} is gross national product last year, Y_{t-2} is GNP two years ago, C_t is consumption spending in year t, and I_t, is investment spending. If $Y = 105$ in 1989 and $Y = 95$ in 1988, what will Y be for each year for the next 20 years? (In economics this type of model is called a *multiplier accelerator* model.) How will the results change if the third equation becomes as follows?

$$I_t = 0.65 * (Y_{t-1} - Y_{t-2})$$

8. Modify the planet program included in the chapter to also tell in what zodiac constellation the planet will appear.

9. When parallel light rays strike a parabolic mirror, they will be reflected back. Write a program that reads in the distance of a particular light ray from the axis of the parabola and then calculates where that light ray will cross the axis after it has been reflected.

10. Write a program similar to the one for exercise 9, but have the light rays strike a spherical mirror.

11. Ohm's law says that $I = V/R$, where V is the voltage in an electronic circuit, R is the resistance (in ohms), and I is the current

(in amperes). Write a program that reads in values for V and R and then calculates I.

12. Write a program that calculates the total impedance in an ac electrical circuit that has frequency f, a capacitor of capacitance C, and an inductor with inductance L. (Refer to a book on electronics.)

13. Write a program that prints a triangle such that each number in the triangle is equal to the sum of the two numbers above it. (This arrangement is known as Pascal's triangle.) The top part of the triangle looks like this:

$$
\begin{array}{c}
1 \\
1\ 1 \\
1\ 2\ 1 \\
1\ 3\ 3\ 1 \\
1\ 4\ 6\ 4\ 1
\end{array}
$$

14. Some gases obey the van der Waals equation of state, which tells the temperature of 1 mole of the gas if the pressure is P and the volume is V:

$$\left(P \ + \ \frac{a}{V^2}\right)(V - b) \ = RT$$

R is the gas constant, which has the value 8.31; a and b are two constants that depend on the type of gas. Write a program that reads in the values of P, V, a, and b and then calculates the temperature.

15. Write a program that reads in the mass of two objects (in kilograms) and their distance apart (in meters) and then calculates the force of gravity between them from the following formula:

$$F \ = \ \frac{Gm_1 m_2}{r^2}$$

where $G = 6.67 \times 10^{-11} m^3/\text{kg--sec}^2$.

16. Write a program that reads in the longitude and latitude of two points on the surface of Earth and then prints the longitude and latitude of five points along the shortest route between them. (The shortest distance is known as the great circle distance.)

17. Write a program that calculates the correlation coefficient between the measurement of two variables. (Refer to a book on statistics.)

18. Write a program that reads in the mass of an object in

grams and then calculates the equivalent energy from the formula $E = mc^2$. Here c is the speed of light, which is 3×10^{10} cm/sec. The result for energy will be measured in a unit called the erg.

19. The theory of relativity says that, if an object is traveling past you at a high speed, it will appear shorter to you than it would if you observed it when it was at rest. If the length of a rod at rest is L and it is moving with velocity v, then its length as it will look to you is given by the following formula:

$$\frac{L}{\sqrt{1 - v^2/c^2}}$$

Write a program to calculate its length.

20. Write a program that calculates how much the frequency (i.e., the color) of light will shift because of the Doppler effect when the light source is moving away from you at velocity v. (Refer to a physics book.)

APPENDIX 1

SUMMARY OF BASIC

PART 1   BASIC TO ENGLISH DICTIONARY

SYMBOLS

Letters
A, B, C, D, E, F, G, H, I, J, K, L, M, N, O, P, Q, R, S, T, U, V, W, X, Y, Z

Digits
0, 1, 2, 3, 4, 5, 6, 7, 8, 9

Operations

+	Addition
−	Subtraction
*	Multiplication
/	Division
↑ or ** or ^	Exponentiation

Other symbols

=	Equals in assignment statement or condition
( )	Parentheses for grouping
'	Separator
;	Separator
"	Quotation mark to enclose character strings
:	Separator for two statements on the same line
$	Symbol for character string variables
<	Less than
>	Greater than
>=	Greater than or equal to
<=	Less than or equal to
<>	Not equal

Exponential notation
Example: 5.4 E 6 means $5.4 \times 10^6 = 5,400,000$

COMMANDS

Items in italics can be replaced by appropriate items of your choosing. Lower-case *x* and *y* stand for variable names; *n* stands for numbers. Items in capital letters must be typed exactly as shown. Only commands that are standard in almost all systems are included. In particular, character string functions will depend greatly on the specific computer being used; therefore, check a manual for your computer.

ABS(*x*) Built-in function: absolute value

ATN(*x*) Built-in function: arctangent (the result is in radians)

COS(*x*) Built-in function: cosine of *x* (*x* must be in radians)

DATA *n1,n2,...* Creates a data stack of the values *n1,n2,....* The values in the stack will be assigned to variables by the use of the READ command.

DEF FN*x*(*y*) = *expression* The DEF command creates a user-defined function with the name FN*x(y)*. (See Chapter 6.)

DIM *x*(*n*) Declares that *x* will be a one-dimensional array with *n* elements.

DIM *x*(*n1,n2*) Declares that *x* will be a two-dimensional array with *n*1 rows and *n*2 columns.

END The statement at the end of the program that tells the computer that the program is completed.

EXP(*x*) Built in function: e^x.

FOR . . .The first statement in a loop. See general form, Chapter 4.

GOSUB *sn* Tells the computer to begin executing a subroutine that starts at statement number *sn*.

GOTO *sn* Tells the computer that the next statement to be executed is the statement with the number *sn*.

IF *condition* THEN *action*

The *condition* is a statement involving comparison symbols (such as =, >, or <) that is either true or false; if the condition is true, then the *action* is performed; otherwise the *action* is not performed.

INPUT *x* Command causes the computer to stop, display a question mark, and wait for the user to type in a value; it then assigns that value to the variable *x*.

INPUT *x,y* Same as above, except two values must be typed in.

INPUT *"message";x* Same as INPUT *x*, except *message* will be displayed instead of the question mark.

INT(*x*) Built-in function: greatest integer smaller than *x*.

LET *x* = *expression* Calculates the value of *expression* and then assigns that value to *x*. (The use of LET is optional.)

LN(*x*) Built-in function: logarithm to the base *e*.

LOG(*x*) Built-in function: logarithm to the base 10. [On some computers LOG(*x*) will be the log to the base *e*.]

NEXT *x* The last statement in a loop. (See Chapter 4.)

PRINT *x* Causes the value of *x* to be printed (or displayed on the screen if you are using a television terminal.)

PRINT *"chars"* Causes the characters *chars* to be printed.

PRINT *item1, item2* Causes the two items to be printed, separated by a standard amount.

PRINT *item1;item2* Causes the two items to be printed right next to each other.

READ *x* Causes the top value of the data stack to be assigned to the variable *x*. (Data stacks are created with DATA statements.)

REM Causes the computer to ignore the rest of that line, thereby allowing a messsage for the programmers to be included in the program.

RETURN The statement at the end of a subroutine. See Chapter 6.

SGN(x) Built-in function: SGN(x) is 1 if $x > 0$; SGN(x) is 0 if $x = 0$; SGN(x) is -1 if $x < 0$.

SIN(x) Built-in function: sine of x (x must be in radians)

STEP Used with FOR-NEXT loop. (See Chapter 4.)

SQR(x) Built-in function: square root of x.

TAB Used as follows:

PRINT TAB(x); item causes item to be printed starting at column x of the screen.

TAN(x) Built-in function: tangent of x (x must be in radians)

TO Used with FOR-NEXT loop. (See Chapter 4.)

USING Used as follows:

PRINT USING"###.##";x means that x is to be printed with two digits to the right and three digits to the left of the decimal point. In general, the USING command is followed by a format string, which tells the computer what format to follow when printing the output. In the format string, # represents a digit, and . represents a decimal point.

PART 2   ENGLISH TO BASIC DICTIONARY

addition Addition is symbolized by +, as in 2 + 2 or A + B.

array An array is a collection of numbers or character strings stored by the computer under a single name. The size of an array is determined by the DIM command.

character string variable A character string variable is a variable that represents a group of characters. Character string variable names end with a $ sign. For example, A$ = "JOHN JONES" and X2$ = "EARTH" are both character string variables.

comment A comment is a statement beginning with the keyword REM that explains what a program does.

conditional command A conditional command is a statement that begins with the keyword IF. The command will be done only if the specified condition is true.

division Division is symbolized by /, as in 25/5 or A1/H.

exponentiation Exponentiation is symbolized by an arrow, ↑ (or by ∧ on some computers), as in 2 ↑ 10, or X ↑ 2.

function, built-in   BASIC comes with many built-in functions, including ABS, ATN, COS, EXP, INT, LN, LOG, SGN, SQR, and TAN. Character string functions available on some systems include LEN, LEFT\$, RIGHT\$, MID\$, ASC, CHR\$, VAL, and STR\$.

function, programmer-defined   A programmer-defined function is created with a DEF statement, such as:

$$DEF\ FNA\ (X) = X \uparrow 2 + 3 * X.$$

grouping   Parentheses, ( ), are used for grouping. When parentheses enclose an operation, that operation is done before operations that are not enclosed by parentheses.

input   "Input" refers to the data that are read into the computer. In BASIC the commands INPUT and READ are used for input.

letter   A letter can be used as a variable name. A variable is a symbol that represents a value, as in X = 10. A letter followed by a \$ sign stands for a character string variable.

loop   A loop is a sequence of statements that will be executed a specified number of times. A loop begins with a FOR statement and ends with a NEXT statement.

multiplication   Multiplication is symbolized by $*$, as in 4 $*$ 4 or 10 $*$ N.

output   "Output" refers to the results communicated from the computer to the programmer. In BASIC the command PRINT is used to direct output.

random number   The RND function in BASIC generates a random number between 0 and 1.

string variable   A string variable is a group of characters. See **character string variable.**

subroutine   A subroutine is a segment of a program that starts being executed when a GOSUB command is encountered. The subroutine ends with a RETURN statement, at which point the computer goes back to executing the main program.

subtraction   Subtraction is symbolized by –, as in 10 – 7 or U–V.

word A word can be stored as a character string variable, which is named by a letter or a letter and one digit followed by a \$ sign. Here are examples of words stored as character string variables:

A\$ = "UNITED STATES OF AMERICA", C2\$ = "BASIC".

PART 3: Advanced Versions of BASIC

It can be difficult to write complicated programs using traditional versions of the BASIC language (such as those described in this book). As a result, in recent years some advanced versions of BASIC have been introduced that include some features often found in other programming languages that make it easier to develop large programs. These versions include QuickBASIC from Microsoft and Turbo BASIC from Borland International. This section will discuss some of the distinctive features of Quick-BASIC:

1. Line numbers are not required. When writing a program using traditional versions of BASIC, it is a good idea to use line numbers that are multiples of 10 so that there is room to insert new lines into the program later. However, it is very difficult to insert a long block of statements between two existing program lines. This problem is avoided in QuickBASIC since line numbers are not needed. However, QuickBASIC does allow line numbers to be used, which makes it easier to run a program that has been written with another version of Microsoft BASIC (such as BASICA on the IBM PC).

2. Subroutines can be given names. We have seen that the variable names that you use in a program should give some indication of the meaning of each variable. For the same reason, it helps if a subroutine has a name that describes what the subroutine does. When you are writing a program in a traditional version of BASIC and you come to a place where you need a GOSUB statement, you might not know the line number where the subroutine will start. Then you will have to leave the space for the line number blank, filling it in later after you have written the subroutine. This makes the process of writing the program more difficult.

In QuickBASIC, the first line of a subroutine contains the word SUB, followed by the name of the subroutine and a list of variables whose values are to be passed to the subroutine (called the list of parameters). The end of the subroutine is marked by the line END SUB. (In traditional BASIC, the command RETURN marks the end of a subroutine, but there is no command that is required to mark the beginning of a subroutine. We have seen that the beginning of a subroutine should be marked with a REM statement indicating what the subroutine does.) The CALL command is used to tell the computer to begin executing a QuickBASIC subroutine. The CALL command is similar to the GOSUB command.

In QuickBASIC, it is also possible to include user-defined functions that require several lines for the function definition. (Remember that functions defined using the DEF command in traditional versions of BASIC are limited to definitions that consist of one line; thus, for example, they may not include IF statements.)

3. The variables that appear in a QuickBASIC subroutine are local variables, which means that they will be recognized only within the subroutine where they belong (unless they are specifically declared to be global variables.) The same variable name might be used for another local variable in another subroutine. Traditional versions of BASIC do not allow for local variables, which means that if you use a variable name I at one point in the program, it will refer to the same variable as does the name I anywhere else in the program. This can make it very difficult to construct large programs, because you have to worry about the fact that assigning a value to a variable in one subroutine will assign the same value to that variable throughout the entire program. It is easier to write a large program if each subroutine can be written independently, without worrying about the effects it might have on other subroutines.

4. QuickBASIC operates as a compiler, which means that programs can run much more quickly. A compiler translates the entire program into machine language before it begins to execute it. By contrast, most versions of BASIC use an interpreter, which has to decipher the meaning of each program line each time it reaches it. A compiler also makes it possible to prepare a machine language version of the program which can be run independently, even if you don't have the disk containing BASIC with you.

5. QuickBASIC comes with a full-screen editor to type your programs into the computer. A full-screen editor makes it possible for you to type at any location in the screen, which helps considerably if you decide to change something on a line other than the line you are currently typing. It uses a system of menus, which makes it easy to switch between editing the program and running it. If you are using a computer that comes equipped with a mouse, you can take advantage of the mouse's ability to move the mouse pointer around the screen to make selections from the menus.

It is quite possible that the version of BASIC you have already learned will be adequate for all the programs you will ever need to write. As we have shown in this book, it is possible to write complex programs in traditional versions of BASIC, provided that you are careful to include GOSUB and REM statements to break the program into smaller sections. Even though a compiled program can run faster than a program that is run with an interpreter, an interpreter is usually a bit easier to use. However, if you will be spending a lot of time writing very complicated programs, you will probably find that you should learn a version of BASIC better suited for that purpose, such as QuickBASIC, or else learn another programming language, such as Pascal.

ANSWERS TO SELECTED EXERCISES

$\mathbf{I}$n this section are given possible solutions to some of the exercises at the ends of the chapters. To save space, the programs shown here often do not print labels. When you write a program that you are actually going to use, you should always include labels for the input and output. Also, a program in regular use should contain a way to test for bad input data. For example, if a program that is going to calculate the balance in a bank account finds that the value read in for the interest rate is negative, the program should ask for a new number.

CHAPTER 1

1. $(10/4)/(16/3)$

2. $12/(3/2)$

4. $1/(1 + X \uparrow 2)$

5. $A * X \uparrow 2 + B * X + C$

7. $1/((1/A) + (1/B))$

21. No. The parentheses are mismatched.

23. No. A negative number cannot be raised to the $\frac{1}{2}$ power. (Many BASIC systems do not allow any negative number to be raised to a power.)

31. No; 4A and 10B are both illegal expressions.

33. 0.416667

34. 6.6667

35. 0.416667

36. 0.416667

37. 6.66667

38. 346

39. ZABCZ

    ABCDEFZABCZ
40. 250

    25
41. HELLO GOODBYE.HELLO GOODBYE.
42. FEBRUARY

    FEBRUARY
43. .333333

    .857143

CHAPTER 2

4.
```
1   REM  PROGRAM TO CONVERT K KILOMETERS
2   REM     INTO M MILES
10  INPUT K
20  M = K * 0.621
30  PRINT M : END
```

5.
```
1   REM  PROGRAM TO CONVERT P1 $ PER LITER
2   REM     INTO P2 $ PER GALLON
10  INPUT P1
20  P2 = P1 * 3.785
30  PRINT P2 : END
```

7.
```
10  INPUT "MONTHLY INFLATION RATE:" ;M
20  Y = (1 + M) ↑ 12 − 1
30  PRINT "ANNUAL INFLATION RATE:" ;Y
```

8.
```
10  INPUT X$
20  Z$=X$+X$+X$
30  PRINT Z$
```

14.
```
10  INPUT "PREV MILEAGE:";X1
20  INPUT "CURRENT MILEAGE:";X2
30  INPUT "AMOUNT OF FILLUP:";A
40  M = (X2 − X1)/A
50  PRINT M
```

15.
```
10  INPUT "HOURLY WAGE:";W
20  Y = 52 * 40 * W
```

Continued

```
            30   PRINT "ANNUAL INCOME:";Y
20.    10   PRINT "ENTER P AND Q FOR ITEM 1"
       20   INPUT P1,Q1
       30   PRINT "ENTER P AND Q FOR ITEM 2"
       40   INPUT P2,Q2
       50   PRINT "ENTER P AND Q FOR ITEM 3"
       60   INPUT P3,Q3
       70   PRINT "ENTER P AND Q FOR ITEM 4"
       80   INPUT P4,Q4
       90   T = P1 * Q1 + P2 * Q2 + P3 * Q3 + P4 * Q4
      100   PRINT T
```

(In Chapter 4, we will learn about loops, which make it much easier to write programs that perform this type of calculation.)

CHAPTER 3

```
1.   1   REM    PROGRAM TO COMPARE CEREAL BOX PRICES
    10   B = 10000 : REM    B IS THE BEST UNIT PRICE
    20   INPUT "PRICE:";P:INPUT "QUANTITY:" ;Q
    30   IF P = 0 GOTO 60
    40   X = P/Q
    45   IF X < B THEN P2 = P : B = X
    50   GOTO 20
    60   PRINT P2 : END
4.  10   INPUT T
    20   IF T <32 THEN PRINT "IT'S FREEZING"
    30   IF (T>=32) AND (T<60) THEN PRINT "TOO COLD!"
    40   IF (T>=60) AND (T<80) THEN PRINT "JUST RIGHT!"
    50   IF T>=80 THEN PRINT "TOO HOT!"
5.  10   INPUT "SECRET NUMBER:";N
    20   PRINT:PRINT:PRINT:PRINT:PRINT:PRINT:PRINT:PRINT:PRINT:PRINT
    21   PRINT:PRINT:PRINT:PRINT:PRINT:PRINT:PRINT:PRINT:PRINT:PRINT
    22   PRINT:PRINT:PRINT:PRINT:PRINT
    25   REM    YOU MAY LOOK IN YOUR MANUAL TO FIND THE COMMAND
    26   REM     THAT CLEARS THE SCREEN AND USE THAT COMMAND INSTEAD
```

```
27    REM      OF ALL THOSE PRINT STATEMENTS.
30    INPUT "YOUR GUESS:";G
40    IF G=N THEN GOTO 90
50    IF G>N THEN PRINT "YOUR GUESS IS TOO BIG"
60    IF G<N THEN PRINT "YOUR GUESS IS TOO SMALL"
70    GOTO 30
90    PRINT "THAT'S RIGHT!":END
```

6. and 7.

```
 1    REM    TEAM 1 HAS W1 WINS AND L1 LOSSES
 2    REM    TEAM 2 HAS W2 WINS AND L2 LOSSES
 3    REM    G IS THE NUMBER OF GAMES TEAM 2 IS
 4    REM       BEHIND TEAM 1
10    INPUT W1,L1,W2,L2
20    S1 = W1 – L1
30    S2 = W2 – L2
40    G = (S1 – S2)/2
50    PRINT "GAMES BACK:";G
60    INPUT "GAMES REMAINING FOR TEAM 1:" ;N1
70    INPUT "GAMES REMAINING FOR TEAM 2:" ;N2
80    N = (N1 + N2)/2
90    C = N – G + 1
100   IF C < 1 THEN PRINT "TEAM 1 HAS CLINCHED FIRST PLACE"
110   IF C > 0 THEN PRINT "CLINCHING NUMBER IS:" ;C
120   END
```

9.
```
100   REM    FIRST WAY — WITH ON/GOTO
110   INPUT N
115   N2=N – 2
120   ON N2 GOTO 130,140,150
125   GOTO 110
130   PRINT "TRIANGLE"
135   GOTO 190
140   PRINT "QUADRILATERAL"
145   GOTO 190
150   PRINT "PENTAGON"
190   END
```

```
200   REM — SECOND WAY — WITH GOTOS
210   INPUT N
220   IF N=3 THEN GOTO 260
230   IF N=4 THEN GOTO 270
240   IF N=5 THEN GOTO 280
250   GOTO 210
260   PRINT "TRIANGLE"
265   GOTO 290
270   PRINT "QUADRILATERAL"
275   GOTO 290
280   PRINT "PENTAGON"
290   END
300   REM — THIRD WAY — WITH NO GOTOS
310   INPUT N
320   IF N=3 THEN PRINT "TRIANGLE"
330   IF N=4 THEN PRINT "QUADRILATERAL"
340   IF N=5 THEN PRINT "PENTAGON"
350   END
```

13.
```
  1   REM    PROGRAM TO TEST IF Y IS A LEAP YEAR
 10   INPUT Y
 20   IF (Y/4)<>INT(Y/4)GOTO 50:REM    NOT
 21        REM            A LEAP YEAR
 30   IF (Y/100)<>INT(Y/100)GOTO 60:REM    Y IS
 31        REM               A LEAP YEAR
 40   IF (Y/400)=INT(Y/400)GOTO 60:REM     Y IS
 41        REM            A LEAP YEAR
 50   PRINT Y;"IS NOT A LEAP YEAR":GOTO 70
 60   PRINT Y;"IS A LEAP YEAR"
 70   END
```

14.
```
  1   REM    PROGRAM TO CALCULATE NUMBER OF
  2   REM        TRAILING ZEROS IN N
  5   T = 0
 10   INPUT N
 20   N = N/10
 30   IF N <> INT(N) GOTO 60
```

```
40   T = T + 1
50   GOTO 20
60   PRINT T : END
```

16.
```
1   REM   PROGRAM TO PRINT PRIME FACTORS OF N
10   INPUT N
20   P = 2 : Q = 1
21   REM   P IS THE LARGEST PRIME NUMBER WE HAVE
22   REM       TESTED SO FAR
30   IF (N/P) <> INT(N/P) GOTO 80
39   REM — N IS DIVISIBLE BY P ——
40   PRINT P
50   N = N/P
60   IF N = 1 GOTO 110: REM   WE'RE DONE
70   GOTO 30
79   REM — N IS NOT DIVISIBLE BY P ——
80   P = P + Q
90   Q = 2
100   GOTO 30
110   END
```

CHAPTER 4

3.
```
1   REM   PROGRAM TO CALCULATE MONOPOLY PROFITS
5   B = 0
10   FOR P = 0 TO 200
20      Q = 100 – P/2
30      C = Q * Q/2 + 10
40   REM   Y IS THE AMOUNT OF PROFIT
50   Y = P * Q – C
60    PRINT P,Q,Y
70   IF Y > B  THEN B = Y : P2 = P
80   NEXT P
100   PRINT "BEST PRICE:";P2:END
```

6.
```
1   REM   PROGRAM TO CALCULATE BATTING AVERAGE
10   FOR P = 1 TO 9
```

Continued

```
20  PRINT "HITS FOR PLAYER" ;P
30  INPUT H
40  PRINT "AT BAT FOR PLAYER" ;P
50  INPUT B
60  A = H/B
70  A = (INT(A * 1000 + 0.5))/1000
80  PRINT "AVERAGE IS:" ;A
90 NEXT P
```

8. Not valid. The NEXT I statement comes before the NEXT J statement.

9. Not valid. There are two NEXT I statements for the same loop.

10. Valid. It is all right to have a GOTO inside a loop.

11. Not valid. Statement 30 contains a GOTO into a loop.

12. Valid. The B loop is properly nested inside the A loop.

13. Valid. It is all right to have a GOTO that leads out of a loop.

14.
```
 1  REM   WINNING PERCENTAGE TABLE
10  FOR N = 1 TO 20
20     PRINT N;"GAMES PLAYED"
30     FOR W = 1 TO N
40        P = W/N
50        P = (INT(1000 * P + 0.5))/1000
55        PRINT W,P
60     NEXT W
70  NEXT N : END
```

15.
```
 1  REM   PROGRAM TO CALCULATE N FACTORIAL
10  INPUT N
20  Z = 1
30  IF N = 0 GOTO 70
40  FOR I = 1 TO N
50     Z = Z * I
60  NEXT I
70  PRINT N;"FACTORIAL IS:";Z
80  END
```

18.
```
 1  REM   PROGRAM TO CALCULATE STANDARD
```

```
 2  REM     DEVIATION
10  A = 0 : REM   A IS E(X)
20  B = 0 : REM   B IS E(X ↑ 2)
30  INPUT N
40  FOR I = 1 TO N
50     INPUT X
60       A = A + X
70       B = B + X ↑ 2
80  NEXT I
90  A = A/N
100  B = B/N
110  S = SQR(B – A ↑ 2)
120  PRINT "STANDARD DEVIATION IS:" ;S:END
```

CHAPTER 5

```
3.  1  REM   PROGRAM TO TEST IF THE ELEMENTS OF
    2  REM      A ARE ARRANGED IN ASCENDING ORDER
   10  L = A(1)
   20  FOR I = 2 TO N
   30     IF L > A(I)PRINT "NOT IN ORDER":GOTO 70
   40     L = A(I)
   50  NEXT I
   60  PRINT "THE LIST IS IN ORDER"
   70  END
5.  1  REM   PROGRAM TO CALCULATE LONGEST STRETCH
    2  REM      OF CONSECUTIVE GAMES WITH AT LEAST 1
    3  REM      HIT IN EACH GAME
   10  S = 0 : L = 0
   20  FOR I = 1 TO 162
   30     IF H(I) = 0 THEN S = 0
   40     IF H(I) > 0 THEN S = S + 1
   50     IF S > L THEN L = S
   60  NEXT I
   70  PRINT L
```

Continued

```
80   IF L > 56 THEN PRINT "DIMAGGIO RECORD"
81   IF L > 56 THEN PRINT "HAS BEEN BROKEN!"
```

6.
```
1   REM    C TELLS HOW MANY TIMES EACH DIGIT
2   REM        OCCURS IN N
10   DIM C(9)
20   FOR J = 0 TO 9: C(J) = 0 : NEXT J
30   FOR I = 1 TO S: REM    S IS THE NUMBER OF
31   REM    ELEMENTS IN N
40      C(N(I)) = C(N(I)) + 1
50   NEXT I
60   FOR J = 0 TO 9 : PRINT J,C(J):NEXT J
70   END
```

7.
```
1   REM    PROGRAM TO CALCULATE HOW MANY TIMES
2   REM        A NUMBER OCCURS IN THE LIST M
10   DIM C(50,2)
11   REM    COLUMN 1 OF C CONTAINS THE NUMBERS
12   REM        CONTAINED IN M
13   REM    (WE ARE ASSUMING THERE ARE NO MORE THAN
14   REM        50 DISTINCT ELEMENTS IN M)
15   REM    COLUMN 2 OF C TELLS HOW MANY TIMES
16   REM        EACH NUMBER OCCURS IN M
20   FOR I = 1 TO 50:C(I,1) = 0:C(I,2) = 0:NEXT I
30   FOR I = 1 TO S: REM    S IS THE TOTAL NUMBER OF
31   REM    ELEMENTS IN M
40      B = M(I)
50      FOR J = 1 TO 50
60   IF C(J,2) = 0 THEN C(J,1) = B: C(J,2) = 1: GOTO 90
70   IF C(J,1) = B THEN C(J,2) = C(J,2) + 1: GOTO 90
80      NEXT J
90   NEXT I
100   END
```

9.
```
1   REM    PROGRAM TO REMOVE ZEROS
10   FOR I = 1 TO N
20      IF A(I) <> 0 GOTO 60
30      FOR J = I TO N − 1
```

```
40          A(J) = A(J + 1)
50      NEXT J
60  NEXT I : END
```

17.   1 REM   PROGRAM TO MULTIPLY TWO
       2 REM   4 × 4 MATRICES A AND B
       3 REM   ASSUME THAT THE VALUES FOR A AND
       4 REM   B HAVE ALREADY BEEN READ IN
       5 REM   C WILL BE THE RESULT
      10 DIM C(4,4)
      50 FOR I = 1 TO 4
      60   FOR J = 1 TO 4
      70   T = 0
      80   FOR K = 1 TO 4
      90   T = T + A(I,K) * B(K,J)
     100   NEXT K
     110   C(I,J) = T
     120   NEXT J
     130 NEXT I
     140 END

CHAPTER 6

1. DEF FNA(I) = I/39.38

7. If p is the parallax and d is the distance in parsecs, then $d = 1/p$. (Parallax is the angle that a star is observed to shift during the year because of the orbital motion of Earth. It is measured in seconds of arc, where 1 second equals 1/3600 of a degree. One parsec is about 3 light years).

8. One volt RMS is equal to 1/2.8 volt peak to peak.

12. Not valid. After the computer executes line 40, it will enter the subroutine starting at line 50 without being sent there by a GOSUB command, so the result will be a RETURN without GOSUB error message.

13. Valid. It is all right to have more than one RETURN in a subroutine. However, if you are not careful, it can be confusing when there is more than one RETURN for a single subroutine.

14. Valid.

15. Not valid. Subroutine 100 calls subroutine 200, but subroutine 200 calls subroutine 100. Therefore the computer will be trapped, moving back and forth between the two subroutines until it runs out of memory.

16. This program will not generate any error messages, but it will not do anything useful. One of the statements in subroutine 100 is GOSUB 100, so this subroutine is calling itself. The term *recursion* is applied when a subroutine calls itself. Recursion is a useful technique for some problems. Some other languages allow for recursion, but BASIC generally does not.

17. 101.025

24.
```
 10   REM    HYPERGEOMETRIC DISTRIBUTION CALCULATION
 15   PRINT "ENTER N,R,B:"
 20   INPUT N,R,B
 30   FOR J = 0 TO B
 40   A1=R:A2=J:GOSUB 100:X=Y
 50   A1=N–R:A2=B–J:GOSUB 100:X=X * Y
 60   A1=N:A2=B:GOSUB 100:X=X/Y
 70   PRINT J,X
 75   NEXT J
 80   END
 99   REM ****************************
100   REM    SUBROUTINE TO CALCULATE BINOMIAL COEFFICIENT
105   REM       A1!/[A2! * (A1–A2)!]
106   REM       STORE THE RESULT AS Y
110   M=A1:GOSUB 200:Y=Z
120   M=A2:GOSUB 200:Y=Y/Z
130   M=(A1–A2):GOSUB 200:Y=Y/Z
140   RETURN
199   REM ***************************
200   REM    SUBROUTINE TO CALCULATE M!
205   REM       STORE THE RESULT AS Z
210   Z=1
220   FOR I = 1 TO M
230    Z = Z * I
240   NEXT I
250   RETURN
```

CHAPTER 7

1.
```
10   INPUT X$
15   INPUT N
20   Z$=LEFT$(X$,LEN(X$)–N)
30   PRINT Z$
```

3.
```
10   INPUT X$
20   FOR I = 1 TO LEN(X$)
30   PRINT LEFT$(X$,LEN(X$)–I)
40   NEXT I
```

7.
```
1    REM    PROGRAM TO CONVERT AN INTEGER
2    REM       N INTO A CHARACTER STRING Z$
3    REM       WITH COMMAS INSERTED BETWEEN
4    REM       EVERY 3 DIGITS
10   INPUT N
20   X$=STR$(N)
25   IF LEFT$(X$,1)="" THEN X$=RIGHT$(X$,LEN(X$)–1)
30   Z$ = ""
35   J = 0
40   FOR I = LEN(X$) TO 1 STEP –1
50   IF J=3 THEN Z$=","+Z$:J=0
60   J=J+1
70   Z$=MID$(X$,I,1)+Z$
80   NEXT I
90   PRINT Z$
100  END
```

9.
```
10   INPUT X$
20   PRINT ASC(X$)–64
```

12.
```
10   INPUT X$
20   FOR I = 2 TO LEN (X$)–1
30   IF MID$(X$,I,1)<>"E" THEN GOTO 90
40   IF MID$(X$,I+1,1)<>"I" THEN GOTO 90
50   IF MID$(X$,I–1,1)="C" THEN GOTO 90
60   PRINT "ERROR"
70   PRINT MID$(X$,I–1,1);MID$(X$,I,1);MID$(X$,I+1,1)
90   NEXT I
```

17.

```
1 REM THIS PROGRAM READS IN A PARAGRAPH AND COUNTS HOW MANY
2 REM   TIMES EACH WORD OCCURS IN THAT PARAGRAPH.
3 REM   THIS PROGRAM ASSUMES THERE IS NO PUNCTUATION.
4 REM   THE WORDS ARE SEPARATED BY BLANKS
5 DIM A$(20),W$(300),WL$(300),CT(300)
10 INPUT "NUMBER OF LINES:";N
20 FOR I=1 TO N:INPUT A$(I):A$(I)=A$(I)+" ":NEXT I
30 K=0
40 FOR I=1 TO N
45    B=1
50    FOR J=1 TO LEN(A$(I))
60       IF MID$(A$(I),J,1)<>" " THEN GOTO 100
70       K=K+1
80       W$(K)=MID$(A$(I),B,J-B)
90       B=J+1
100   NEXT J
110 NEXT I
120 NW=K :REM NUMBER OF WORDS
130 REM -- COUNT WORDS
135 ND=0 :REM ND IS THE NUMBER OF DISTINCT WORDS
140 FOR I=1 TO NW
145     W1$=W$(I)
150    FOR K=1 TO 300
160       IF W1$=WL$(K) THEN CT(K)=CT(K)+1:GOTO 180
170       IF WL$(K)="" THEN WL$(K)=W1$:CT(K)=1:ND=ND+1:GOTO 180
175    NEXT K
180 NEXT I
200 REM -- SORT WORDS
210 FOR I=1 TO ND
220   FOR J=1 TO ND-I
230     IF WL$(J)<WL$(J+1) THEN GOTO 260
240       T$=WL$(J+1):WL$(J+1)=WL$(J):WL$(J)=T$
250       T=CT(J+1):CT(J+1)=CT(J):CT(J)=T
260    NEXT J
270 NEXT I
300 REM -- OUTPUT
310 FOR I=1 TO ND
320   PRINT WL$(I),CT(I)
330 NEXT I
340 END
```

18.

```
1 REM   THIS PROGRAM CODES AND DECODES MESSAGES.
2 REM   TO ENCODE A MESSAGE FIRST TYPE IN A SEQUENCE OF
3 REM   CAPITAL LETTERS AS THE KEY.   THEN TYPE THE MESSAGE.
4 REM   THE PROGRAM ASSUMES THE MESSAGE CONSISTS SOLELY OF
5 REM   CAPITAL LETTERS WITH NO PUNCTUATION MARKS.
6 REM   THE PERSON WHO DECODES THE MESSAGE MUST TYPE IN
7 REM   THE SAME KEY THAT WAS USED WHEN THE MESSAGE WAS
8 REM   ENCODED.
12 DIM CM$(50),M$(50)
15 INPUT "TYPE D TO DECODE OR E TO ENCODE OR S TO STOP";Q$
20 IF Q$="D" THEN GOTO 500
```

```
30  IF Q$="E" THEN GOTO 100
35  IF Q$="S" THEN END
40  GOTO 10
99  REM************************************
100 REM ENCODE
110 INPUT "KEY:";K$
120 INPUT "NUMBER OF LINES LINES IN MESSAGE:";N
125 FOR I=1 TO N
130    PRINT "INPUT LINE ";I;
140    INPUT M$(I)
150 NEXT I
160 K=0
170 FOR I=1 TO N
175    CM$(I)="" :REM CM$ HOLDS THE CODED MESSAGE
180    FOR J=1 TO LEN(M$(I))
185      IF MID$(M$(I),J,1)=" " THEN GOTO 250
190      IF K=LEN(K$) THEN K=0
200      K=K+1
210      C=ASC(MID$(K$,K,1))-64
220      D=ASC(MID$(M$(I),J,1))-64
230      E=D+C: IF E>26 THEN E=E-26
240      CM$(I)=CM$(I)+CHR$(E+64)
250    NEXT J
260 NEXT I
270 FOR I=1 TO N
280    PRINT CM$(I)
290 NEXT I
295 GOTO 15
499 REM************************************
500 REM DECODE
510 INPUT "KEY:";K$
520 INPUT "NUMBER OF LINES:";N
530 FOR I=1 TO N
540    PRINT "ENTER LINE ";I;
550    INPUT CM$(I)
560 NEXT I
570 K=0
580 FOR I=1 TO N
590 FOR J=1 TO LEN(CM$(I))
600    IF K=LEN(K$) THEN K=0
610    K=K+1
620    C=ASC(MID$(K$,K,1))-64
630    E=ASC(MID$(CM$(I),J,1))-64
640    D=E-C: IF D<1 THEN D=D+26
650    PRINT CHR$(D+64);
660    NEXT J
670    PRINT
680 NEXT I
690 GOTO 15
```

CHAPTER 8

1. SQR(X^2 + Y^2 + Z^2)

3. (−B+SQR(B^2 − 4 ∗ A ∗ C))/(2 ∗ A)

5. SIN(A) ∗ SIN(B) + COS(A) ∗ COS(B)

8. A^2 + B^2 − 2 ∗ A ∗ B ∗ COS(C)

9. B1 ∗ SIN(A)/(SIN(B))

14.
```
1   REM   COORDINATE ROTATION PROGRAM
2   REM   X,Y ARE THE INITIAL COORDINATES
3   REM   THE AXES ARE ROTATED BY AN ANGLE T
4   REM   X2,Y2 ARE THE NEW COORDINATES
10  INPUT X,Y,T
20  X2 = X ∗ COS(T) + Y ∗ SIN(T)
30  Y2 = Y ∗ COS(T) − X ∗ SIN(T)
40  PRINT X2,Y2 : END
```

16. Use Hero's formula. If a,b, and c are the lengths of the sides, and $s = (a + b + c)/2$ then

$$A = \sqrt{s(s-a)(s-b)(s-c)}$$

18.
```
1    REM   PROGRAM TO SOLVE A QUADRATIC EQUATION
10   PRINT "INPUT A,B, AND C:"
20   INPUT A, B, C
30   D = B ∗ B − 4 ∗ A ∗ C
40   IF D = 0 GOTO 120
50   IF D < 0 GOTO 150
60   PRINT "THE EQUATION HAS TWO REAL ROOTS"
70   PRINT "ROOT ONE"
80   PRINT (−B + SQR (D))/(2 ∗ A)
90   PRINT "ROOT TWO"
100  PRINT (−B − SQR(D))/(2∗A)
110  GOTO 200
120  PRINT "THE EQUATION HAS ONE REAL ROOT"
130  PRINT −B/(2∗A)
140  GOTO 200
150  PRINT "THE EQUATION HAS TWO COMPLEX ROOTS"
```

```
        160   PRINT "REAL PART"
        170   PRINT –B/(2∗A)
        180   PRINT "IMAGINARY PART"
        190   PRINT "+OR – ";SQR(–D)/(2∗A)
        200   END
21.       1   REM    PROGRAM TO PRINT THE
          2   REM        RIGHTMOST B DIGITS OF N
         10   INPUT N,B
         20   K = N/(10 ↑ B)
         30   L = K – INT(K)
         40   M = (10 ↑ B) ∗ L
         50   PRINT M : END
22.       1   REM    N IS A NUMBER LESS THAN 64
          2   REM    THIS PROGRAM WILL PRINT THE DIGITS
          3   REM        OF THE BINARY REPRESENTATION OF N
         10   B = 32
         20   IF N < B THEN PRINT 0
         30   IF N > = B THEN PRINT 1 : N = N – B
         40   B = B/2
         50   IF B > = 1 GOTO 20
         60   END
23.       1   REM    PROGRAM TO CALCULATE
          2   REM        A ∗ X ↑ 4 + B ∗ X ↑ 3 + C ∗ X ↑ 2 + D ∗ X + E
         10   INPUT A,B,C,D,E
         20   Y = E + X ∗ (D + X ∗ (C + X ∗ (B + X ∗ A)))
         30   PRINT Y : END
24.       1   REM    THIS PROGRAM CALCULATES THE
          2   REM        ARCTANGENT OF Y/X AND PLACES THE
          3   REM        RESULT IN THE CORRECT QUADRANT.
         10   INPUT X, Y
         20   Q = ATN(Y/X)
         30   IF X < 0 THEN Q = Q + 3.14159
         40   IF Q < 0 THEN Q = Q + 2 ∗ 3.14159
```

Continued

```
              45   Q = 180 * Q/3.14159
              50   PRINT Q : END
        25.    1   REM    PROGRAM TO USE NEWTON'S METHOD
               2   REM        TO FIND ONE SOLUTION OF THE EQUATION
               3   REM    A * X^3 + B * X^2 + C * X + D = 0
              10   INPUT A,B,C,D
              19   PRINT "ENTER INITIAL GUESS:"
              20   INPUT X
              30   Y=A * X^3 + B * X^2 + C * X+D
              40   IF ABS(Y) <.001 THEN GOTO 80
              50   Y2=3 * A * X^2 + 2 * B * X + C
              60   X=X–Y/Y2
              70   GOTO 30
              80   PRINT X:END
        29.    1   REM    AREA UNDER NORMAL PROBABILITY CURVE
               2   REM        BETWEEN 0 AND X
               5   T = 0
               7   C=100 * SQR(2 * 3.14159)
              10   FOR X=0 TO 3 STEP .01
              20   Y=EXP(–((X+5E–03)^2)/2)
              30   T=T+Y
              40   A=T/C
              50   PRINT USING "#######.####";(X+.01),A
              60   NEXT X:END
        33.    1   REM    APPROXIMATION FOR SIN X
               2   REM    X IS IN RADIANS
              10   INPUT X
              20   S = 1
              30   N = 1
              40   Y = 0
              50   FOR A = 1 TO 10
              60      T = 1
              70      FOR B = 1 TO N
```

```
    90    NEXT B
    100   Y = Y + S * T
    110   S = –S
    120   N = N + 2
    130   NEXT A
    140   PRINT "SIN";X;"IS:";Y:END
37.  10   INPUT X
     20   GOSUB 100
     30   PRINT X,Z
     40   END
     100  REM   SUBROUTINE TO CALCULATE SQUARE ROOT OF X
     101  REM     USING AN ITERATIVE METHOD CALLED
     102  REM     NEWTON'S METHOD
     110  Z=X/2
     120  IF ABS(Z * Z – X)<.0001 THEN RETURN
     130  Z=(Z+X/Z)/2
     140  GOTO 120
```

CHAPTER 9
8.

```
1 REM     MICROSOFT BASIC PROGRAM MAP
2 REM        This program makes a list of
3 REM        all variables and key words
4 REM        used in a program and tells what
5 REM        line numbers they are used in.
6 REM        To use this program you must
7 REM        save the program you are using
8 REM        as an ASCII file, by putting ,A
9 REM        at the end of the SAVE command
10 REM       for example,  SAVE "PROG",A
35   MAXVAR=300:DIM MP%(2*MAXVAR,2)
36     DIM VAR$(MAXVAR),PL%(MAXVAR)
40 DIM A$(5*MAXVAR),B$(5*MAXVAR)
45 FILES "*.BAS"
50 INPUT "FILE NAME:";F$
60 F$=F$+".BAS"
99 REM ******************************
100 PRINT "Reading in file"
105 OPEN "I",#1,F$
110 I=0
115    REM - START LOOP
117      IF EOF(1) THEN GOTO 180
120      I=I+1
125      LINE INPUT#1,A$(I)
```

Continued

```
130      GOTO 115
180   CLOSE#1
190   N=I
199 REM ******************************
200   PRINT "Breaking apart multi-statement lines"
205   I=0:J=0
210   REM - START LOOP
215     I=I+1
217     IF I>N THEN GOTO 290
220     A1$=A$(I)+":"
237     L2=INSTR(A1$," "):LNUM$=LEFT$(A1$,L2-1)
238     A1$=RIGHT$(A1$,LEN(A1$)-L2)
239     L1=INSTR(A1$,":")
240     J=J+1
242     B$(J)=LNUM$+"|"+LEFT$(A1$,L1-1)
250     A1$=RIGHT$(A1$,LEN(A1$)-L1)
255     IF LEN(A1$)>1 THEN GOTO 239 ELSE GOTO 215
290     N=J
299 REM ******************************
300 PRINT "Removing excess blanks"
310   FOR I=1 TO N
311     GOSUB 1000   'CONVERT ALL SEPARATORS TO BLANKS
312     A2$=""
320     FOR J=1 TO LEN(A1$)
325       A3$=MID$(A1$,J,1)
330       IF A3$<>" " THEN A2$=A2$+A3$:GOTO 370
340       IF RIGHT$(A2$,1) <>"|" THEN A2$=A2$+"|"
341       REM  The | character is used here as a separator
342       REM  Assume that the program itself does not contain |
370     NEXT J
380     A$(I)=A2$
390   NEXT I
399 REM ******************************
400   PRINT "Removing comments"
405   FOR I=1 TO N
410       A1$=A$(I)
415       L1=INSTR(A1$,"REM")
420       IF L1>0 THEN A1$=LEFT$(A1$,L1+2)
425       L2=INSTR(A1$,"'")
430       IF L2>0 THEN A1$=LEFT$(A1$,L2-1)
435       A$(I)=A1$
440   NEXT I
449 REM ******************************
450 PRINT "Removing material in quotation marks"
455   FOR I=1 TO N
460       IF INSTR(A$(I),CHR$(34))=0 THEN GOTO 497
465       A2$=""
467       A1$=A$(I)
468       SC=1
470       FOR J=1 TO LEN(A1$)
475         A3$=MID$(A1$,J,1)
480         IF (A3$<>CHR$(34)) AND SC=1 THEN A2$=A2$+A3$
485         IF (A3$=CHR$(34)) THEN SC=1 - SC
490       NEXT J
492       A$(I)=A2$
497   NEXT I
499 REM ******************************
500 PRINT "Begin map"
```

```
502      M=0:NUMVAR=0
505   FOR I=1 TO N
507      A1$=A$(I)
508      IF RIGHT$(A1$,1)<>"|" THEN A1$=A1$+"|"
510      GOSUB 2000 'BREAK APART AT | MARK
515      LNUM%=VAL(A2$)
520      WHILE LEN(A1$)>1
530         GOSUB 2000
540         IF VAL(A2$)<>0 THEN GOTO 520
550         FOR K=1 TO MAXVAR
555            IF VAR$(K)=A2$ THEN GOTO 600
560            IF VAR$(K)="" THEN VAR$(K)=A2$:NUMVAR=NUMVAR+1:GOTO 600
570         NEXT K
580       PRINT "MORE THAN ";MAXVAR; " VARIABLES ":END
600      M=M+1
605        MP%(M,1)=K
610        MP%(M,2)=LNUM%
620      WEND
630   NEXT I
699 REM ********************************
700 PRINT "Sorting"
702   FOR I1=1 TO NUMVAR:PL%(I1)=I1:NEXT I1
705   FOR I1=1 TO NUMVAR
710      FOR I2=1 TO NUMVAR-I1
715         IF VAR$(I2)<VAR$(I2+1) THEN GOTO 740
720         SWAP VAR$(I2),VAR$(I2+1)
725         SWAP PL%(I2),PL%(I2+1)
740      NEXT I2
745   NEXT I1
800   FOR I1=1 TO NUMVAR
802   LPRINT:LPRINT "---------"
805    LPRINT VAR$(I1)
810      K=PL%(I1)
820      FOR I2=1 TO M
830      IF MP%(I2,1)=K THEN LPRINT MP%(I2,2);"   ";
840      NEXT I2
850   NEXT I1
998 END
999 REM *********************************
1000 REM CONVERT ALL SEPARATORS TO BLANKS
1010    A1$=B$(I)
1020    FOR J=1 TO LEN(A1$)
1025    A3$=MID$(A1$,J,1)
1030    IF (A3$=",") OR (A3$=";") OR (A3$="+") OR (A3$="=") THEN GOTO 1060
1035    IF (A3$="-") OR (A3$="*") OR (A3$="/") OR (A3$="(") THEN GOTO 1060
1040    IF (A3$=")") OR (A3$=">") OR (A3$="<") THEN GOTO 1060
1050    GOTO 1070
1060    MID$(A1$,J,1)=" "
1070    NEXT J
1095 RETURN
1999 REM *********************************
2000 REM BREAK APART AT | MARK
2010    L1=INSTR(A1$,"|")
2015    IF L1=0 THEN A1$="":RETURN
2020    A2$=LEFT$(A1$,L1-1)
2030    A1$=RIGHT$(A1$,LEN(A1$)-L1)
2040    RETURN
```

CHAPTER 11

5. Here is an Apple IIe program to calculate financial tables:

```
1    REM   FINANCIAL TABLE PROGRAM
2    REM   THIS PROGRAM CALCULATES
3    REM   6 DIFFERENT FINANCIAL TABLES
4    REM   THIS PROGRAM IS FOR AN APPLE IIE
50 GOSUB 9000 : REM INITIALIZE
60 CW = 8 : REM COLUMN WIDTH
100   REM MAIN PROGRAM
110   GOSUB 1000 : REM READ IN TABLE SPECIFICATIONS
120   GOSUB 2000 : REM DISPLAY TABLE
130   INPUT "TYPE R TO DO ANOTHER TABLE:";Q$
140   IF Q$ = "R" THEN GOTO 100
150   END
999   REM ********************
1000   REM   READ IN TABLE SPECIFICATIONS
1010   FOR I = 1 TO 6
1015   PRINT I;" - ";TT$(I)
1020   NEXT I
1030   PRINT "ENTER YOUR CHOICE FOR"
1035   PRINT "THE TABLE NUMBER"
1040   INPUT TN
1045   PRINT "INPUT ";A$(TN)
1046   INPUT A
1047   IF TN = 6 THEN INPUT "COUPON RATE:";CR
1050   INPUT "INT RATE -   LOW VALUE:";R0
1055   INPUT "INT RATE - HIGH VALUE:";R9
1060   INPUT "INT RATE - STEP SIZE:";RS
1070   PRINT "ENTER COMPOUNDING PERIODS"
1075   INPUT "PER YEAR:";P
1077   IF TN = 6 THEN C = CR*A/P : REM COUPON AMOUNT
1080   INPUT "PERIOD -   LOW VALUE:";N0
1085   INPUT "PERIOD - HIGH VALUE:";N9
1090   INPUT "PERIOD - STEP SIZE:";NS
1100   RETURN
1999   REM **************************
2000   REM  DISPLAY TABLE
2005   HOME
2010   PRINT TT$(TN)
2020   PRINT A$(TN);" = ";A
2030   IF TN = 6 THEN PRINT "COUPON RATE = ";CR
2035   PRINT "COMPOUNDING PERIODS PER YEAR:";P
2037   PRINT "              INT RATE"
2040   NN = INT((N9 - N0)/NS + .5) + 1
2045   NR = INT((R9 - R0)/RS + .5) + 1
2050   PRINT "    N";
2051   REM  IF THERE ARE 12 COMPOUNDING PERIODS
2052   REM  PER YEAR THEN N IS MEASURED IN MONTHS.
2053   REM  IF THERE IS 1 COMPOUNDING PERIOD PER
2054   REM  YEAR THEN N IS MEASURED IN YEARS
2060   R = R0
2062   FOR J = 1 TO NR
2065   ND = 3 : X = R : GOSUB 2900 : REM OUTPUT
2070   R = R + RS
```

```
2075    NEXT J
2080    PRINT
2085    N = N0
2090    FOR I = 1 TO NN
2095    R = R0
2100    N$ = STR$(N) : PRINT SPC(5 - LEN(N$));N$;
2110    FOR J = 1 TO NR
2115    R1 = R/P
2118    REM   NOW PERFORM CALCULATIONS:
2120    ON TN GOSUB 3100,3200,3300,3400,3500,3600
2130    ND = 2 : X = Z : GOSUB 2900
2135    R = R + RS
2140    NEXT J
2150    PRINT
2155    N = N + NS
2160    NEXT I
2170    RETURN
2899    REM ************************
2900    REM   OUTPUT A NUMBER
2905    NK = 10 ^ ND
2910    X = (INT(X*NK+1/2))/NK
2915    X$ = STR$(X)
2917    IF LEN(X$) < 3 THEN X$ = " " + X$
2921    IF ND<>2 THEN GOTO 2925
2922    IF MID$(X$,LEN(X$)-1,1)="." THEN X$=X$+"0":GOTO 2925
2923    IF MID$(X$,LEN(X$)-2,1)<>"." THEN X$=X$+".00"
2925    PRINT SPC(CW-LEN(X$));
2926    REM   CW IS THE COLUMN WIDTH
2930    PRINT X$;
2935    RETURN
3099    REM ******************************
3100    REM    -- COMPOUND INTEREST TABLE
3110    Z = A * (1 + R1)^N
3120    RETURN
3199    REM ******************************
3200    REM    -- COMPOUND INTEREST WITH CONSTANT
3201    REM    DEPOSIT --   A IS THE AMOUNT THAT YOU
3202    REM    ARE ADDING TO THE ACCOUNT EACH PERIOD
3210    R2 = 1 + R1
3220    Z = A * (R2^N - 1)/(R2 - 1)
3230    RETURN
3299    REM ************************
3300    REM   PRESENT VALUE TABLE
3310    Z = A/(1 + R1)^N
3320    RETURN
3399    REM ***********************
3400    REM    ANNUITY TABLE
3410    R2 = 1 + R1
3420    Z = A*(R2^N - 1)/(R1*R2^N)
3430    RETURN
3499    REM ***********************
3500    REM   MORTGAGE PAYMENT TABLE
3510    R2 = 1 + R1
3520    Z = A*R1*R2^N/(R2^N-1)
3530    RETURN
3599    REM ***********************
```

Continued

```
3600   REM    BOND PRICE TABLE
3610   R2 = 1 + R1
3620   Z = C*(R2^N-1)/(R1*R2^N)
3630   Z = Z + A/R2^N
3640   RETURN
8999   REM ***********************
9000   REM  INITIALIZE
9010   DIM TT$(6),A$(6)
9020   FOR I = 1 TO 6
9030   READ TT$(I),A$(I)
9035   NEXT I
9040   DATA "COMPOUND INTEREST"
9045   DATA "INITIAL AMOUNT"
9050   DATA "COMP. INT. WITH CONST.DEPOSIT"
9055   DATA "AMOUNT SAVED EACH PERIOD"
9060   DATA "PRESENT VALUE"
9065   DATA "AMOUNT AFTER N PERIODS"
9070   DATA "P.V. OF ANNUITY"
9075   DATA "AMOUNT RECEIVED EACH PERIOD"
9080   DATA "MORTGAGE PAYMENT"
9085   DATA "INITIAL PRINCIPAL AMOUNT"
9090   DATA "BOND PRICE"
9100   DATA "PAR VALUE"
9110   RETURN
```

The array TT\$ holds the six table titles. Each table requires you to enter one quantity needed for the calculation of that particular table. For example, the present-value table requires you to read in the amount received at the end of *n* periods, and the mortgage-payment table requires you to read in the initial principal amount. The bond-price table needs one additional quantity: the coupon rate.

The interest rate is always given as an annual rate, but you may choose monthly, quarterly semiannual, or annual compounding by changing the number of periods per year. The formulas used for the calculations are contained in the six subroutines located between lines 3100 and 3640.

CHAPTER 14

20.

```
1     REM  This program draws a ring on the screen.
2     REM  The user enters the angle of tilt (in degrees)
3     REM   and the relative size of the inner edge and the
4     REM   outer edge (both of which are numbers between 0 and 1).
20    SH=200 : REM screen height
25    SW=320 : REM screen width
30    H2=SH/2 : W2=SW/2
100   INPUT "ANGLE:";AN
110   AN=3.14159*AN/180
120   INPUT "Size of outer edge:";S1
125   INPUT "Size of inner edge:";S2
127   SCREEN 1   : REM initialize graphics --
```

```
128                    REM include the appropriate
129                    REM command for your computer
130 A1=SH*S1/2
135 B1=A1*SIN(AN)
140 A2=SH*S2/2
145 B2=A2*SIN(AN)
150 FOR X1=-A1 TO A1
160    Y1=B1*SQR(1-X1*X1/(A1*A1))
165    D=1-X1*X1/(A2*A2)
170    IF D<0 THEN GOTO 240
175    Y2=B2*SQR(D)
185    FOR Y3=Y1 TO Y2 STEP -1
187      GOSUB 1000  : REM plot point
190    NEXT Y3
200    FOR Y3=-Y2 TO -Y1 STEP -1
210      GOSUB 1000
220    NEXT Y3
230    GOTO 280
240    REM -- AT EDGE OF RINGS
250    FOR Y3=Y1 TO -Y1 STEP -1
260      GOSUB 1000
270    NEXT Y3
280 NEXT X1
290 END
1000 REM  PLOT POINT
1010    X=X1+W2
1020    Y=H2-Y3
1030    PSET(X,Y)  : REM This is the command for IBM PC BASIC
1040    RETURN
```

24.

```
1  REM  THIS MICROSOFT BASIC PROGRAM DRAWS A CUBE ON THE
2  REM  SCREEN AND THEN MAKES IT POSSIBLE FOR THE USER TO
3  REM  ROTATE THE CUBE TO SEE HOW ITS APPEARANCE CHANGES
100 DIM A(8,3) ' THE ARRAY A CONTAINS THE COORDINATES
101            ' OF THE 8 VERTICES OF THE CUBE
110 REM -- READ IN INITIAL COORDINATES
120 FOR I=1 TO 8:FOR J=1 TO 3:READ A(I,J):NEXT J:NEXT I
129 REM    X  Y  Z
130 DATA  1, 1, 1
140 DATA -1, 1, 1
150 DATA -1,-1, 1
160 DATA  1,-1, 1
170 DATA  1, 1,-1
180 DATA -1, 1,-1
190 DATA -1,-1,-1
200 DATA  1,-1,-1
210  H=140 : SCALE=50   'THE VALUE OF SCALE CAN BE ADJUSTED TO
211                      'CHANGE THE SIZE OF THE CUBE
220 FOR I=1 TO 8:FOR J=1 TO 3:A(I,J)=A(I,J)*SCALE:NEXT J:NEXT I
230    GOSUB 300  'DRAW CUBE
240    GOSUB 400  'INPUT COMMAND
250    GOSUB 500  'PERFORM ROTATION
260    GOTO 230
300 REM -- DRAW CUBE
```

Continued

```
305 SCREEN 1:CLS
306 REM  IT TAKES 12 LINES TO DRAW THE CUBE
310  FOR I=1 TO 3
320    LINE ((H+A(I,1)),(H+A(I,3)))-((H+A(I+1,1)),(H+A(I+1,3)))
330    LINE ((H+A(I+4,1)),(H+A(I+4,3)))-((H+A(I+5,1)),(H+A(I+5,3)))
340  NEXT I
350    LINE ((H+A(1,1)),(H+A(1,3)))-((H+A(4,1)),(H+A(4,3)))
360    LINE ((H+A(5,1)),(H+A(5,3)))-((H+A(8,1)),(H+A(8,3)))
370  FOR I=1 TO 4
380    LINE ((H+A(I,1)),(H+A(I,3)))-((H+A(I+4,1)),(H+A(I+4,3)))
390  NEXT I
395 RETURN
400 REM INPUT COMMAND
401 LOCATE 24,1
410 REM THESE ARE THE ALLOWABLE COMMANDS:
411 'R : ROTATE RIGHT BY A CERTAIN ANGLE    EXAMPLE: R 10
412 'D : ROTATE DOWN BY A CERTAIN ANGLE     EXAMPLE: D -20
420 INPUT X$
430 IF X$="S" THEN END  'S MEANS TO STOP
440 DIRECTION$=LEFT$(X$,1)  'DIRECTION OF ROTATION, R OR D
450 ANGLE = (3.14159/180)*VAL(MID$(X$,2,LEN(X$)-1))
451 REM  NOTE - THE ANGLE IS READ IN DEGREES AND
452 REM          THEN CONVERTED TO RADIANS
460 RETURN
500 REM PERFORM ROTATION
510 IF DIRECTION$="R" THEN GOTO 520 ELSE GOTO 600
520  REM - ROTATE TO THE RIGHT
530  FOR I=1 TO 8
540    X=A(I,1):Y=A(I,2)  'Z COORDINATE IS UNCHANGED
550    X2=X*COS(ANGLE)+Y*SIN(ANGLE)
560    Y2=Y*COS(ANGLE)-X*SIN(ANGLE)
570    A(I,1)=X2:A(I,2)=Y2
575  NEXT I
580  RETURN
600  REM - ROTATE DOWN
610  FOR I=1 TO 8
620    Y=A(I,2):Z=A(I,3) 'X COORDINATE IS UNCHANGED
630    Y2=Y*COS(ANGLE)+Z*SIN(ANGLE)
640    Z2=Z*COS(ANGLE)-Y*SIN(ANGLE)
650    A(I,2)=Y2:A(I,3)=Z2
660  NEXT I
670  RETURN
```

CHAPTER 15

1. The new value of $P(1)$ will be the number of people born that year. Then, for $I>1$, $P(I)$ will equal the value of $P(I-1)$ for last year minus the number of people of age $I-1$ who died last year.

7. The value of GNP exhibits cycles in this type of model.

9. All the light rays will be reflected back to the same point when they strike the parabolic mirror.

INDEX

MOVE TO THE HEAD OF YOUR CLASS

THE EASY WAY!

Barron's presents THE EASY WAY SERIES—specially prepared by top educators, it maximizes effective learning, while minimizing the time and effort it takes to raise your grades, brush up on the basics, and build your confidence. Comprehensive and full of clear review examples, **THE EASY WAY SERIES** is your best bet for better grades, quickly! Each book is $9.95, Can. $13.95 unless otherwise noted below.

4187-9	**Accounting the Easy Way, 2nd Ed.**
4194-1	**Algebra the Easy Way, 2nd Ed.**
4625-0	**American History the Easy Way—$9.95, Can. $12.95**
4197-6	**Arithmetic the Easy Way, 2nd Ed.**
4286-7	**Biology the Easy Way, 2nd Ed.**
4371-5	**Bookkeeping the Easy Way, 2nd Ed.**
4626-9	**Business Letters the Easy Way, 2nd Ed.**
4627-7	**Business Mathematics the Easy Way, 2nd Ed.**
4078-3	**Calculus the Easy Way, 2nd Ed.**
4198-4	**Chemistry the Easy Way, 2nd Ed.**
4253-0	**Computer Programming In Basic the Easy Way, 2nd Ed.**
2800-7	**Computer Programming In Fortran the Easy Way**
2799-X	**Computer Programming in Pascal the Easy Way— $11.95, Can. $15.95**
4081-3	**Electronics the Easy Way, 2nd Ed.**
3347-7	**English the Easy Way, 2nd Ed.**
4205-0	**French the Easy Way, 2nd Ed.**
4287-5	**Geometry the Easy Way, 2nd Ed.**
2719-1	**German the Easy Way**
3830-4	**Italian the Easy Way**
4079-1	**Mathematics the Easy Way, 2nd Ed.**
4390-1	**Physics the Easy Way, 2nd Ed.**
4204-2	**Spanish the Easy Way, 2nd Ed.**
3346-9	**Spelling the Easy Way, 2nd Ed.**
4196-8	**Statistics the Easy Way, 2nd Ed.**
4389-8	**Trigonometry the Easy Way, 2nd Ed.**
4080-5	**Typing the Easy Way, 2nd Ed.—$10.95, Can. $14.95**
4615-3	**Writing the Easy Way, 2nd Ed.**

BARRON'S EDUCATIONAL SERIES
250 Wireless Boulevard • Hauppauge, New York 11788
In Canada: Georgetown Book Warehouse • 34 Armstrong Avenue
Georgetown, Ontario L7G 4R9

Prices subject to change without notice. Books may be purchased at your local bookstore, or by mail from Barron's. Enclose check or money order for total amount plus sales tax where applicable and 10% for postage and handling (minimum charge $1.75, Canada $2.00). All books are paperback editions.
ISBN Prefix 0-8120